Kevin Rafferty CM

GW00670464

# Fragments of a Life

the columba press

First published in 2009 by
the columba press
55A Spruce Avenue, Stillorgan Industrial Park,
Blackrock, Co Dublin

Cover by Bill Bolger
Origination by The Columba Press
Printed in Ireland by ColourBooks Ltd, Dublin

ISBN 978-1-85607-621-0

# Table of Contents

# Foreword

As a close friend of Kevin, it is a privilege to contribute this foreword. With many others I can say that Kevin has touched and changed me deeply. This was his greatest gift to the world, his ability to relate with ease and to nurture growth in others.

This book is not about Kevin, but it is a uniquely personal contribution giving us his observations on, and describing his contribution to, Irish church life in a time of great change.

The sociologists tell us that the past fifty years have seen more social change than ever before in the developed world as they still try to date and define concepts like modernity and post modernity. Whatever these words mean and however we define them, there has been massive cultural and social change in Europe. And it continues.

The church has inevitably been part of this change. Many have theorised about this religious transition, but Kevin has been an active part of it. In this book, he privileges us with a reflective description and a personal experience from the front line.

Among Kevin's gifts was his ability to observe, to look forward and to respond with gentle courage while others just wrote about, discussed or hesitated before what was happening. Kevin combined close and careful observation with equally profound reflection on religious change. He then responded, particularly in naming the deeper purpose of All Hallows, bringing it even beyond being a great centre for educating missionary priests to what it is today. Mission theology has developed the concept of mission as sending priests to other countries to the recognition that the church is on mission everywhere and in every one of its members. Recognising this before many others did, Kevin transformed All Hallows. Following him, others have made great contributions to bringing All Hallows to its present great missionary service in adult Christian education to Irish Catholic men and woman, to lay students from other churches and many from other countries. Each year, Kevin's forward vision continues on Graduation day in Woodlock Hall.

As he and I talked over our monthly three-hour meal in the National Art Gallery – afterwards he would have me read the captions under his favourite paintings – it became clearer to me that Kevin was a great listener and a ready learner everywhere he went, and with all whom he met.

I asked him one day how he would describe himself. His answer: 'I suppose you could describe me as a searcher.' What this great searcher found is now our privilege to read and I am confident that his greatest search as a Vincentian priest has now ended in God.

*Desmond O'Donnell* OMI

# *Preface*

In my final year in the provincial office, 2001, I learned that I had developed macular degeneration. Doctors in Dublin and Belfast did their best to halt the progress of the disease but by the month of May I had great difficulty reading letters and documents. With the help of Una, my secretary, I struggled through the last few months in the provincial office. I retained reasonably good peripheral vision but the centre of the retina ceased functioning. Everything became slightly fuzzy. My greatest fear was that I was going blind.

In the Autumn I flew to Australia and stayed for the following six months in Perth with my friend, Fr Joe Walsh, in the parish of Subiaco. I enjoyed the beautiful weather, swimming in the ocean a short distance away, and meeting parishioners who invited me to their homes for a meal. This was the first time that I had the space to think back over turning points in my life and the people who had influenced me. For a few hours each day I put memories and reflections on tape. At first this was a therapeutic exercise but as time went on I began to put order into these fragments. This helped me to reflect on some of my deeper convictions which had been swallowed up in the heavy administrative work I had been immersed in over the previous 25 years. It also gave me the freedom to articulate some of my views on aspects of the church which up to now I had to keep to myself for political or other reasons.

Before I left Australia, an eminent eye specialist told me that he had good news and bad news for me. The good news was that I should hold on to my peripheral vision for the rest of my life. The bad news was that he could do nothing to restore my central vision. Hearing that I was not going blind lifted a great black cloud which had been hanging over me for the previous twelve months.

As soon as I returned to Ireland I acquired two computer programmes which enabled me to read large print on a computer screen and with the help of a scanner to listen to books and articles being read to me. I felt that I was rejoining the human race once again. Over the following years I reworked the memories and reflections I had put on tape in Australia into nine chapters corresponding to nine periods of my life. In Chapter 10, I concentrate on experiences and conversations I have had over the last five years about the present state of the Catholic Church in Western Europe and the challenges facing it today.

In recording these memories I kept the mention of names to a minimum. It was the easiest way for me to avoid 'leaving people out'. However, I do want to thank with gratitude Margaret Doyle here in Dublin and Anna Germana in Perth who typed the hard copies of this text for me. They helped to put order into my fragments.

I would like to dedicate *Fragments of a Life* to my sister Mary Shortall. Mary died two weeks before I flew to Perth in November 2001. I can imagine her reading these memories and telling me, from time to time, to come off my high horse.

*25 January 2008*
*Conversion of St Paul*

# CHAPTER 1

# Growing Up in Glenamaddy
## 1936-1949

*Family Background*

My mother's name was Mary Connolly. She was one of three daughters born at the beginning of the 20th century. Her eldest sister, Agnes, was born in September 1900. My mother Mary, or May as she was called, was born in October 1901 and her youngest sister, Kathleen, was born in December 1902. Their father, James Connolly, came from a farming family in Park West a few miles from Glenamaddy and had married into the family business, located in one of the corner houses in the square of Glenamaddy. His wife, Margaret Keaveney, was the daughter of Malachy Keaveney, a substantial land and property owner in the town. Apart from his own premises he had built two properties for his two daughters, one for Margaret, my maternal grandmother, and another for her sister, who married a Patrick McDermott who lived next door.

My father, Martin Rafferty, was born in 1904 and was the third eldest son in his family of four brothers and three sisters. His father owned a hotel and a business in Castle Street, Roscommon Town. His father had spent some time in the United States and returned to Roscommon to buy this business and develop it. My father's mother, Margaret Connolly, came from a village called Foughil, situated between Williamstown and Ballymoe, County Galway. My father was 28 years old when he married my mother, who was two years older than him. Coming to the sleepy town of Glenamaddy from the thriving town of Roscommon must have been a challenge for him. When he arrived the Connolly business was in decline and all his energies now went into breathing life into this 'merchant business' once again.

My mother went to school with the Dominican sisters in

Taylor's Hill, Galway, as did her two sisters. I never got the impression that passing examinations was important for her. Becoming a woman of refinement and taste ranked much higher on the scale of values in girls' secondary schools in those days. My father did not complete his secondary school education. This may very well have been one of the reasons why he wanted his children to have all the benefits of education. As he grew up he had an interest in farming and buying and selling cattle. On 2 February 1932 my parents were married in the Pro-Cathedral in Dublin and had their reception in the Gresham Hotel. They then settled down in Glenamaddy where my father gradually took over the business from my grandfather and also began to work a small farm of about twenty to thirty acres, which the family possessed on the edge of the town.

In my family there are six children. My eldest brother, Martin, born in 1933; Jim, born in 1934; twins, Malachy and Kevin, born in 1936; my sister, Mary, born in 1938; and my youngest sister, Margaret, born in 1942. In the economic depression years of the 1930s and 1940s it must have been a daunting task for my parents to be faced with bringing up a family of six children in a remote and emigration-hit area of North East Galway. From 1820 to 1940 the population of the parish of Glenamaddy had fallen from nearly 8,000 to 2,000 people. To make a business pay in this area of small landholdings was quite a task.

*Merchant – Licence to sell beer and spirits*
The family home, built in the 1880s, comprised a shop, a bar, kitchen, and a dining room on the bottom floor with a drawing room and a number of bedrooms on the first floor. At the back of the house was a courtyard and outhouses for a car and storerooms. The outhouses contained anything from wool to coffins, seed and grain. At one time there had been a bakery which had supplied bread to the local workhouse. The shop consisted of a grocery, a bar and a fairly extensive hardware business. The bar had a snug attached. The amount of Guinness consumed in the bar, especially on fair days, led me to have an abiding detestation for this drink which I have never been able to overcome. I could see from my earliest years that drinking to a point of

inebriation was the main form of recreation for many people who frequented our pub on Fair days. At the back of the shop and outhouses was a garden with a fairly big hayshed and another outhouse where turf was stored.

Some of my earliest memories are associated with climbing the trees in this garden. Very often very competitive football matches took place in this garden with anything from six to ten youngsters on each side. The annual threshing of the oats and wheat, which had been harvested from our small farm on the outskirts of the town, also took place in this garden in early autumn.

Having a shop and a pub meant that we got to know many people in the area who were 'our customers'. With our regular customers there would be the expectation of a 'Christmas box' every year. Indeed some of the debts of these customers would be paid when the emigrant members of their families returned home for Christmas or summer holidays. This did not stop my father from putting up a notice in the grocery business, which said 'No credit – we never get it – therefore we can't give it.' The bar came into its own on Fair days when it was packed with farmers and cattle dealers. There was a pig fair once a month and a cattle fair once a month and these took place in the middle of the town until sometime in the late fifties when a cattle mart was set up outside the town. There was a terrible mess after the Fair. Owners of the shops would spend a good deal of time at the end of the day or the next day hosing down the outside of their premises getting rid of the cattle dung.

The dining room and kitchen were private areas. One of my earliest memories is having to eat porridge for breakfast, which I never took to, even when it had cream added to it. I also have memories of counting the money taken in the shop on fair days. The youngest children would be allowed to count copper and silver. I also remember the family rosary which I found very boring.

Rural electrification did not reach Glenamaddy until 1949. Prior to this time, most of the reading was done by candle light. As my brothers and I were keen on reading comics, it is surprising the house did not go on fire at one stage or another. In the dining room we had an Aladdin lamp and I was always intrigued by the lighting of the lamp itself.

The main source of entertainment in the evening, especially at the weekends, was listening to the radio. I have distinct memories of listening to Joe Linnane's *Question Time*. Attending recently a performance of Brian Friel's *Dancing at Lughnasa*, I was reminded of the way the radio set used to crackle and our reliance for power on a wet battery. I also have memories of listening to GAA football and hurling finals on the radio and Micheál O'Hehir's big build up to the match itself. Because of the interest of my elder brother in cricket we would tune into Test matches between England and Australia. We played 'Test matches' against one another in the cement courtyard at the back of our house. On good days we would run up a century or more against one another.

I have also memories of going for walks through the farm we owned on the outskirts of the town. On the few days where we 'saved the hay' it was all hands on deck. During one particular summer, I also got involved in 'footing turf' in a bog near Kiltullagh Lake and enjoyed catching the wet turf as it was thrown up to me from the turf bank below.

## North East Galway

Glenamaddy was a town of about 200 people, situated midway between Roscommon and Tuam. The countryside all around was flat, consisting of small farm holdings. There was a steady stream of emigration to England and the United States in the 1930s, 40s and 50s. Many families were sustained by the money that was sent back home from their emigrant relatives. There were twelve pubs, six hardware shops, two banks and two chemists in the town. The presence of two substantial banks, with large premises for the banks themselves and extensive upper floors for the resident bank manager, was always a kind of mystery to me. Some of the mystery was resolved recently when I heard that when one of the directors of one of these banks was visiting the town in the early part of the 20th century he decided that if the town had such an impressive church – built in 1904 – it would be able to sustain a bank in the town. Glenamaddy was known in Irish as *Gleann na Mada*, although most people knew the town as Glan. To the south of Glenamaddy were the towns of Kilkerrin, Moylough and Mountbellew. To the north Williamstown and Ballymoe. To the west Dunmore and Tuam, and to the east Creggs and Roscommon. Roscommon was the town we got to know best because of our aunts, uncles and cousins living there. Due to the lack of transport during the war and post-war period it was very seldom that we visited the other towns. It was many years later before I got to know the beautiful landscape in the West of Ireland – the Galway and Mayo coastlands. The nearest train station was at Ballymoe some nine miles away and the only bus service was to and from Galway through the towns of Dunmore and Tuam. This daily bus service delivered the daily newspapers to the town. Because of petrol rationing, cars were off the road during the war. People came to town either by foot or by pony and trap. It was well into the 1950s before the car became a common form of transport.

It was sometime in 1946, '47, '48 that a number of the residents in the town got telephone lines. The post office itself was the telephone station. The parish priest and the doctor were amongst the first to get telephone lines installed. We followed fairly early and if my memory serves me right our number was Glenamaddy 6.

There were two primary schools in the town, one for boys and one for girls, and three sets of schools for boys and girls in Clondoyle, Stonepark and Lisheennahelta. These were relatively small schools with two teachers in each. The war years from 1939 to 1945 were a time of great shortage of luxury goods. However, I have no memory of there ever being a shortage of basic foods, but because my family owned a grocery business we were cushioned from real hardship during these war years. I have no doubt that some families lived on the breadline in dire poverty.

Some of my earliest memories are of playing cowboys and Indians in the local graveyard, being enthralled by the local blacksmith shoeing horses in his forge and using his bellows to bring the coal fire to red hot heat, and being bewitched by the stonemasons, Martin and Dan Murphy, using their hand tools to cut script on headstones.

*Uphill to School*

Because of some misgivings about the teaching in the local primary school, our parents very bravely decided to send my two older brothers, Martin and Jim, to the Franciscan Brothers in Kilkerrin, three miles from Glenamaddy. Before the war began my mother drove them in the car we owned and then during the war years four boys, sometimes joined by a few other boys from other parts of the town of Glenamaddy, were driven in a pony and trap to this monastery school in Kilkerrin. This was done to the great chagrin of the local parish priest. I heard recently that my parents were denounced from the altar shortly after they sent my elder brothers to Kilkerrin. He was obviously afraid that we would start a trend. However, this did not deter my parents. The 'Monastery School', as we called it, was a two-teacher school with one brother looking after each section. Malachy and I were enrolled in the school on 6 May 1940 – six days after our fourth birthday. During most of my time in the lower school I was taught by Brother Leonard and in the upper school by Brother Philip. From today's perspective the school was quite primitive. Heating was from two turf fires, one in each section of the school. The school itself had been built around 1870. It was quite an innovation in the area. The brothers were pioneers in agricultural development and they had an extensive farm at the back of the monastery itself. The brothers generated their own electricity from a wind propeller at the top of a mast, which could be seen from a long distance.

The school provided a good grounding in basic subjects, Irish being the medium for the teaching of all subjects. I remember learning my maths tables and also the chief cities and main rivers in Ireland and the capital cities of Europe. At the end of the 6th class we did the primary certificate and I did reasonably well in all subjects. During my final year in school Brother Philip invited a number of pupils to Saturday morning class for those who were going to secondary school and gave us a basic training in algebra and geometry and I think a little French also.

For the last three or four years in primary school my brother and myself cycled to school each day. This was quite a journey for a 7/8-year-old and in winter it was particularly cold so that when we arrived in the school itself we were very often famished and sometimes wet. The brothers took good care of us, making sure that we dried out properly. We and other boys who travelled long distances to school were invited to have our lunch in the monastery kitchen. This consisted of sandwiches, which we brought in ourselves, and tea provided by the brothers. I have one very distinct memory of a particular day in May 1945 when there was a big headline in the *Independent* newspaper announcing the end of the war. The journey from Kilkerrin monastery school to Glenamaddy was usually much easier because one was going downhill and I often remember that if one had a good wind from behind, one got home very quickly in a matter of twenty minutes. Cycling to and from school was certainly an experience. It was physically quite demanding for my brother and myself and it certainly toughened up both of us for experiences that later would require a good deal of physical effort.

*Local Church and Parish Community*

A natural background to all our lives was regular attendance at Mass on Sundays and sometimes on weekdays. There were two Masses on Sunday, one at nine o'clock and the second at eleven. Communion could only be received at the first Mass. Like other youngsters in the town we became altar servers at quite an early age, learning the responses in Latin. At first we were quite nervous about missing out or stumbling over words, especially if we were serving the elderly and grumpy parish priest, Fr Kelly. Very quickly we got into the run of things. I can still remember the hush that came over the packed church on a Sunday morning as we neared the words of consecration. Belting the gong three times with the sound ringing around the church was a privileged moment for an altar server, and we had many battles before and after in the sacristy deciding who was going to take on this task.

The preaching tended to be moralistic and for a youngster it came across as tedious. It was only when a parish mission took place in Glenamaddy and another in Kilkerrin that I have any memories of sermons. This is because the priests who were preaching preached in a dramatic way that certainly held the attention of everybody attending Mass. My brother and I made our First Communion at the age of six which was probably too young. This took place after we made our first confession in Kilkerrin parish church. My only memory of my First Communion is having a bottle of lemonade in the Glynn family home in Kilkerrin. The three Connolly brothers, who joined the Columbans, would sometimes knock on our door early in the morning looking for a server, which of course they were required to have at that time. The only memory I have of Holy Week ceremonies is the very jejune Holy Saturday morning service. I can still remember the saintly Canon Joseph Walsh thumbing his way through the Latin missal with a small scattering of people attending. These ceremonies which took place in the morning seemed to me to be interminable. With Sunday Mass I associated crowds of people coming into our shop for an hour or so after Mass and of course there would be some regular customers in the pub as well. In the late 1940s my mother opened a small confectionery shop on one side of our property and I remember helping out there on most Sundays to cope with the Sunday rush, one of the attractions to our shop being the availability of whipped ice creams.

The Gothic church, built in 1904, was quite an imposing building. I was to learn later that it was built through the phenomenal energies of Fr Walter Conway who collected the £9,000 needed to construct it from contributions both inside and outside Ireland. I also learned later that my grandfather, James Connolly, contributed £200 to its construction and later paid for the installation of the central Harry Clarke window at the back of the altar in memory of his parents and relatives. Some people today would say that the building of this fine church in 1904 by Fr Walter Conway put the town on the map. He was also responsible for building the parochial house and a number of schools in the parish. A sad postscript is that Fr Conway, because of a dispute with his curate and the Archbishop of Tuam, left the town overnight in 1919 and spent the rest of his life as a chaplain to a convent near Dundee in Scotland. It has been said that all his energies now went into becoming a champion golfer. He never came back to visit the town and he died in 1943.

One feature of life in Glenamaddy was the annual Corpus Christi procession led by the first communicants, the boys smartly turned out and the girls in their white dresses strewing flowers before the Blessed Sacrament. Each house in the town decorated its doorway with a little altar of statues and flowers. This public manifestation of Christian belief was taken very much for granted and continued right up to Vatican II and for some years afterwards.

The outside of the church was crowded by men awaiting the two Sunday Masses despite the best efforts of various priests to encourage the people into the church itself. Some would venture into the side aisles and during the consecration would kneel on their handkerchief or on their cap – one knee that is. An early break for the pubs before Mass was over was part and parcel of life through these years. Trying to stay on the right side of the mortal sin line as regards arriving before the gospel and not leaving before the priest's communion, was an art cultivated by quite a few.

*Extended Family*

An important part of our growing up in Glenamaddy were visits to aunts, uncles and their families in Tycooly, Ballinrobe, Roscommon and Dublin. We were very close to the Connolly family and there were regular visits once or twice a year to the large farm they owned three miles on the other side of Mountbellew. The fifteen mile journey must have been done in less than an hour but to me, who found car journeys very difficult, it seemed to take an eternity. The long road through to Tycooly to the back entrance of a well developed farm, and arriving in a courtyard with many buildings, was always intriguing. One of the attractions of course was the tennis court which this family had, and the beautiful meal which we were provided with in the course of the afternoon or evening. Very often there were priests visiting this family. These included Mgr John McCarthy, who taught moral theology in Maynooth for many years and who was later Parish Priest of Athlone. Another visitor was Canon Malachy Brennan, who was a Parish Priest in Ahascragh.

Another family which we visited on an annual basis was the O'Rorke family in Ballinrobe. Again the journey to Ballinrobe appeared to me to be endless and brought us through towns which we scarcely ever visited such as Dunmore and Claremorris. The father of this family was working in a bank and died in his early forties in 1945. I will never forget the afternoon that word came through by telephone of his sudden death. The tragedy which hit the O'Rorke family was palpable to us forty miles away. ·

Our most frequent visits to relatives were to the Rafferty clan in Roscommon where we visited two of my uncles, John and James, living beside one another on Castle Street, and my aunt, May O'Reilly, in another part of the town. Again these visits were marked by attractive meals and also by interaction with our cousins in the different households, with our parents comparing notes with their brothers and sisters about each other's families. One of my aunts, Gretta, who had always been very ill, died around 1948. She had a respiratory disease so her death was not unexpected.

*Holidays*

Most of our holidays through our primary school years were in Galway. We often went to the same hotel, Osterley House, and hired a few rooms there over a one or two week period. We got to know the sea front very well and often enjoyed meals in Lydon's Restaurant on the main street of Galway. My mother would usually take the younger members of the family on these holidays and our father would remain at home to mind the shop.

In the summer of 1947 there was a break from this and, with the exception of my elder brother Martin and my father, the rest of us went to Bray. We stayed in a number of rooms in the terrace at the end of the esplanade. I have a very distinct memory of eating loads of banana sandwiches during this particular holiday. However, my appetite for climbing was whetted by climbing Bray Head. I did this on a number of occasions during that visit. There was a fantastic view of the coastline north and south. On one of these climbs I came across a couple engaged in some heavy petting, necking and kissing and for the first time I began to awaken to what the possibilities of human physical love might be all about.

*An Ordination in St Patrick's, Carlow*

In the summer of 1949 I accompanied my mother to the ordination of Father Martin Connolly in St Patrick's College, Carlow, where he had just completed his six year course. I remember staying in a hotel in Bagnelstown overnight and moving on from there to the college chapel in Carlow early the next morning. The Connolly and O'Rorke families were there, of course, and very proud of this special day for the eldest son of the Connolly family. There must have been fifteen or twenty families packed into the small college chapel and I watched for the first time the ordination rite with all the triumphalism of liturgy in those days. Martin was his usual friendly self, bubbling with enthusiasm, and the intense joy of all the families present was shared by all. The reception took place afterwards back in Bagnelstown. The following day Martin said his first Mass in his parish church in Caltra, Co Galway and, as far as I remember, I was one of the servers. This was followed by family and friends returning to the Connolly homestead in Tycooly for a great meal.

I have no doubt that, when the time came for me to make a decision about what I was going to do with my life, memories of this joyful occasion lingered on in my mind.

### Significant Events

*The reality of death:* My memories of growing up in Glenamaddy in the 1940s were marked by the drowning of two young people. The first was of a boy of nine or ten, my own age, Noel Mannion. In the middle of a beautiful summer while swimming in the lough (a small lake on the Roscommon Road) he was pulled out of the lake and great efforts were made to revive him. My memory is of messages coming in from the lake to groups of people in the town discussing the tragedy. The second drowning was of one of the McFadden brothers, a group who travelled around from town to town showing films of the 1930s and 1940s. He was drowned in Kiltullagh Lake and again I have very distinct memories of gloom descending on the town when the efforts to save or revive him petered out. The reality of death, in this case the deaths of two young people, is etched in my mind.

*The Second World War:* Sometime in the middle of the Second World War a German plane crashed not far from Glenamaddy.

The bodies of crew members were brought in four or five coffins in a lorry through our town and this sight has stayed with me. The reality of what was happening in England and on the Continent through the Second World War did not impinge very much on me. Although I have memories of local defence forces training from time to time to prepare for an invasion if it came our way, I certainly had no memory of people saying that Hitler was about to invade Ireland nor indeed did I have memories of the famous exchange between De Valera and Churchill about the use of Irish ports.

*The winter of 1947:* A very significant snowfall took place in Ireland in 1947, probably in January or February. I have memories of our town being snowed up and of being confined to the house for a two to three week period. I have an idea that most of our family contracted colds or flu during this period. My guess is that our schools were closed also during this time. There was an air of relief when eventually the snow lifted and life returned to normal.

*Influences*
In reflecting on the significant events and influences on me through the years growing up in Glenamaddy through the 1940s, my mind focuses on a number of events and influences that certainly left a mark on me.

*Locality:* Growing up in this small town in north-east Galway through the war years and its immediate aftermath could be painted in very negative terms. We were certainly quite isolated. Local news was the big news. Great events were taking place elsewhere – Germany, France, and England – but these made little impact on me at the time. With the unavailability of transport – petrol was rationed, especially during the war years – it was very seldom that we travelled out of Glenamaddy. The routine life of a relatively small and unknown town was the boundary of our existence. The domestic tragedies were the only tragedies we knew at first hand. Newspaper headlines or news coming through the radio had very little impact on young people growing up in Ireland at that time. In comparison to many families in the area, our family was well off. We were never short of food and having a shop meant that we had first call on tea, butter and

Cadbury's chocolate. Our world was the world of a rural farming community – there was a time for sowing and a time for reaping – which we got to know through the interaction with our customers, most of whom were small landowners, and through the cultivation of our own small farm. Because we were living in the middle of the town, this farming life was one or two removes from us.

*Education:* Our primary school education was reasonably good. The consequences of having poor primary school teachers could have had very far reaching effects but we were saved from that by being sent to the monastery school in Kilkerrin. Brother Leonard was a fretful, nervous and fussy teacher. Brother Philip had the ability to get the best out of his pupils, not ever having to take a heavy hand to keep discipline in the classroom. Seeing so many of his pupils end their education at primary school level must have been heart-rending to him. He saw the ability that existed in many pupils coming from poor families who would have no opportunity of getting secondary school education. Brother Philip had high expectations at every level. He knew how to motivate youngsters to set high goals for themselves. The physical inadequacies of the school by today's standards, and the unavailability of textbooks and teaching aids, were of secondary importance in comparison with the quality of the teaching itself. Going to school in Kilkerrin meant that my brothers and I had a good grounding in the essentials when we were ready to go to secondary school.

*Peer Group:* As often happens in small towns, a whole generation of young families were growing up in Glenamaddy in the 1940s. Youngsters saw a good deal of one another especially on the football pitch, which often happened to be the back garden of our house. Life and death contests were played late into summer evenings, with six to ten youngsters on each side. Sometimes we attracted an adult audience who would urge on one side or the other and add a little spice to these epic contests. Through the energy and enthusiasm of an altruistic assistant manager of the National Bank, Jerry Curtin, a grass tennis court was built on one of our fields at the edge of the town and this also became a meeting point for both boys and girls in the town.

*Church:* The Catholic Church was an ever-present reality in the background to all our activities. The weekly round of Sunday Masses and the great church feastdays marked our existence from year to year and from week to week. The church's influence was always seen as positive and there was great respect for our parish clergy despite the odd lapse here and there. A lot of our families had priest friends. They were in fact the key community leaders and the fortunes of the town depended in some measure on the calibre and initiative of either the parish priest or curate assigned to the parish. Most of our parish priests were on their last assignment, which meant that the impetus for church or community development often came from the curates or administrators as they were sometimes called. There were a number of aunts and cousins in convents in Boyle, Galway, Roscommon, Athlone and Sligo whom we called to see from time to time.

In this pre-Vatican II era we were instructed in the eternal truths of death, judgement, hell and heaven. It was a religion of fear rather than a religion of love that motivated most people. The diocesan priest who influenced me most in the 1940s was a Father Malone. He was a kind and a gentle man who later moved on to become Administrator in Knock. The Catholic Church at this time was moving into a golden age of its missionary activity. The stories in *The Far East* magazine, whose editor was one of the Connolly brothers, certainly fired our imaginations, even as primary school children. The visits of the two other Connolly brothers, who were missioners in South America, also kept the missionary perspective alive. We came in contact with them through serving their Masses during their holidays from their missions.

*Family:* The example of our parents, who worked extremely hard to provide a livelihood for all of us, was taken for granted. In retrospect we realised how many sacrifices they had made to give us a good start in life. The fact that they worked around the clock meant that there was not that much time for family reunions or get-togethers. The harmony of our family background would have manifested itself from time to time, especially on Sundays when we would be gathered around the radio listening to one programme or another, or helping to count the proceeds at the end of a busy fair day. Regular demands were made on us to help out in the home and in the shop. Overall, we grew up on a very loose rein, being given plenty of freedom to explore our interests. Our father would have given all of us 'a talking to' from time to time after one or other misdemeanour. I can remember only one occasion when I got a severe beating for missing music lessons with a Miss McGuinness. It was the element of deception rather than the wasting of money that got to my Dad. Our mother more often than not would take a more gentle approach and encourage us to do what our father had told us.

There were plenty of sibling rivalries especially between the boys in the family and if there was a row peace was restored fairly quickly. I have never tried to fathom too deeply the implications of being one of twin boys. I would have accepted from an early age that I was the introvert whereas my brother was universally recognised as the extrovert. I am certainly more at home staying in the background trying to influence things from a distance.

*Postscript: Growing Up in Rural Ireland in the 1940s*
As I reflect on my memories of growing up in rural Ireland in the 1940s, I am conscious of seeing the world with the freshness of a child's eyes – the rhythm of the four seasons, the fields being ploughed by teams of horses in the spring, footing the turf and saving the hay in the summer, the excitement of a day's threshing in the autumn when the '*meitheal*' came together, the darkness and short days of winter when we would be gathered around the dining room fire in the evening and wrapped up in bed sometimes with winds blowing across our flat landscape outside. Our 'merchants' business status cushioned us from some of the harsher aspects of the depressed Irish economy of the 1940s, and going to school in Kilkerrin made us outsiders among our own peer group in the town, although this did not stop us playing football together, especially in the summer time. The church and priests played a big part in our lives. They were our mediators with a God who in theory was a loving God but in practice this God could turn into a judging God who could send us to hell for all eternity if we crossed the mortal sin divide.

There is no doubt that 1940s Glenamaddy was a narrow provincial world. Our outlets to an outside world were through the radio – Radio Éireann and BBC and the daily newspapers and our returning emigrants – Yanks from the US and labourers

– skilled and unskilled – from cities and towns all over England. Their arrival boosted our sales in both our pub and grocery business and in some cases paid off bills that had mounted up for a particular family over the year. From one point of view, growing up in Glenamaddy was idyllic – we were as children on a very loose rein. Not having an outgoing personality like my twin brother, I had to live with the taunt 'You could not sell a box of matches!' However, apart from there being a policy of 'all hands on deck' on fair days, one was free as a bird to roam the town or its environs or to get stuck into comics in an upstairs room undisturbed.

Today, over fifty years later, we tend to see rural Ireland of the 1940s in black and white – more black than white. For me it was the golden age of childhood – a time of exciting discoveries – learning the names of the great rivers and capital cities of Europe – before the Iron Curtain fell, listening to the sound a downpour of rain made on the corrugated iron roof of one of our outhouses, looking out over the town from the topmost branch of one of the mature trees in our back garden, tasting a banana for the first time after the first consignment arrived in our shop at the end of the war, learning that I was good at mental arithmetic after I started to come top of the class in this kind of mental gymnastics, watching one of our cows calving and beginning to suspect that babies were not just delivered by a stork, neatly wrapped in tissue paper, struggling with the difference between right and wrong when my Dad told me to correct some bit of information I had passed on to Brother Philip about why I had not attended school on a particular day. The beginnings of a fundamental option for goodness and for truthfulness and for integrity were being laid down, in our home, in our school, and in our church, but of course I was not fully aware of this until much later.

# CHAPTER 2

# Up to School in Dublin
## 1949-1954

*Up to School in Dublin – Castleknock College*
Joining our two elder brothers in Castleknock College in September 1949 was taken for granted. When my twin brother Mal and I joined our two older brothers, I'm sure it must have put tremendous financial pressure on my parents. I'm not sure what dictated the choice of Castleknock in 1946. My guess is that it was either because an uncle of ours, James Rafferty from Roscommon, had gone there for a number of years or because of contact with one or other family in the west, probably a solicitor's family called Meaghers of Tuam, who may have encouraged my father to go down this road. I do not know if he ever seriously considered some of the local schools in the west of Ireland such as St Jarlaths, Tuam or Garbally in Ballinasloe where our Connolly cousins had gone but, whatever the reason, the choice was Castleknock. At that time, no secondary education was available in Glenamaddy or any of the surrounding towns. Fifteen years later in 1964, the O'Malley Education Act introduced free secondary education in Ireland. The Christian Brothers, of course, and the Mercy, Presentation, Loreto and St Louis sisters were providing what must have amounted to free education in the major towns in Ireland but Glenamaddy was too small for consideration. Through the good offices of Msgr Charlie Scahill, a very able administrator in Glenamaddy from 1957–1967, three Mercy sisters from Tuam were sent to Glenamaddy in 1958 to open a secondary school the following year 1959 – too late for the Rafferty clan to take advantage of this development.

I have no doubt that my parents made great sacrifices to send us to Castleknock, which opened up opportunities for us in later life. I did not realise until later that this move to Dublin was going to cut me off from my Glenamaddy roots which in my own case I never made up later on, partly because of living out-side Ireland for twenty years and only returning very rarely to Glenamaddy. Going up to school in Dublin in September 1949 marked quite a turning point in my life but I did not understand the implications of all this until much later.

*First Impressions*

Founded in 1835 by the Vincentian Fathers, Castleknock College had a long, proud tradition. It was one of the oldest boarding schools in the country. Situated in spacious grounds, west of the Phoenix Park, it had extensive playing fields and what then ap-peared to be ample dormitory and study space. There were 240 boarders in the school in 1949. About half of them came from Dublin with the other half from towns and villages all over Ireland. These boys were the sons of businessmen, doctors, farmers, solicitors and bankers.

My earliest memories of Castleknock College are finding my bed in Francis Clet's dormitory looking out on the old castle building. The autumn scenes from this dormitory, and a similar view from the large study hall nearby looking out on mature trees shedding their leaves in the autumn of each year, has al-ways remained with me – an annual reminder of the transitory nature of this world – a theme often taken up in our school re-treats. New arrivals into Years 1 and 2 had their own beginning-of-the-year three-day retreat in the front avenue area and, unlike the rest of the boys in the school, we were allowed to talk to one another and to play conkers with the chestnuts falling from the trees. Over the first few days in the school there was a 'period of grace' during which the college rules were not fully in oper-ation. This meant that the older boys engaged in all kinds of gambling games, including poker and 'pitch and toss', which took place under the trees near the ball alley and college farm-yard. However, at the end of the retreat the rules were read out very solemnly by the Dean and from then on one ran the hazard of being punished if school rules were infringed. These rules outlawed gambling, smoking, being late for class or meals, and not getting up in the morning. One of my earlier shocks in school was learning that there was such a thing as corporal pun-ishment. One day in my first week or so I heard the swishing of a cane in a room around the corner of a corridor. Seeing some boys coming down the corridor in some pain, gasping and holding their hands after a 'four shot' or 'six shot', made me realise that this place was not as idyllic as I thought it was going to be.

My brother and I were assigned to 2B, a classroom in the depths of an area known as the 'catacombs'. It was a class of about twenty to twenty-four boys. My brother and I coasted along very freely for the first month or six weeks, having no difficulty in completing our school work in the first hour or so of study time. We could have coasted on quite easily in this class through our years in Castleknock but for the fact that we both had been found reading comics after an hour in the study hall on one particular study period. Our only excuse for doing so was that we had completed our homework. When I was called to see the Dean of Studies, he quizzed me about what I was learning from one class to another. Then quite suddenly he told me to go back down to the 2B classroom, collect my brother and our books, and proceed to the 2A classroom located in another part of the school. From then on neither my brother nor I had very much spare time in study periods.

My brother and myself were assigned to what were known as the 'scuts' tables in the dining room. These were three tables at the bottom end of the large dining room – at least it appeared large to us at that time. Looking down on us was a large painting of St Vincent de Paul tutoring two of the children of the de Gondi family, and portraits of some of the famous 'old boys 'of the college. We very quickly grew into the ritual of the school regime: the devouring of meals three times a day with an afternoon snack thrown in known as 'stale bun'. We all had assigned positions in the dining room. From the word go we could see our future for the next five years mapped out before us as we proceeded along the sequence of tables from first to sixth year. My memories of school meals were dominated by the annual ritual of our senior and junior rugby football teams walking into the refectory after the matches and being cheered uproariously by the whole school. Of course if we had won or beaten one of the other big teams in the competition there were extra decibels to the applause. Unfortunately for me, I experienced four finals during my five years in Castleknock but no victory through any of those years. I had to live vicariously on the folklore of what it was like to be in the school when one of our rugby teams won the Senior or Junior Rugby competitions.

In the college chapel we were also assigned positions at the start of each year, beginning near the door and moving up year by year nearer the sanctuary. Mass on feastdays stands out because of the solemnity of the High Mass: Deacon, Sub-Deacon, singing and a procession in and out of the church with sometimes a priest from outside preaching. With about seventeen priests working and living in the school, there was always a multiplicity of private Masses early in the morning. Pupils took their turn in serving Masses in the oratories in the school chapel area and elsewhere. Early morning Mass, weekday Mass at 7.20am and rosary at 4.15pm or thereabouts, punctuated each day. We spent a significant amount of time in the college chapel each week, all of which we appeared to take for granted.

### The Rhythm of the Seasons

As I look down now through the arches of the years I can sense that each year had its high points and low points. As 'scuts' in the lower part of the school we looked up to the seniors in every sense. As seniors we looked down on the juniors, expecting them to make way for us if we encountered them walking around the grounds. The school provided a very safe environment to mark our passage from childhood to adolescence to young adulthood. In contrast to the situation today, we were living in a quasi-monastic setting and were monitored in all kinds of ways by the Dean and the other priests on the staff. Passing from one year to another were kinds of 'rites of passage'. We were certainly protected from the harsher aspects of life but from time to time there were outbreaks of bullying, especially at the end of the summer term, which the school authorities came down hard on. Boys could also be very vindictive in the nicknames they gave to one another. My brothers and I seemed to escape this and we were known individually as 'Raff'.

The autumn, spring and summer terms had their own moments of excitement and moments of depression and boredom too. Coming back to college after three months' holidays was always exciting – linking up with school friends once again, finding out what teachers we were going to have for each class subject, getting our first game of football after the long summer break and so on. The silence during the three day school retreat was taken quite seriously by most of the boys. The retreat givers were usually seasoned Vincentian parish missioners with good stories to tell.

On the morning after the retreat was over, the school rules were read out with great solemnity. There was some benign encouragement – if you keep these rules, these rules will keep you innocent and happy – but there were also some severe warnings, especially to the seniors about the consequences of breaking bounds. The rules outlawing games of chance – 'pitch and toss' and poker – were in full force once again. Smoking was banned both inside and outside the house. We did not see much inconsistency in the prefects not being bound by this rule – smoking for the prefects was confined to the prefects' room, which always seemed to be filled with smoke.

Mid-term breaks had not arrived during my time in Castleknock but what we called Union Night did mark a midway stage through the autumn term. Our dining room was taken over by a few hundred pastmen to mark the birthday of the college. The boys were issued with 'bat and ball' – a slab of fruit cake and an orange' and some other fare which we devoured in the study hall. This was followed by class plays or sketches in which boys went as far as they could go to lampoon and caricature priests, teachers and some of the unpopular prefects. The writers of these sketches used all their ingenuity to escape the censorship of the Dean and hit hard at the eccentricities of the staff.

Coming near the end of the autumn term our actors and singers had an opportunity to express their talents in a Gilbert and Sullivan opera – *Iolanthe*, *The Gondoliers*, *H.M.S. Pinafore* and one year *The Student Prince*. Many hours of rehearsal took place before staging these productions. Younger boys, with their soprano voices intact, played the female parts. Running a co-operative venture with girls from Mount Sackville School nearby does not seem to have been considered as an option in the 1950s.

Coming back to Castleknock in early January brings back memories of arctic winds blowing across the campus. We did our best to keep wrapped up in overcoats, scarves and headgear as we walked around the grounds. Most years brought flu epidemics when there could be fifty or sixty boys in the infirmary. One bonus from all this was that we usually got up later through such times. Most of the excitement of the spring term was bound up with going to cup matches in Donnybrook or International matches in Lansdowne Rd. Memories of bouts of depression after cup defeats in Donnybrook and four cup final defeats in Lansdowne Rd linger on in my mind. I belonged to one of the first generation of boys that did not experience the euphoria of winning a rugby cup during my five years in 'Knock.

To some extent Castleknock College came into its own in the summer term – rolling green spaces dotted with mature trees in full bloom, the ivy façade of the old buildings nestled between the castle and the hill, summer games, tennis, basketball and the completion of the college leagues. Through four of my five years in Castleknock I had public exams to contend with – the Intermediate exam, which we did twice in 3A and 4A, the University Matriculation exam, which we did in fifth year, and the Leaving Certificate in sixth year. These exams were preceded by Union Day, which came at the end of May. Parents of the boys were milling about and the afternoon was interspersed with a gymnastics display, various sports events and the music of the No I Army Band. The day was rounded off by open air Benediction at the foot of the Castle with someone like the Papal Nuncio presiding. It was not a day I enjoyed very much. To some extent parents took over and it was more a day for the display of the latest fashions in dress or cars. As we moved into the senior house, boys' conversations would have been taken up with comments on the good looking sister of so and so or boasting about a date in the making, especially among the more sophisticated Dublin boys.

When the exams were over we gathered our goods and chattels together, made our early morning taxi journeys across the Phoenix Park, along the banks of the Liffey to Westland Row, boarded our steam trains to our various destinations, having notched up another 'successful year' at school. Three months holidays stretched out before us.

*Class, Study and Curriculum*

The teaching staff was composed of about twelve priests and twelve lay professors. There were no women teachers teaching major subjects in my time. With one notable exception there was very little pressure in the classroom. One completed one's study assignments and got a certain amount of verbal praise or blame for one's efforts. The notable exception I referred to above, taught through instilling fear and was in fact a bully. To escape his wrath or fear of being sent to see the Dean of Studies, one spent a disproportionate amount of study time making sure that his school assignments were complete. I will never forget the day in 4A when a burly student scowled back at this teacher after he had missed out on four or five topics and automatically found himself on four or five different lists: 'X, if you don't stop giving me looks of death I will bring you down to see the President', he bellowed at him.

In my early years I opted for physics rather than French, something I regretted later, and in my Leaving Certificate I took technical drawing by dropping history. My best subject in the Leaving Certificate was mathematics, in which I surprised myself and others by coming within a hair's breadth of 80%. My worst was Latin, which I just about passed. I progressed through the school, somewhere in the middle of the A stream, gaining book prizes in one particular year when I must have come in fifth or sixth place. The school reports were fairly reasonable all through school and I got used to taking public examinations from third year onwards. In fact, to some extent, I liked the challenge of the examinations.

There were quite extended study periods every day of the week, including Sunday, and certainly it was relatively easy to fall into a pattern of study in Castleknock, where the study periods were supervised by the priests of the college. In the Castleknock of the 1950s we didn't have the pressure of gaining a certain number of points to gain university entrance. It was in fact relatively easy to get university entrance either through the Matriculation exam, which many of us took in fifth year, or in buying the Matriculation off the Leaving Certificate. The overall attitude amongst the boys was not to take study too seriously. The ideal inculcated was someone who did his work in the classroom and who spent a good deal of time in various sporting, recreational activities. Many of the boys who did well in later life in various professions were late developers.

One of the most humorous teachers was Mr Albert Kearney, known as APK, the pseudonym he used as a regular contributor to *Dublin Opinion*. He taught mathematics and every so often he would carry on a conversation about a fictitious student called 'Noodle' who found difficulties. Noodle's problem was that he saw complexities where there were no complexities. In a famous article he wrote for the *Castleknock Chronicle* about Noodle, he said he often met this student in later life and that he was now employing ten mathematical experts in his business to deal with matters mathematical. The implication was that not being too successful in maths would not stop Noodle getting to the top of the financial ladder. Mr Kearney had a constant look of bewilderment on his moustached face – bewilderment at the constant responses of his pupils to mathematical problems. At a house exam at the end of the autumn term in my second year in Castleknock he marked 'copied' at the end of one of my answers. He also wrote the same on a similar answer in my brother's answer book. He suspected that one of us had copied from the other and his way of finding out was to wait and see which of us would protest most.

Another of our teachers was Mr Gerry Muldowney, known to all of us as 'the Jer'. His classes were also pretty lively. We copied down maps he drew of France and Italy on the large blackboard in the 4A classroom in which he inserted symbols for the various kinds of produce, such as wine, coal and manufacturing. His constant refrain to individual pupils was, 'Murphy, if you cannot look intelligent do try to look happy.'

Other teachers included Mr Michael Ferriter who hailed from the Galway Gaeltacht. He did his best to communicate his love for the Irish language to us. (I learned later that he had played football for the Galway Senior team in 1938.) In my case my command of spoken Irish diminished year by year and I never recovered the facility I had in this language when I was leaving the National School at the age of twelve.

Among the best priest teachers in my day were Larry O'Dea for science, Brendan Steen for maths and Tom O'Flynn for

English. Tommo's classes would go off in all kinds of directions. He did not believe in sticking to a syllabus but he did cover the essentials. His pupils did in fact get very good results in examinations. The second half of most of his class would end up in a lively debate about some current political topic. The more opposition he could provoke on a particular topic the better he liked it. He had the reputation of being absent-minded and would turn up for class, it was said, with two different coloured socks, leading to the appellation 'Tom Sock' from one particular class of pupils. He would arrive and leave early for cup matches in Donnybrook, leading to the disclosure on one particular day after a cup match that he thought the opposing side had won. He was not aware that Knock had scored a winning try in the last minute of the game. From one point of view, Tom O'Flynn's classes were chaotic, but I would take the view that he and Fr Donal Cregan were two of the best educationalists in the school and were responsible for many of the developments in the school through the 1950s.

My brother and I moved in our own different circles in Castleknock. My brother tended to be part of the core gang in the year, boys who mixed around a lot and the centre of most activities on the sport pitch and elsewhere. I tended to link up with a small group of three boys who were more or less on the margin of things and we walked around the grounds together. Sometimes on free days we would go to a movie in town together. Our class and year group had a number of very bright boys not all of whom came top of the class. We also had a number of 'characters' with a very lively sense of humour that kept teachers on their toes with all kinds of questions. Most of the teachers knew that they were being taken for a ride and played along with the game.

*Sports: Rugby, Soccer, Basketball, Tennis ...*

All pupils were expected to tog out and play football twice a week on Wednesdays and Saturdays, which were half days. Frequently one would also play football on Sunday afternoons. Recreational activities took place inside school grounds and it was only if one was representing the college in one or other sport that one left the college grounds. Because I never made any of the college teams under thirteens, under fourteens, junior or senior, I never had the experience of going to other schools playing competitively against them. In my early years in the school I played soccer a good deal with a group of boys who were keen on this game but in my final years I played on the seconds and played out-half and in some of the internal college league matches. Basketball was a game which I enjoyed very much. I was very keen on tennis. Because there was a limited number of courts available, one had to be lucky to get matches through the summer term. My best achievement was beating one of the college prefects in the senior competition when I was in fourth year, taking him to three sets and beating him. Quite a few people gathered around to watch the upstart from fourth year defeating this particular character. I got great pleasure out of this. With regards to indoor sports, billiards was a game most of us liked to play but again because of the limitation of billiard tables one was lucky to get a game from time to time. I can remember senior boys playing some games of cricket against another school – I think it was Belvedere – in my early years at school. I don't think the notion that one would be regarded as 'West British' if one played cricket had much to do with its demise in Castleknock. With the short summer term, and increasing emphasis on examination successes, cricket faded out.

As I was slightly built as a school boy, I accepted quite easily the fact that I was in the second league in regard to rugby football. I came to admire those with greater skills than I had and their courage in all the give and take of rough and tumble competitive matches.

The memory of my brother playing full-back against the team that A. J. O'Reilly led at semi-final level in 1954 lingers on in my mind, as do the efforts of a shoulder-padded Barney Brogan to pin down Tony O' Reilly through most of the match. My brother put up a reasonably good performance playing full-back, although O'Reilly sent him diving the wrong way at a key moment in the latter part of that particular game. On another occasion in this match my brother and a winger hesitated between them as to who was going to field a ball. The delay led to the winger's kick being blocked down and one of the Belvedere backs went through to score. The final result of this match was

Belvedere 11, Castleknock 3. Belvedere were defeated by Niall Brophy's Blackrock team in the final. Tony O'Reilly got his place on the Irish team the following year.

Was the school too orientated to rugby in the 1950s? It is true that boys who had no interest in football had very limited opportunities in how they would use their free time. I think too much pressure was put on them to turn out on the football pitches twice a week. However, there is a lot to be said for a certain amount of good physical exercise for young people and being given an opportunity to participate in team sports. Boys themselves have ways of curbing excessive individualism. This could happen on the sports pitch as well as in other contexts too.

*Religious and Church Influences*
Apart from Sunday Mass and daily Mass on five or six days each week, each academic year in Castleknock was punctuated by religious feastdays. These feastdays were either feastdays of the church, such as November 1st, All Saints, December 8th, The Immaculate Conception, March 17th, St Patrick's Day, Ascension Thursday, or Vincentian feastdays such as that of Blessed John Gabriel Perboyre and Blessed Francis Clet – both martyred in China and recently canonised, St Catherine Labouré, The Translation of the relics of St Vincent de Paul, marking the installation of the mortal remains of St Vincent in the Chapel of the Congregation's headquarters on 95 rue de Sevres, Paris. These feastdays were celebrated by a solemn High Mass with all the pomp and circumstance of the pre-Vatican II liturgies – processions, incense, priest, deacon and sub-deacon and very often a special sermon given by a visiting priest. The 'sacred dance' of these High Masses, with some beautiful singing from the choir, enthralled our minds and senses. The fact that these feastdays were free from the drudgery of class, a slap-up meal with lemonade and tipsy cake and a movie in the evening, were added reasons why we looked forward to these feastdays.

The three-day retreat at the beginning of each year and a one-day retreat in the spring term were taken very seriously. Boys would walk around the grounds on their own, read Catholic Truth Society pamphlets or the life of some saint, have our meals in silence and attend all the religious services and talks conducted by the retreat giver. Small radios had not yet arrived to distract us. These retreats must have been particularly difficult for the extroverts amongst us and I am sure they found ways of passing the time. The sermons would have played variations on the eternal truths of death, judgement, hell and heaven – most of the retreat-givers were seasoned parish missioners. They may not have reached the intensity of James Joyce's sermon on hell in *The Portrait of the Artist as a Young Man*. Nevertheless, we were confronted with a world of good and evil and instructed that the only worthwhile thing in life was to save our immortal souls.

Backing all this through our first three years in the college was our initiation into various sodalities. The first was the sodality of the Sacred Heart, which we were admitted to in our first and second years. There was a monthly meeting on the first Friday of each month in which we were strongly urged to make reparation for our own sins and the sins of others.

In our 4th year we were admitted to the Children of Mary sodality, each of us being given a sizeable silver Miraculous Medal with a blue ribbon. We were encouraged to regard this medal as our most proud possession for the rest of our lives. The Vincentian priests introduced us to the origin of the medal in the apparitions to St Catherine Labouré in the rue du Bac in the middle of the 19th century and the subsequent promulgation of the dogma of the Immaculate Conception by Pius IX in 1854.

The third group some of the boys were admitted to was that of the Pioneer Total Abstinence Association. My own motives for joining were a little bit suspect because I knew that members of this association in the college got out to town on a particular Sunday in October for a rally in Croke Park. I have some memories of going out to town but no memories of going to the rallies. I kept this pledge until the day I knew I was going to spend three years in continental Europe, doing postgraduate studies in philosophy. I convinced myself that keeping the pledge was not feasible as wine would be the customary drink at meals in Belgium where I was going. The drink on offer turned out to be table beer. However, I found myself living right beside the Stella Artois factory and with fellow Louvain students learned how to sample this brew in double quick time. Anyway, I was to discover later that there were very few religious actions that I took that were not shot through with a good deal of self-interest.

Two incidents of a religious nature took me outside the college during my five years there. The first took place in my first year when myself and my brother and two other boys were confirmed by Archbishop John Charles McQuaid in the parish church in Celbridge. The college Dean, Fr Kevin O'Kane, drove the four of us down to Celbridge and then gave us permission to go into Dublin that afternoon to celebrate. I can remember very little about the confirmation ceremony or of feeling any euphoria about becoming a 'soldier of Christ'. The second incident took place in my final year in Castleknock in 1954, which had been declared a Marian Year by Pius XII. To gain the plenary indulgence the whole school marched to the church in Porterstown, a mile and a half from the college. I can remember that it was a beautiful spring day. We filled up the small church in Porterstown and were led in prayer to fulfil the required Our Fathers and Hail Marys to gain the plenary indulgence.

Beginning on Ash Wednesday and running through the Wednesdays of Lent, we had a special spiritual pep talk about either Christian virtues to be acquired or vices to be avoided. This took place at the unearthly hour of 7.00 am and meant getting up twenty minutes ahead of schedule. I have a vague memory of all of us going bleary eyed into the college study hall to listen to this talk and then heading off for Mass in the college chapel. Was this practice an offshoot of some religious practice Vincentian priests engaged in or a carry over from some Minor Seminaries in France? I am not sure. I think it had the effect of leaving some of us in bad form for the rest of the day, having missed twenty minutes of our beauty sleep.

With all of the above there is no doubt that a strong religious framework ran through our lives in Castleknock. With 16 or 17 priests on the staff from year to year and with the strong religious sensibility in Ireland through these years, this is not surprising. Were we force-fed with religion or was there religious indoctrination? Things did not come across to us like that. In the country at large the Catholic religion was part of the air we breathed and there was a unity of purpose between home, parish and a school like Castleknock. Secondly, though the priests could be demanding in the classroom, or even on the rugby pitch, they did not come across to us as arrogant or heavy handed. There was in fact a very easy relationship between most of the priests and the boys in the school. The fact that many of them were between the ages of twenty-five and forty and the fact that there were always a few 'scut Vins', Vins recently ordained, on the staff of the college, some of whom played Rugby with the seniors on a few occasions through the year, helped to build up good relationships between the boys and the priests on the staff of the college.

*Movies*
In the Ireland of the early 1950s we were living in a pre-TV age. At home we may have had access to radio but as far as Castleknock was concerned we also lived in a pre-radio stage. The only group who had access to radio was the prefects and some technologically minded boys who could tune into Radio Luxembourg on transistor radios underneath the bedclothes at night. In post-war Ireland the world of film had opened up in a big way with cinemas in nearly every town in the country and a continual stream of movies coming in from Hollywood and Ealing Studios in London. Through my time in Castleknock we must have had on average 20 to 25 movies each year. These movies lifted us out of the mundane world of school life and fed our fantasy world. After supper on a Sunday evening or on a free day, we carried chairs from the dining room into the play hall and watched an evening's entertainment which usually consisted of a *Tom and Jerry* cartoon, a twenty or thirty minute documentary and a feature film. The films were projected onto a reasonably large screen from a projection box outside the play hall. The quality of sound was also reasonably good.

From the *Castleknock Chronicles* of my time, 1949-1954, I learned that the movies shown in my time could be divided into five categories:
- War Movies: *The Wooden Horse; Objective Burma; Operation Pacific*
- Westerners: *She wore a Yellow Ribbon; High Noon*
- Humour: Marx Brothers – *A Day at the Races;* Alec Guinness – *The Man in the White Suit*

- Thrillers: Spencer Tracy in *North West Passage*; Alan Ladd in *Appointment with Danger*
- Others: *Bambi; Fr Flanagan's Boys Town; Tom Brown's School Days; Lorna Doon; Quo Vadis*

From this cross section of movies one can see that there was a good representation of movies that have stood the test of time. These movies fed our imaginations. Sometimes they led to a prefect earning another nickname. One of our tallest prefects earned the name of Bambi. They introduced us to British and American brands of humour. They brought alive some of the horrors of the Second World War though many of these movies glamorised the allied victories and demonised Germans. The Westerns fed our hunger for heroes – macho though many of these heroes may have been.

Some of our English teachers did some analysis of these movies in class afterwards, helping us to formulate criteria to distinguish between good and bad movies. However, I believe educational opportunities were missed to take film appreciation further, which I believe did come about a decade or so later.

Looking forward to a good evening's movie entertainment was one of the delights of life in Castleknock. Recovering from the depression that hit us when the movie was over and a week's class stretching out in front of us was one of the low points of our days in school.

*Holidays from School*

Holiday periods from school were eagerly looked forward to, as indeed were getting back to school especially when the long summer holidays were over. I have very vivid memories of leaving Castleknock in taxis at six or seven o'clock in the morning to get trains from Westland Row to the West of Ireland. The Dean was in his element marshalling the troops to get them away in time to catch their trains. I forget how long the journey took across Ireland. Our train travelled through Mullingar, Roscommon and Ballymoe station, which has since closed. One or other of our parents was there to meet us at Ballymoe. This train would go on further to Castlebar, Ballina and Westport. My memories of the journey are of a continuous poker school beginning in

Westland Row and tapering off as we lost a few students at each station.

It was quite a change returning to small town life in Glenamaddy, contrasting as it did with the new life opening up for us at school in Dublin. We were a bit of a novelty in the town because most of our peer group were going to St Jarlath's in Tuam or Garbally in Ballinasloe. A little more pressure was put on now to help out in the shop or in the bar, especially at busy times. My overall memory is that we had an enormous amount of free time to use in whatever way we wanted. Reading and going to the cinema in Roscommon town, partly owned by my uncle, John Rafferty, were our main pastimes during these holiday periods. At a very young age we were trusted to drive the family car and with so little traffic on the roads at that time it was quite easy to navigate the roads to Roscommon, Galway and sometimes to Dublin. Having just acquired a driving licence at the age of seventeen, I have very distinct memories of my father asking me to drive him across part of the city of Dublin, negotiating traffic lights. This was a real baptism of fire for me.

During the summer holidays we got involved quite a bit in farming activities, making the hay and, in one particular year, cutting turf. I remember spending three or four days in a very warm summer footing turf in a bog near Kiltullagh Lake and feeling great afterwards having engaged in this manly activity. I remember going out to shoot for the first time with a rifle and having very mixed feelings after I shot a rabbit that probably had myxomatosis and couldn't move very rapidly. I had no hankering for shooting animals after that.

On one particular summer holiday, when I was aged fifteen or sixteen, I took off with three or four others to climb Croagh Patrick at night. The attraction for me was climbing a mountain and I don't think I had any whiff of religious motivation in doing this. It was a tough climb and it rained on the way up. Seeing the sunrise at dawn from the top certainly gave me a great attraction for mountain climbing from then on. One of the girls in the group was a seventeen or eighteen year old who later joined the Ursuline Sisters. My memory is that two adult members of the group practically carried her up the mountain. My own self interest at this particular time probably obscured the relevance of what I was doing as a pilgrimage experience but I have clear memories of the crowds of people that were on the mountain that particular night and jostling for climbing space on both the ascent and descent. Over the last forty years I have climbed Croagh Patrick about ten times and on about half those occasions I marvelled at the view one gets of the islands in Clew Bay.

On another occasion during my summer holidays, probably when I was fourteen or fifteen, I went with my mother, an aunt from Dublin, her daughter Margaret and my sister Mary on a tour of Connemara. We began by visiting some friends in the Ursuline Convent in Sligo. That particular day we travelled out to Lough Gill to what today is the site of St Angela's College. For the very first time I was struck by the physical beauty of the scenery. I'm not sure that I was familiar with W. B. Yeats' *Lake Isle of Innisfree* at this time, but the beauty of the wooded scenes beside the lake certainly stayed with me ever afterwards.

From Sligo we travelled west to Belmullet and from there down the west coast to Mulrany. Eventually we finished up in the Ashford Castle area. I forget where we stayed that night but we certainly had a meal in Ashford Castle. Again I was over-awed by the splendour of the dining room looking out on the lakes.

Early in September 1952 I accompanied my mother to the Sacred Heart School in Roscrea with my sister Mary who was just about to begin school there. Some years later when I read Edna O'Brien's *A girl with green eyes* it reminded me of this school and I could not get away from seeing my sister's life there, in terms of the three youngsters in the novel and the pranks they got up to, especially their clashes with the authorities. For whatever reason I could only imagine my sister's life in the Sacred Heart convent school in Roscrea through the eyes of Edna O'Brien.

Another summer holiday I spent in Dublin, staying with my aunt and uncle in Terenure. Through a two or three week period I cycled all over Dublin: to the Phoenix Park and the Dublin mountains where I climbed up to the Hellfire Club. A good deal of that holiday was spent in the Leinster cricket grounds where I played cricket with my cousin and some of his friends. I was about the age of fifteen or sixteen at this time. I also cycled out to Bray where I climbed Bray Head once again. I had been there three or four years previously.

In the early 1950s an enterprising assistant bank manager came to Glenamaddy and built a tennis court on a field owned by my parents. This grass court was never up to Wimbledon standards but it provided a number of summers of very good tennis for me and my brothers and our age group around the town. In my final year at home before I left for Blackrock, my brother and I played for a team in a competition in Galway city in a tennis club on Threadneedle Road, near Taylor's Hill. My memory of this occasion was that I was beaten in a singles match.

In the summer of 1954 I went on a pilgrimage to Lourdes with my mother and my sister Mary. We flew Aer Lingus to Paris where we spent a few days and took the train from there down to Lourdes. It was quite a traumatic time for me because I was still in the throes of trying to firm up my decision to join the Vincentians. I had indicated to a number of people that this is what I had intended to do but I realised that I still had room for manoeuvre before taking the final step. Of course, I was en-thralled by the processions in Lourdes and the display of popu-lar piety, the choreography of the daytime procession and of the candlelight procession in the evening, but I was also attracted to the fact that Lourdes was near very high mountains. I did a little bit of exploring in Lourdes but not that much because it was hard to know at that time how one could get near the very high mountains. I took all the pilgrimage activities in my stride: Stations of the Cross, processions, but I baulked at taking the customary ice-cold bath near the Grotto. However, without telling anybody, I did do so on my last day in Lourdes and felt chuffed with myself afterwards.

### The World at Large:1949-1954

From 1949 through the first part of the 1950s Europe was being reconstructed after the wartime destruction of many cities. Germany was going forward economically at a great rate under the leadership of Chancellor Konrad Adenaeur. The Conservative Government in Britain had come back into power under the leadership of Winston Churchill. The Suez Crisis occurred in which Anthony Eden lost his head in nearlt every sense of the word. The Royal Festival Hall was opened in London in 1953. In the same year, the young Queen Elizabeth took over the throne in England on the death of her father. Hillary and Tenzing climbed Mount Everest. Stanley Matthews won a football cup medal for the first time. In Ireland the Mother and Child scheme of Doctor Noël Browne got the thumbs down from the bishops, and John Charles McQuaid was in full flight with his various social work schemes as well as beginning to build a whole string of new churches and schools around the city of Dublin. Under pressure from Archbishop McQuaid, the Vincentians opened St Paul's College, Raheny, in 1950 and sent some of their newly ordained men of that year to staff the college. The numbers coming into seminaries was still very high and many seminaries and religious orders were planning and beginning to build new houses of formation or new houses of studies, all of which were becoming 'white elephants' some fifteen years later. One could see this period of the 1950s in Ireland as the golden age of triumphalist Catholicism. It was a church with a very centralised authority at every level, with enormous control over people's lives. Its missionary endeavours were expanding on all fronts all over the world.

The following were discussed at the meetings of the college Senior Debating Society and reflect the political, economic and social concerns of the time:

- Strikes should be decreed illegal
- That foreign games should not be played in Ireland
- That the old school tie is out of date in the modern world
- That those suspected of communism be deprived of positions of influence in society
- That the building of a new road from Dublin to Bray is an unwarranted extravagance
- That the importing of English Sunday newspapers should be stopped
- That patriotism in the Irish character leaves much to be desired
- That Britain should get out of Egypt
- That Irishmen are unfairly presented in films

- That a new approach to the Irish langage revival is necessary
- That American influence in Europe is damaging

I have drawn the above from the *Castleknock College Chronicles* 1949-1954. I was astonished by how relevant some of these topics are to us today – American influence in Europe, a new road from Dublin to Bray, Irish identity and so on. We continue to debate some of these topics in a new social, economic and political context. In the framing of some of the motions, one can detect that some of the issues under discussion are being seen from the angle of some of the privileged groups in Ireland of that time rather than from the side of the under-privileged and impoverished people of the 1950s. The accounts of these school debates make fascinating reading and it would be an interesting exercise to compare the views of some of these 16, 17, and 18 year olds with their career options and views they have held in later life.

There are also a number of interesting views expressed in the accounts of the Castleknock College Pastmen's Union through these years. A Discussion Circle seems to have flourished through the 1950s in which aspects of the relationship between church and state were discussed. A moral theologian from Maynooth, Dr John McCarthy, read a paper on the *Role of Church and State in relationship to marriage* and a Vincentian, Dr Gerard Shannon, read a paper on the *Strengths and Weakness of Communism*. A number of pastmen took part in a public march in O'Connell Street to protest at the imprisonment of Archbishop Stepinac in Hungary. There was an awareness among the members of this Discussion Circle of the importance of bringing 'the light of the gospel to bear on their professional activities' and all this was seen in the framework of what was called Catholic Action at that time. One can sense a desire among a number of pastmen, especially men in the legal and medical professions, to raise the level of discussion about a number of social and political matters in the Ireland of the 1950s. One would love to know where a number of them stood when the proverbial matter hit the fan after the debacle of Noël Browne's Mother and Child scheme!

*Decision for Priesthood*

The decision to become a priest had been maturing slowly in my mind through my time in secondary school. The example of some idealistic seminary students from my hometown of Glenamaddy a few years older than me, who had gone to Maynooth, Clonliffe and Dalgan Park, would certainly have influenced me. So many of us during the 1950s were drawn naturally into priesthood because it was regarded as a very worthwhile way to spend our lives. There was plenty of scope for idealism of all kinds in the priesthood. In my final year I discussed with Father Tom O'Flynn my decision and he encouraged me to go forward. Through my last year or two in Castleknock I committed myself to going to daily Mass through Lent and kept this up when I was at home on holidays. This was not too unusual. Boys from across the spectrum in Castleknock, including some of the good rugby players, did this too.

I never considered joining any order other than the Vincentians. The natural thing seemed to be to join the group of priests who were running Castleknock. Of course it would have been said to me that Vincentians in the Irish province were engaged in all kinds of work which would suit me. I would also have been influenced by Castleknock boys in the years ahead of me joining the Vincentians. Through the 1950s there was an average of four or five boys entering the Blackrock novitiate from Castleknock each year. In my year, 1958, this increased to eight. However, there was also a notable drop out of Castleknock boys from the seminary in Blackrock at this time too.

Looking back on my decision, it would probably have been better if I had gone to the university for a few years. The question never even arose in my mind at the time and nobody encouraged me to think along those lines. It seemed to be the natural thing to make this decision at the age of eighteen and, to some extent, to burn one's boats. At the same time we all knew that there was a considerable amount of risk in all this – what would have been perceived as the risk of failure. I had a final interview with the President of the school, Father Donal Cregan. He asked me what I was going to do and I told him that I was hoping to join the Vincentians. He did not seem to be too surprised and my guess is that he had learnt about this from other quarters. I had visited the novitiate in Blackrock a number of times because my elder brother had joined the Vincentians in 1952. I had an idea of the regime there. However, what lay ahead was quite unknown to me.

If I had to go through the battery of tests that seminarians have to go through today, I doubt very much if I would have got through. I'm very sure I would have been told to see a bit more of life before making this decision for priesthood. At the same time I have always been convinced that, even at the age of eighteen, one can still make a good decision for priesthood. Looking on things now, I would see the decision as making a fundamental option for truth and beauty and goodness or indeed endorsing a series of fundamental options I had already made. It was a decision to spend one's life idealistically rather than a religiously motivated decision to promote the kingdom of God. It was like climbing Croagh Patrick once again but now there was some religious motivation involved. In the Ireland of 1955 Christianity was the framework of our existence. Being an active member of the church was taken for granted. In that context, opting for priesthood was seen as an honourable and praiseworthy way to spend one's life. In my family circle there was a great esteem for priesthood and religious life and there were enough good role models around, both at home and at school, who convinced me that it was a worthwhile path to follow.

*Retrospect: Looking back 50 years later*
Throughout my time in Castleknock College I felt privileged in being a pupil of the school. We were aware that the school had a long tradition and that it had a good reputation. For over 100 years Vincentians had worked hard to build up this tradition. During my school days there were up to sixteen young Vincentians on the staff who shared in all aspects of the life of the school: teaching, football and debating. The relationship between the boys and the priests was a very friendly one. There was always good banter or exchange in the classroom. By 1950s standards, there were very good sports facilities in the school. Mixing with pupils from all ranges of professional life and the business world certainly broadened our horizons about what we might do in our lives. I played around with the idea of becom-

ing an architect for a number of years in the senior school and this was the reason I chose to do technical drawing. At the same time, in the Ireland of the mid 1950s so much would have depended on whether one's parents could have supported one in the university or in gaining entry into one of the professions. In my case, opting for priesthood bypassed these kinds of questions.

By the time I got to Castleknock it had clocked up over 100 years of tradition. It was one of the oldest secondary boarding schools in the country, in competition with six or eight other fee-paying boarding schools run by religious orders. What we did not realise at the time was that the school was coming near the end of its successes on the rugby pitch – only two cups were to come its way through the following fifty years. But more seriously, it was going to have to take a hard look at its curriculum and teaching methods if it was to remain in competition for university and third-level colleges. Looking back now with the perspective of fifty years, one can see the Castleknock of the 1950s as a kind of golden age. It was in fact to be the end of an era. In a relatively short time the college would be faced with a whole set of new challenges from a rapidly changing society and from a church shaken to its roots by the Second Vatican Council.

At this stage it would be very easy to evaluate the school of the 1950s by our standards fifty years later. The advantages or disadvantages of it being a single sex school, the merits and demerits of boarding schools, the quality of education, the choice of subjects, the monitoring of progress, over-emphasis on rugby or outdoor sports. By the standards of the 1950s it measured up quite well. And under the outstanding leadership of Fr Donal Cregan, I can very well understand how many of my contemporaries might regard the 1950s as the golden age of the school. Be that as it may, perhaps there is a sense in which our school days are everybody's golden age. For each one of us our schooldays are unique. There is a sense in which we never escape them. As we look back we sense that there were opportunities grasped and opportunities missed. It is a time of soul making. As we look back we can sense moments of achievement. Moments of euphoria and moments of genuine well-being. We can also sense moments of failure or moments where tragedy lurked around the corner. The illustrations depicting the 'Road to Ruin' on one of the walls of the senior play hall were joked about. Now and again a little information would leak through about a former pupil 'crashing' in one way or another.

We had a reunion of our class in 1985 and 2007. It was fascinating to see the variety of professions that my class had joined: Psychiatry, Legal Profession, Barrister/Solicitor, Farming, Horse breeding, Teaching, Veterinary Medicine, Dentistry, Property Developer, Auctioneer, University Administrator, Bank Manager, Hotelier, Company Director, Publican, University Lecturer, Anaesthetist, Accountant, The British Navy, Priesthood, Investment Banker, and businesses of all kinds, inside and outside of Ireland. The fact that our class group only met twice meant that the friendships between boys in my class year were more on a one-to-one basis than on a group basis. Other class groups meet more regularly, some annually and others on a five or ten year basis.

As regards my own personal development in the school, I could probably have acquired more confidence in public speaking situations and in being able to hold my own in a group. As an eighteen year old I tended to be shy and retiring, yielding the floor on most occasions to my twin brother and others. At the same time I had acquired a degree of independence to make my own decision about what I was going to do with my life. When I left school a whole new world was opening up before me. To a great extent it was going to be a journey inwards – at least for the first year or two.

With the passage of the years memory begins to fade and my five years in the school begin to coalesce into one another. Nevertheless some images and memories do linger on:

- seeing Bro Michael O'Sullivan in his well-worn black clothes cycling across the crease, brandishing a stick at his turkeys and followed by his faithful dog called 'Rebel'
- hearing the Guinness Clock chiming out the time on a summer's night when everyone had quietened down in the dormitory and sleep was slow in coming
- being tongue-tied at a Senior Impromptu Debating Society meeting when not a syllable would cross my lips
- inhaling the strong scent coming from the refrigerator in the

Pavilion building as the doors opened for an ice cream sale

- Listening to Fr Kevin O'Kane announcing in a strong voice *Bendicamus Domino* as he came swishing through the door into Holy Angels dormitory and watching him sailing through with his cape half hanging off his shoulders

As the years come and go I am left with a deep sense of gratitude to my contemporaries – fellow pupils, teachers and staff – for opening up a variety of worlds to me and for giving me a sense of being at home there. It is fashionable today to look back on the 1950s as a grim grey decade. From our perspective it was a time of frugal living for many people. In Castleknock we were protected from the harsher aspects of Irish society – unemployment, emigration and lack of educational opportunities. There was a certain carefree quality to our lives in the school. We were not pushed too hard academically or in any other way. We got a good start along the path of discovering our true talents and gifts.

# CHAPTER 3

# Into Blackrock/Out to University College Dublin
# 1954-1958

*Joining the Vincentians*

My decision to join the Vincentian Congregation was based on very little hard information about their works universally or in the Irish Province. I was not encouraged to read a life of Saint Vincent de Paul or any other literature before entering, and apart from knowing that they taught in places such as Castleknock and St Paul's College, Raheny, I had no knowledge of their works in Ireland or England or elsewhere in the world. Nor indeed had I any knowledge of other orders or congregations. It would be true to say that 'I drifted into the Vincentians' and it seemed at the time to be the natural thing to do. The fact that one of my elder brothers had already joined two years earlier may have had some influence on me. Completely independently of me, my twin brother also decided to join the Vincentians. It was quite late in the summer of 1954 when I became aware of this and like many others I was surprised. Each of us had gone our own way in Castleknock, mixing with different groups of friends, and I doubt if there was any secret telepathic communication between us.

The fact that I was leaving home in September and not likely to be returning for eight years until I was ordained – this was the rule at the time – certainly added a good deal of nostalgia to this final summer in Glenamaddy. There was a party on the night before we left in which the O'Regans and McDermotts participated – one member from each of these families also entered seminaries in the autumn of 1954, Michael McDermott going to Holy Cross College, Clonliffe and Barney O'Regan coming late to join the Vincentians in Blackrock. The last film I went to with one or two others was *Shane* in the Astoria Cinema in Galway. I remember going to Tycooly a few days before 3 September and saying goodbye to the Connolly family. I also did the same in Roscommon with my relatives there. Even though I was only going as far as Dublin, there was something of the American wake about the departure of my brother and myself from Glan to the Vincentian seminary a hundred miles away on the outskirts of Dublin city.

*Entering a clerical world ...*

Our cousin, Danny Connolly, drove my parents, my brother and myself to Dublin on 3 September 1954, the day we were due to check into the seminary. We arrived there in the evening around six or seven o'clock and were met by Father James Cahalan, the Director of Students at the time. There were a lot of people milling around because twelve students, a bumper number for the Vincentians, were due to begin the two year novitiate. The group included six school leavers from Castleknock, a number from St Patrick's College, Armagh and other schools. One of the men expected from Armagh did not arrive because his mother could not live with the idea of him leaving home without returning for this eight year stretch. His name was Arthur McCrystal. He joined All Hallows and was ordained seven years later for an English diocese. However, our number was supplemented by one or two more in the following weeks, enabling us to hold onto the title of the twelve apostles – the title given us by the priest who directed our opening retreat. A constant theme in conversations amongst us over the next few months was which of us was going to play Judas.

Later that evening we were installed in cubicles in a very Spartan dormitory and the next day we began a five day retreat. The emphasis over these first few months was on 'leaving the world' and burning our boats. Each of us had bought a new soutane in Clery's but we were all given a second-hand soutane which we wore every day apart from Sunday. God knows how many people had worn it before we did. We were also issued with birettas. Learning how to wear it properly and learning also how to take it off when being addressed by one of the priests was one of the first lessons we learned over the first few days. On 8 September we met the rest of the student group who were on an eight day retreat. By the time all of us had arrived our number amounted to between thirty-five and forty. I knew a number of the students who had been ahead of us at Castleknock College. It took our group quite a while to settle down because we had a few jokers in our midst who enabled us to see the funny side of things.

On the afternoon of 8 September we all donned our black suits and hats for the first time, including two-inch Roman collars, and walked two by two to the Forty Foot. On the way many people saluted us and we found this very hard to get used to. Wearing all this black gear it is not surprising that we were treated as a race apart – out of touch in every sense of the expression.

*'Re-birth – Finding oneself and God'*
All through this first year, which was an intensive year of spiritual formation, there was a very detailed programme of spiritual exercises to be followed each day. There was an hour's prayer, beginning at six o'clock in the morning, then Mass, followed by various spiritual exercises, classes, spiritual reading, with periods in the afternoon of working on the farm or around the grounds. We worked out our frustrations on the football pitch on two occasions each week, playing either rugby, Gaelic football or soccer. These games were played with great intensity and vigour. There were no newspapers or radio available. Television had not yet arrived and we had to work out various ways of amusing ourselves. There was very little contact with our families or friends and visiting times were restricted, particularly in the first year, to a few occasions. Apart from the cooking of food, all the domestic tasks of keeping the house clean were looked after by the students themselves. The only books available to read were of a spiritual or self-improving nature. There was a good cross-section of spiritual classics but there was also some pious hagiography which should have been consigned to the dustbin. We were encouraged to read the various lives of Saint Vincent de Paul by Bougaud, Calvet, Maynard and Coste. Each year we had an eight day retreat in early September and over the first two years of the novitiate period there was a five day retreat at Easter. We met the Director of Students on a regular monthly basis to review our spiritual progress and address aspects of our behaviour that he might have concerns about. The rule of silence

was strictly observed, especially in the evenings, all of this having the purpose of inculcating a contemplative attitude to life. At various times during the day we could hear the bells of the Carmelite Convent next door to us calling the sisters to prayer, and on foggy evenings we could hear the Dún Laoghaire harbour fog horn warning ships about a fog descending. The nearest we came to 'sowing cabbages upside down' was copying the rules of the *seminaire* in Latin, known as the *Regulae* and reading Rodriguez each day, a distillation of the writings of the desert fathers on the spiritual life. Rodriguez was dry as dust and some of the stories he told about the ascetical practices of these monks beggared belief. Each week the Director gave us a spiritual conference for thirty to forty minutes which, in Father Cahalan's case, tended to be drawn from the letters of St Paul, of whom he was an enthusiastic student.

The Provincial and the Superior of the house lived in another part of the building and there were two or three other priests living in Blackrock in semi-retirement for health or for other reasons. One of them was a returned missioner from China who glided silently along the corridors and admonished us by whispering 'noisy brush' if he thought we were hitting the pipes too hard. We came to the conclusion that he had been living on his own for too long on a lonely mission in the Chinese countryside.

His eccentricities were a matter of amusement to us but deep down we were probably saying to ourselves, 'maybe we could go this way too'. The poor man died quite suddenly in 1957. The hour's Morning Prayer with his coffin in front of us between the choir stalls in the Blackrock chapel provided us with plenty to reflect on regarding the eternal verities.

In the autumn of 1956 our Superior General, Fr William Slattery, came to visit the Irish Province and he used Blackrock as his base of operations. He was accompanied by a small squat Frenchman called Fr Dulau. Fr Slattery was a saintly man who spoke to us about the importance of our spiritual preparation for our ministry as priests . As the successor of St Vincent he was held in great esteem by the Vincentians and Daughters of Charity who came to visit him. He was the first non-Frenchman to be elected as Superior General. The politics of an American presiding over the Maison Mère in Paris was lost on us students.

*Stoking the furnace*

First year seminarians usually took on the task of starting the furnace in the morning around five or five fifteen when it was desperately cold both inside and even more so outside during the winter months. The dust was horrific in this underground boiler room area below what we used to call the new wing. It took about ten minutes to light the two coal furnaces. For any-one with asthmatic problems this cannot have been too healthy. In my second or third year I found myself on the rota for this task two or three times in a short space of time. Deep down I felt it was unfair but said nothing about it. I had an idea that one of the directors was testing me out and I was not going to wilt under this kind of pressure. There may have been a more exalted motive that I was making giant strides along the 'road to sanctity' by enduring in silence.

*Projects and Diversions*

Throughout my four year period in Blackrock the students were always engaged in one or other development programme on the farm, or the walks, or something to do with the buildings. In my first and second year, my year group virtually took over the run-ning of the farm – milking cows, feeding pigs, looking after the poultry farm and so on. I have very distinct memories of learn-ing how to ring a hen's neck before plucking her feathers for the dinner table on a feastday. All this activity certainly provoked the comment from some of our priest visitors that we were more an agricultural college than an ecclesiastical seminary. It is true that our Director of Students for our first two years, Fr James Cahalan, had leanings towards being a farmer but I think that he also realised that this kind of activity was a good outlet for many of the students and it helped many of us to retain our sanity, helping us through the intense hothouse spiritual atmosphere that was Blackrock in our days. It was also an escape route for Fr Cahalan himself who carried nearly all the responsibility for the forty students in Blackrock.

These activities on the farm followed the rhythm of the sea-sons. We saved the hay and the corn in the summer, dug the potatoes in the autumn and sowed and planted in the spring. I remember some very cold days in October when we were digging potatoes in Stradbrook Hall nearby which at that time was the novitiate house of the Presentation Sisters. The novices brought out to us mugs of tea half way through the afternoon which helped us to keep body and soul together . Each of us was assigned a section of the grounds to look after, clipping bushes and planting flowers. To make sure we did not get too attached to these flowerbeds we switched around every six months. We also engaged in various building and renovating programmes, especially during holiday periods. 'Operation Lodge' – a complete overhaul of the entrance lodge at the main gate – was one task we engaged in.

I also have memories of being involved in the building of a tarmacadam walk along the river stream from Brookfield to the lake area through the month of August 1956. We had a Polish confrère, Fr Stawvorski, and a French confrère, Fr Bringer, joining us over these weeks who were learning English. Memories of putting down posts in concrete for a wire fence and tarring over the stones remain vividly in my mind. I can still remember the smell of the creosote we put on the wooden posts and the fumes that came from the heated tar. During that summer too we had a visiting confrère from Egypt who belonged to our Lebanese Province. He was an expert on Arabian philosophy, especially on Averroes and Avicenna. He had written a doctoral thesis on this subject in the Sorbonne in Paris. With my newly found interest in philosophy I was keen to learn more about Aristotle's influence on these Arabian philosophers which I was to learn more about later when I read Fernand van Steenberghen's *Aristotle in the West*.

On other occasions during these summer months we would have had young Vincentian priests from Colombia, S America or from Australia, staying at Castleknock or Blackrock when they were on holidays from their studies in Rome. Their main interest was learning English. In chatting to them we learned more about what the Congregation of the Mission was doing in a variety of countries throughout the world. One very memorable occasion in 1955 was listening to an Irish Vincentian, Fr Maurice Kavanagh, talking about his experiences as a prisoner in a Communist jail in Beijing after the takeover.

*Summer Holidays in Castleknock College*

We spent the month of July on holidays in Castleknock and we had the run of the grounds and sporting facilities. I have very good memories of intense competitive football matches between seminarists and the rest of the student group as well as between the Blackrock students and the Glenart students in Gaelic football. There were some epic matches and no quarter was given by either side.

During the summer of 1955 I spent a lot of time on the river Liffey, down below the Glenmaroon Guinness House beside the Strawberry Beds where I learned to swim. It was easy to be carried along by the current and eventually I learned how to stay afloat in the slow-moving river. This was good practice for swimming in the Forty-Foot in Sandycove. July 1955 was a glorious summer and we made the most of it.

Apart from the summer of 1958, which I spent preparing for my final BA autumn examinations, most of July and August was spent in Castleknock or Blackrock. Looking back on it, it is amazing that we were not asked to learn languages, especially French, during this time. One of my greatest regrets is that I was not permitted to go to France, and possibly Germany, to learn French and German. During these years the only people that went to learn French were Vincentian students who were doing French in their BA programme. It was a requirement of their university course that they spent some of the summer months in France. The intense physical and sporting activities we engaged in during three months of each summer were no doubt good for body and spirit but much more could have been done to enlarge our horizons culturally and pastorally. All of this was to come for Vincentian students some ten years later. Our lives were enclosed in all kinds of ways. Our only outlets were visits to other Vincentian houses such as All Hallows for plays, or visits to houses of the Daughters of Charity for slap-up meals as in Glenmaroon or St Teresa's, Blackrock, where we put on concerts to pay our way, so to speak. To relieve our isolation, some of the newly ordained Vincentians would come to visit us at Christmas. Sometimes they played a game of rugby with us and brought us up to date about the chances of Castleknock or St Paul's winning Senior or Junior cups in the spring.

*Students leaving the Seminary*

In my time about 30% of the student intake would leave at one or other stage on the way through, usually during their Blackrock days. These were very often the saddest days during our time there. We all felt very threatened when a very good student left and there would be no apparent reason why he did so. The reason why they left was not disclosed to us, presumably in case this would have unsettled the rest of us. Very often the Director of Students would announce that so and so had left. Whether he had left of his own accord or was encouraged to leave was never disclosed to us. We assumed that most of those who left arrived at the decision themselves. Very often when a student was about to leave it might have been preceded by a period of depression or the man being out of sorts. This was often the only way one had an inkling that a student was about to 'throw in the towel'. The cruellest part of all this was that there was no mourning period for friends who had left, people who had travelled with us through thick and thin for three or four years or indeed longer periods suddenly disappeared from our lives. There was something quite inhumane about this and I doubt it did very much for our human or spiritual development.

*Taking Vows*

At the end of our first year in Blackrock we made promises to continue on the path towards Vincentian priesthood and a year later our group took temporary vows for three years – vows of poverty, chastity and obedience. It was a simple ceremony that occurred during Mass on 8 September. The superior of the house was delegated to witness our taking these vows. We were carefully instructed about the implications of taking this step. The vows were being presented to us as ways in which we freed ourselves to engage in proclaiming the gospel in our time. Some Vincentians see themselves as diocesan priests living in community. Taking these vows was another stage on the way to priesthood for me and trying to live the Christian life at a deep level.

In so far as I had any crisis coming up to taking these vows, it was in relation to the dawning realisation that my reasons for being in the seminary and wanting to be ordained a priest contained a measure of self-interest. Whether through my own reading or through dialogue with spiritual directors, I came to realise that everything we do is done for a mixture of motives. The ambiguity in our motivation came home to me through reading Freud, Jung and other psychologists. I became more aware of how complicated our motivation can be in what we think are our disinterested actions.

As time went on I began to realise that 'purity of heart' – the ability to will one thing, as Kierkegaard defines it – was a life-long task.

## Death of my Parents

In the middle of February 1958 my mother was brought to St Luke's Hospital in Dublin. Cancer had been diagnosed and it was decided to operate three or four days later. The surgeon was Dr Eamon De Valera. Gradually my mother weakened and died at twelve o'clock on the morning of 26 February. I rushed over by bicycle from St Joseph's, Blackrock and was one of the last of the family to arrive. At this time my father was also quite ill with a heart condition but all my brothers and sisters were there except for my younger sister Margaret who was at school in the Sacred Heart Convent, Roscrea. Before dying, my mother insisted that the nurses who had looked after her be given a present of nylon stockings to thank them for their kindness to her. Like many mothers at that time she would have looked forward very much to having a son, or sons, ordained to the priesthood but this was not to be. With nurses in tears coming and going from the room, my mother faded into a coma and died a short time later.

A day later the funeral cortege set off from St Luke's. I was given the task of guiding the hearse out of Dublin. Many cars joined the cortege from Roscommon onwards and that evening we arrived in the town of Glenamaddy which was crowded with people who had come for the reception of the remains. Darkness had fallen on the town as the hearse arrived at Glenamaddy church. My brothers and sisters were surrounded by people sympathising with us in our loss. The next day the funeral Mass was celebrated by the Administrator, Fr Charlie Scahill. It was a solemn High Mass with two priests from neighbouring towns acting as deacon and sub-deacon. As was the custom at the time, there was no funeral homily. My mother was buried in a new plot in the new cemetery out beside the Lough on the Roscommon Road. As my father was not well, he did not attend the funeral but watched the funeral procession passing by from a window in his bedroom. After a meal in the afternoon we returned to Blackrock on that same day. That afternoon was the last time I saw my father alive. He had lost a lot of weight and everybody knew that he too was going to die in the fairly near future. My father lingered on until May and died on 13 May, three months later. Again the church was packed for the reception of my father's remains and for the funeral Mass on the following day. Apart from many people sympathising with me, my memories are of walking to the graveyard and myself and my three brothers carrying the coffin to the burial plot beside my mother. My mother was 56 years old when she died and my father was 54. These were very sad days for all our family.

My way of coping was to escape into preparing for my BA examinations coming up in the autumn. The death of my father hit my twin brother very hard. He felt he should have been allowed to visit my father on a number of occasions before he died and he expressed this quite firmly to the Vincentians in charge in Blackrock. I was fairly sure that his decision to leave was influenced by these exchanges.

*Final observations on formation in Blackrock*

Looking back over forty years on my formation in Blackrock is a painful exercise to engage in. I wonder if this is because it was in fact a very painful period in my life in which I was trying to get to know myself better. The lessons I had to learn about myself were not easy to take on board. Was I mature enough to engage in this kind of novitiate experience? I have no doubt I still had an awful lot of growing up to do and by today's standards I certainly would have been encouraged to see a little bit more of life before taking this step. Being of an introspective caste of mind, living through long periods of silence might not have been the best thing for me at the time. There is no doubt that it was a tough regime and quite a number of demands were made upon us in terms of enduring boredom and carrying through tedious exercises. I think the reason why a number of us came through was because of the peer group support that existed in the student body to the extent that somewhere in our psyches we were saying 'we'll defeat the system'. The man who came to be most responsible for our formation was the Director of Students. He was a very experienced and likeable man. However I would say that the Vincentian formation in Blackrock at this time was a very parochial and narrow system. I would sum up the deficiencies of the situation under the following headings:

- There was I think a latent Jansenism in a lot of French spirituality and the spirituality of Vincentians as it was experienced by us in the Blackrock of the 1950s. This could be expressed in terms of dualism or pessimism about human nature. There was very little understanding of spirituality in terms of wholeness – wholeness of mind and body, or what we call holistic spirituality today.
- Vincentian formation in the 1950s was anti-intellectual. Quotations from St Vincent about the dangers of intellectual life were pulled out of context in St Vincent's writings. On the one hand, we were being told repeatedly that our intellectual studies in the university could lead us to be puffed up with pride and, at the same time, we were in daily contact with university professors who were urging us to drink deeply of intellectual traditions in history, English, philosophy and other subjects. A number of them were on ego trips but others came across to us as balanced and humble men and women.
- A parochial spirit prevailed in regard to theological and liturgical developments in Continental Europe. We were cut off from exciting developments there. Vincentians acted in a very 'safe way' which meant that their students were not going to be exposed to anything that might threaten orthodoxy in any way.
- Our formation was a monastic formation and, of course, it wasn't any different to what was going on in many seminaries and houses of formation. It was hard to see any originality in the way retreats were organised. We had to endure so many tedious retreat conferences which did little to open up our minds and hearts to the riches of the Christian tradition.

There were one or two exceptions to this but overall retreats in Blackrock were uninspiring.

- We were asked to spend too much of our time in fruitless kinds of exercises. For instance, through practically every Wednesday in our first year we went for long walks beginning around 8.30 in the morning to destinations like Dalkey, Sandyford, Mount Merrion and Irishtown. We often sat at the back of some of these churches getting through some of our spiritual exercises and watching weddings taking place at the other end of the church and fantasising a little about what we might be missing out on.

- A constant theme running through conferences and retreats was that we were preparing to be 'evangelisers of the poor'. Through these four years of formation in Blackrock we had literally no contact with the poor or marginalised of Irish society. A walk through one of the estates near our house of formation or a bus trip to inner city Dublin could have remedied that. Becoming a Carthusian at home before becoming an apostle abroad appeared to be one of the guiding principles of our formation.

- There was no input on human development. Many of us were adolescent and little was done to promote our emotional development or to make us aware of ourselves as emotional beings. There was a belief that natural instincts could be sublimated – grace would perfect nature. The fact that so many could come through this system without deepening their own self-knowledge led to all kinds of limitations in their pastoral effectiveness later. It also led to less contentment in themselves and in their work.

- Like most of our contemporaries in seminaries, we were cut off from what was going on in the world around us. All this led to us being cut off from events in society. We were sheltered during this formative period in our lives from the harsher aspects of Irish life – the poverty of inner city Dublin, the thousands taking the emigrant boat to England, the United States and elsewhere and the difficulties of making ends meet for fathers and mothers of large families.

One might possibly argue that the essentials were in place in our formation system – an understanding Director of Students, plenty of silence so that we could really reflect deeply within ourselves, guidelines to begin a prayer life that would sustain us through a life of ministry and a sense of identity with a world-wide congregation inspired by the life and teachings of St Vincent de Paul. It is easy to draw up a balance sheet – positive and negative – of my Blackrock period. Our formation, like formation in many seminaries, needed a good shake-up. Vatican II would do exactly that some five years later. We had no idea then that we were the last of an old generation, products of a pre-Vatican II church, full of self-confidence and self-righteousness. The Vincentian ministries in the Irish Province were flourishing – a great demand for parish missions, new education apostolates in Raheny and Coventry, expanding numbers and building projects in Castleknock, All Hallows and Strawberry Hill. We were completely unaware of the storms that lay ahead.

## OUT TO UNIVERSITY COLLEGE DUBLIN 1955-1958

### Going out to the University

I was enrolled as a first year student in University College, Dublin, in October 1955 and I attended lectures there for the following three years. The President of the University was Dr Michael Tierney and the university at this time was located in Earlsfort Terrace. Most of the Vincentian students travelled either by bus to Merrion Square or by train to Westland Row and walked from there to the university which was about a ten to fifteen minute walk. Across the Iveagh grounds was Newman's University Church and it is here that the opening Mass of the academic year took place in the month of October. There were about 4,000/5,000 students in the university at this time. The seminarians and women religious were very conspicuous because of their clerical garb or religious habits. A controversial issue at the time was the provision of morning coffee for the seminarians and religious in the basement of Earlsfort Terrace. One of the students going up for election as Student Union President coined the phrase 'buns for the nuns and esoterics for the clerics'. I am not sure that this won him too many votes from the seminarians or sisters! Many of the clerics would arrive on bicycles from the various religious houses around the city. I can remember the OMI students arriving very often in the winter without any overcoats. The word doing the rounds was that they were preparing for a mission in Alaska and some did end up there. Some of the women religious arrived in large chauffeur driven cars and it was interesting to see them in their long white habits descending from these limousines and making their way into the corridors of the Earlsfort terrace buildings.

*First Arts Subjects*

Fr James Dyer, the Assistant Director of Students, interviewed me before I went to the university in September 1955. He wanted me to take mathematics in my degree as I had obtained 79% in honours maths in the Leaving Certificate the year before. I took the view that this mark overrated me and I encouraged him to consult Fr Brendan Steen, who had taught me mathematics in 5th year in Castleknock. Fr Dyer came back to me a week or so later to say that, after seeking advice, he had decided to ask me to take other subjects in my degree programme in UCD. Fr Steen had some reservations about my doing a maths degree and of course this was great news from my point of view. The maths degree was sometimes known as the suicide degree because of the difficulty of passing the exam. Fr Dyer then 'suggested' that I take the following four subjects: Introduction to Philosophy, Logic, English and Latin. I had no idea what philosophy or logic were all about so my understanding was that they wanted me to specialise in English and possibly teach English and maybe Latin in a secondary school later on.

*Introduction to Philosophy*

These lectures took place in one of the large lecture halls with tiered seating. Introduction to Philosophy was chosen by many Arts students, including Law students. The lecture theatre was packed for most of the lectures. We had two or three lectures a week for this subject, each of them lasting about 50 minutes. The clerics who arrived early were seated in the front rows of the amphitheatre. Law students often arrived late, clattering noisily up the back stairs to the top rows, to the annoyance of the lecturer. Their number often included the red-haired A. J. O'Reilly. There was very little give and take between the lecturer and the students and very seldom would a student ask a question of the lecturer. An American seminarian from Clonliffe did ask questions in the first few weeks. Eventually he quietened down, muzzled either by his fellow students or the seminary authorities.

The course was covered historically. We were introduced to the history of philosophy which was divided into four periods:

- Ancient Philosophy: The Pre-Socratics, Plato, Aristotle and the Stoics;
- Medieval Philosophy: Anselm, Bonaventure and Aquinas;
- Modern Philosophy: Hobbes, Berkeley, Hume, Descartes, Malebranche and Spinoza
- Contemporary Philosophy: Logical Positivism (Ayer), Linguistic Analysis (Wittgenstein) and Existentialism (Heidegger, Sartre, Jaspers and Marcel.)

The only lecturer I remember very well lecturing on this course was Desmond Connell, later to become Archbishop of Dublin. The Introduction to Philosophy course also included lectures from E. F. O' Doherty on some elementary notions in Thomistic psychology and lectures from Conor Martin and Bertie Crowe on basic concepts in moral philosophy.

*Logic*
The logic course was covered by Bertie Crowe who lectured twice a week to a large group in the Physics Theatre. He brought us through all the main parts of Aristotelian logic – the syllogism, induction and different kinds of inference and fallacies.

*English Literature*
We covered a number of topics:
- T. P. Dunning and Professor Hogan on Shakespeare plays. Tom Dunning intrigued us with his cultivated Oxford accent;
- Roger McHugh on Newman's idea of a university;
- Denis O'Donoghue on Pope and Dryden;
- Lorna Reynolds on some topic I cannot remember. She later became Professor of English in UCG.

*Latin*

The subject I was least interested in was Latin which in fact was my weakest subject in the Leaving Certificate. We covered one or two of the Latin classical texts, Livy or Caesar, and Roman history. In this area we had a gifted lecturer called Walsh who later became Professor of Classics in the University of Glasgow. I met him many years later in Glasgow when Strawberry Hill was getting advice to have its degrees validated by the National Council for Academic Awards.

As students we were quite passive, taking notes during lectures, and I have no memory of there being any tutorials in first year. The idea was to absorb the material in each subject and exercises, especially in logic and Latin composition, and give back to the lecturer the substance of his notes in the summer examinations. I acquired the skill of taking reasonably good lecture notes but my writing deteriorated to a point where I was the only person who could decipher what I had written. Along with our work in the university, we had to maintain our commitment to spiritual exercises in Blackrock each day, so there was not that much time to engage in reading around the subjects.

The examinations took place in the great hall in the university, which is now the National Concert Hall. I have no memory of feeling any great tension although I do think I was quite worried about how I had got on in Latin. If one failed a subject, it was repeated in the autumn. When the examination results came out later in the summer I discovered that I got second place in Introduction to Philosophy – Paddy Masterson, who was a Vincentian student, came first. I got first place in logic. Paddy went on to pursue doctoral studies in Louvain. On returning he joined the Philosophy Department. He later became Registrar and President of UCD for a nine-year period and moved from Dublin to become President of the European University in Florence. I got a reasonable result in English and passed Latin. The first lot of philosophy courses awakened my interest in philosophy and I was hoping very much that I might be allowed to continue it in second arts.

## Second and Third Arts

There was some uncertainty during the summer months about what subjects I would take in second and third arts for my degree. Early in September Father James Dyer informed me that I could go ahead and take a philosophy degree. It was a little bit unusual at the time because most Vincentian students took subjects they could teach in secondary school. It was also known that Paddy Masterson had done very well in philosophy and the possibility of the two of us taking philosophy degrees appeared to be unlikely. I was very happy to learn that philosophy was to be my subject. To an extent my future was also decided in my taking this subject, as it was more than likely that I would be sent on for postgraduate studies and be asked to teach philosophy in a seminary or third-level institution.

Nearly all the students taking philosophy in the degree programme in second and third arts were seminarians and the lecturers were priests, most of them from the Archdiocese of Dublin. The Dublin Archdiocese had controlled the philosophy department for many years. The students from Clonliffe dominated the class group but there were also students from various congregations such as Carmelites, Oblates of Mary Immaculate, Spiritans and other groups. We got to know one another reasonably well but lost contact after we finished our degrees in UCD.

The philosophy programme in second and third arts, which ran in a two year cycle, was broken into metaphysics, psychology, ethics and politics and, in the third year, an honours logic module was introduced in my time.

### Metaphysics

The metaphysics course was a very traditional one and the main topics overlapped with what one would find in traditional philosophy textbooks used in seminaries in the 1950s. The two professors who lectured us were Msgr John Horgan and Fr Desmond Connell, both of whom were Louvain graduates. It is not surprising that the Louvain approach to metaphysics extended to UCD, meaning that a good deal of effort was made to put philosophers into their historical context and at the same time the overall approach was that of an enlightened brand of Thomism. The traditional distinction between general metaphysics and special metaphysics was also carried over from Louvain to Dublin. Special metaphysics corresponded more or less to philosophy of religion. It was concerned mainly with the proofs for the existence of God. I have very little recollection of the content of the two year metaphysics course but overall it was uninspiring.

One reason for this is that Professor Horgan tended to treat philosophy as a preparation for the study of theology. For example, he pointed up the importance of the distinction between substance and accident to understand (the theory of) transubstantiation. There was a sense of philosophy being subordinated to theology.

The honours group had special lectures on a number of topics but I cannot remember the details of this course in either second or third arts. It is possible that Desmond Connell lectured us on the area he had specialised in for his doctoral studies in Louvain which was Malebranche's theory of divine illumination in relation to the existence of God. I have no detailed recollection of this, neither have I any recollection of being introduced firsthand to any of the classical texts on metaphysics in the history of philosophy: Plato, Aristotle, Augustine, Anselm, Aquinas, Kant and so on.

Professor Horgan was an eccentric lecturer. He communicated very little enthusiasm for his subject and we were treated like schoolboys. He carried on in a patronising way with students, especially those he singled out for questioning. He also gave us lectures on etiquette from time to time which were triggered off by a Clonliffe student arriving late or banging the door at the end of the room. Desmond Connell was finding his feet as a lecturer in UCD. He prepared his lectures in a conscientious way and the lectures were well ordered and put together, which made it easy for us to take notes. However, he worked completely within a traditional approach to metaphysics and I never got the impression that he was open to contemporary philosophy, e.g. to Heidegger or any other twentieth-century philosopher. The only recollection I have of any reference by Desmond Connell to twentieth-century philosophy was when he announced at the beginning of a lecture that Bernard Lonergan's *Insight* – just published – was one of the most important philosophy books of the twentieth century and he held a copy of the book aloft. He was friendly in his relationship with students.

## Psychology

We had two lectures a week over two years on different areas of psychology. The two lecturers were Professor E. F. O'Doherty, the Head of the Department, and Professor Martin Nolan, who later took over the department. I have only a vague memory of the areas we covered in psychology. The course was divided into rational and empirical psychology. Rational psychology covered what was contained in a number of the topics found in the traditional seminary textbooks on this subject: Aristotle's anthropology, with reference to the *De Anima*; views on the immortality of the soul; Aquinas' synthesis of Aristotle and Augustine as found in the *Summa Theologiae*; and Averroes and Avicenna's interpretation of Aristotle on the immortality of the soul. Professor O'Doherty made no secret of the fact that he deliberately lectured above our heads. It was a question of students rising up to his level rather than he coming down to ours. He also said on a number of occasions that if we gave him back his lecture notes in exams he would give us a pass but to get honours we would have to read around the material he was covering and show evidence of that in the examinations.

Under the heading of empirical psychology we studied various activities of the human person, especially 'remembering'. E. F. O'Doherty had studied in Oxford, under Professor Bartlett who had done pioneering studies in this area.

There was nothing in the course on either Freud or Jung. Professor O'Doherty tended to put-down or dismiss psychoanalysis. He did remark on one occasion that he thought that Jung was a greater threat to the faith than Freud but what the context of this remark was I cannot remember. Professor Nolan, recently returned from his own doctoral studies in Cambridge, covered some topics in the area of the biological roots of human behaviour. He was also finding his feet as a lecturer in UCD.

The courses in psychology were given under the auspices of the Philosophy Department. A short time later, a separate department of psychology was set up which moved far beyond the Thomistic framework of the mid-1950s.

*Ethics*

The lecturers in this area were Conor Martin and Bertie Crowe. I have very vivid memories of Conor Martin bringing us through Aristotle's *Nicomachean Ethics* and staying very close to the text. He gave the impression of grappling personally with the text itself and teasing out its implications. In my mind he was one of the genuine philosophers we encountered in University College Dublin. For me he made Aristotle come alive and I always retained an interest in the *Nicomachean Ethics* which I later lectured on to groups of students in St Mary's College, Strawberry Hill. Themes such as 'the final end of man', 'the nature of friendship', the 'relationship between the active and the contemplative life' provided a framework for one's own searching in these areas. I have also vivid memories of attending lectures by Father Bertie Crowe on natural law. Father Crowe had completed his doctoral thesis in Louvain on an aspect of natural law, with special emphasis on the notion of 'synderesis', and some twenty years later he published a book on natural law.

*Politics*

In third arts we followed a course of lectures by Father James Kavanagh on politics. Father Kavanagh published a small book around this time on social ethics. There was a good exchange between James Kavanagh and the student group, especially a number of the law students including A. J. O'Reilly, about topics of the day. In this course Father Kavanagh covered some classic texts, including Plato's *Republic*, Aristotle's *Politics*, Augustine's *City of God*, texts of Aquinas, Machiavelli's *The Prince*, John Stuart Mill *On Liberty* and Hobbes' *Leviathan*.

In our final year we also got a number of lectures from Gabriel Bowe OP on *The Two Sovereignties*, the separation of church and state in medieval times. Fr Bowe had specialised in this area in his doctoral thesis.

*Logic*

In my final year in UCD Professor O'Doherty, who was the Professor of Psychology and Logic, introduced an honours logic course. This course amounted to an introduction to a Polish logician called Lucasawich who actually was an emigré in Dublin during the second world war. Lucasawich's logic was a very mathematical system and to the best of my knowledge I had no great difficulty in mastering it – my background in mathematics probably helped in this regard.

One of the most memorable moments of my three years in UCD occurred when we were three or four weeks into this modern logic course. One of the Spiritan students was getting more and more frustrated by the succession of logical symbols coming up on the blackboard. Half way through the lecture he could restrain himself no longer so he blurted out 'What use is all this ... going to be to me when I go on the missions to Africa?' Professor O'Doherty did not lose his cool. He sat down and gave us a half hour lecture on Newman's notion of the value of knowledge for its own sake. I am not sure if my red-faced Spiritan friend was satisfied but the rest of us had to admire the Professor's adroitness in taking advantage of a good teaching moment to stretch our intellectual horizons.

*Final exam and Graduation*

I have no memories of my second arts examinations, which I must have coasted through. My guess is that we were all probably given either a pass or fail mark.

I had the long summer of 1958 to prepare for my final exams in September of that year. I tackled my preparation in a very systematic way, spending most of the month of June covering six to eight topics in the history of philosophy and metaphysics and writing essays on them. Doing the same in July for psychology and logic and the same in August for ethics and politics. Going into the exam I had over six essays prepared for each of the six examinations I was about to take. Having studied previous examination papers very closely, I was reasonably confident. Although I felt exhausted when they were over, I was reasonably happy that I had given the examiners a good run for their money. I did not realise that, for most of the students who studied philosophy with me in UCD, these exams would be 'a parting of the ways'. Students who belonged to religious orders were on their way to their houses of theology for the following four years and then after ordination were sent all over the world. I did meet a number of them at 'vicariate' examinations or at ordinations to minor or major orders in Clonliffe College.

A few weeks later, when I had already transferred to Glenart, Father Richard McCullen whispered to me after night prayer one evening that I had obtained a first class honours degree, coming third to Paddy Masterson and Arthur McCrystal. Arthur McCrystal was a student in All Hallows College and he went on to become Head of the Religious Studies Department in Newman College in Birmingham. He had a lot of trouble with arthritis in the 1980s and died quite young in 1990.

I went to the graduation ceremony in University College Dublin in November 1958. It took place in the great hall in Earlsfort Terrace. I think I was in the very first group called up to be awarded degrees on that day. Other Vincentian students were there too, among them were Peter McNamara, Gerry Ferguson and Barney O' Regan. I have no memories of any of my own family of brothers or sisters being with me in UCD on that day. It is more than likely that the group travelled with either Father James Cahalan or Father Richard McCullen up and down to Glenart on that same day. Celebrating intellectual achievement was not in the scheme of things at that time.

*UCD in retrospect*

I have always felt privileged in having the opportunity to study philosophy in University College Dublin in the mid-1950s. It opened the door to first-hand knowledge of writings of some of the important philosophers in each of the great periods of philosophy. Some of the professors, such as Conor Martin, Desmond Connell or E. F. O'Doherty, introduced me to the importance of grappling with the texts themselves; of the importance of logical and clear thinking; and of the importance of stretching one's intellectual abilities.

There were lots of limitations to the degree itself in that a lot of the learning was passive learning. To some extent I overcame this in the final three months of exam preparation when I tried to form my own personal view about a number of issues. I was not expecting to get a first class honours degree but I think the fact that I was prepared to put forward a personal point of view after carefully studying the texts or issues impressed my examiners.

Doing this degree enabled me to see that a number of attitudes inside the Vincentian Province were quite narrow and limited and ever afterwards I was keen to look beyond the traditional sources of information that Vincentians used to form opinions . Contact with first class critical minds at university or elsewhere challenges one to step beyond intellectual mediocrity at certain moments in one's life.

Participating in university life as a clerical student was only half a life. I missed out on all the social interaction between young men and young women and all the activities bound up with the sporting facilities and debating societies. During my three years in UCD, I was unable to attend plays, debates, films or any musical events and this was the same for all the other clerical students in the university. I was aware that Newman's University, founded in the 1850s, was a forerunner of University College Dublin, and visiting Newman's University church was a reminder of this. However, it was only on re-reading Newman's idea of a university some fifteen years later that I really became aware of what Newman meant by a liberal education and the idea of knowledge as an end in itself. This ran counter to the anti-intellectual attitudes that were prevalent in some Vincentian circles during my days in the university.

Through contact with Professor T. P. Dunning, who was lecturing in the English department in UCD and was a Vincentian priest resident in Blackrock, I would have become aware of the notion of Christian humanism in 1957 or '58. He gave the students of Blackrock a series of lectures on this theme. He studied in Oxford where he was a contemporary of Tolkien.

CHAPTER 4

# Glenart: Theology in the Wicklow Hills
# 1958-1962

*Glenart Castle*

Glenart Castle was purchased by the Vincentians in the late 1940s and opened as a House of Theology in September 1949. The property was comprised of 100 acres of farmland and extensive gardens and a castle building dating from the early 19th century. The Vincentians built a new extension with chapel and lecture rooms on the ground floor and bedrooms on the 1st and 2nd floors. In whatever way the extension was constructed the floor-boards were constantly creaking, especially in the summer time when the wood expanded or contracted. Glenart Castle is situated about two miles outside Arklow on the way to Woodenbridge. When I arrived there in mi-September 1958 there were about 25 students, 5 priests, 4 house staff and 2 men working on the farm. The living conditions were Spartan, the meals were wholesome and we got plenty of fresh air working on the grounds, restoring footpaths, reclaiming and replanting flower beds and pruning back shrubs of all kinds. An earlier group of students saw them-selves as trailblazers in this work of reclamation. They were very proud of the fact that they had dredged the lake near the en-trance lodge and re-sown many of the plants and flowers in the three-tiered garden. By the time I arrived in September 1958 the attention of students was turning towards the cultivation of the farmland and the development of poultry enterprises. One notable achievement was the building of a swimming pool using an old gas cylinder twenty feet in diameter and ten feet deep, inserting it into the ground and constructing a diving board. Unfortunately what could not be guaranteed was a con-stant supply of water because of water shortages in the summer.

Some students found the isolation very hard to take. We did not have access to radios or newspapers and our knowledge of

75

what was going on in the outside world was very limited. Now and again there would be a few forays into Arklow on messages, or to see the doctor or dentist, and during holiday times there might be the odd excursion, especially around Easter, to one of the Wicklow mountains nearby or to the strand in Castletown south of Arklow.

There was very little movement out of Glenart or contact with other seminarians. Kiltegan was only 20 miles from Glenart but again during my time I cannot remember any visit to this group. It was very seldom that we visited Dublin, apart from the holiday month of July spent in Castleknock College. We also went to Dublin for Vicariate Examinations and for the conferring of Minor Orders as well as for ordination to Major Orders – Sub-diaconate, Diaconate and Priesthood. We had very little contact with local farmers or with business people in the town of Arklow. The only people we really had contact with, and even this was limited, were the farm hands and the staff looking after the house. From them we learnt a little about what was happening in the Arklow and south Wicklow area.

*First impressions*
Most of the students looked forward to the move from Blackrock to Glenart as it was the halfway stage for most of us on our way to priesthood. We had moved from the novitiate house in Blackrock which dictated the style of life for all of the students living there. Glenart had a freer atmosphere even if the order of the day and general regime were quite demanding. We had the impression that we were being treated in a more mature way.

Looking back on my first two months or so in Glenart, I think it would be true to say that I was quite depressed. There were a number of reasons for this. My twin brother had just left the seminary at the end of August or early September, about three weeks before I arrived. His leaving certainly set me thinking about why I should remain. Secondly, I found it quite difficult to adapt to theology. A number of the lectures were anything but stimulating. The textbook system was a very inadequate way to do theology and to be asked to take so much on faith after spending three years learning to be critical about sources was a shock to my system. A third reason is that I was genuinely very tired after all the effort I had put into preparing assiduously for the final exams in UCD and I was suffering from post-examination blues. Finally, I began to mourn the deaths of my parents who had died three months and six months previously.

A day or two after arriving in Glenart I decided to have a go at chopping through a large tree trunk with a hatchet. It was an opportunity for demanding physical exercise but also a way to work off my frustrations. I laboriously worked my way through this tree trunk, three feet in diameter, during the afternoons of my first two to three weeks in Glenart. A number of people, both staff and students, must have thought I was off my rocker as a much simpler way to do this would have been to use a saw. I was grateful to the priests and students later for the space they gave me in working out my inner frustrations and loneliness on the trunk of this fallen tree.

Glenart was nestled in the Wicklow hills and valleys and I quickly explored the neighbouring area near the Vincentian residence. There were some beautiful walks through forest land in the direction of Arklow, as well as at the back or our property going up to an area called Rustigah. Mature trees – oaks, beeches, chestnuts, Dutch pines – were scattered all over the property. The autumn colours were brilliant as of course were the flowering of rhododendrons and acacia plants some six months later in the spring. Glenart was going to provide me with the soothing balm of nature to help me refocus my energies for the next stage of my journey towards priesthood. There was one cloud on the physical landscape. A short time after my arrival in Glenart a fertiliser factory was built in the river valley, between Arklow and Woodenbridge, and the fumes from this factory would eventually damage the trees all around us. With so much unemployment in the Arklow of the 1950s many people kept quiet about the potential damage to the beautiful valley in setting up this fertiliser factory.

*Theology Curriculum*

The theology curriculum we followed had been laid down for many years by the Roman authorities and comprised major and minor subjects. Major subjects were scripture, dogmatic theology and moral theology and the minor subjects included church history, liturgy, catechetics, pastoral theology and canon law. With a number of exceptions, these major and minor subjects were taught by Vincentian priests. In dogmatic theology and moral theology Latin textbooks were used and an effort was made to keep up the teaching of these subjects in Latin. As facility in spoken Latin was quite difficult, both students and staff were uncomfortable with this state of affairs but an effort was made to comply with the requirements of the Roman Congregation for Education in this regard.

The following is a brief outline of topics taught in the major and minor subjects we dealt with:

### Scripture/Old Testament

Our lecturer in this area was a man in poor health who was living in mortal fear that he was going to communicate erroneous or heretical teaching to us. The riches of the Old Testament writings were never opened up for us. The after effects of the modernist crisis were still in the air, especially after the publication of Pope Pius XII's *Humani Generis*. He lived in mortal fear that he had another Ernest Renan in the class. Some of our questions must have given him many sleepless nights.

### Scripture/New Testament

The Jerusalem Bible had just been published in which there was good material in the introductions and the footnotes. A Catholic commentary had also been published at around this time. We dealt with the synoptic gospels including the synoptic problem and a number of Pauline texts. I have no detailed memory of covering the Johannine writings or the Acts of the Apostles. The subject was taught in an uninspiring way but this was not surprising because this man was also responsible for all of systematic theology or dogma as we called it then.

### Dogmatic Theology

Throughout my four years in Glenart we covered the four volumes of Hervé's *Dogmatic Theology* in Latin. Everything was neatly packaged and suitably labelled in terms of '*De Fide Definita*,' *De Fide Catholica*', etc. A section called *Errores*, in each chapter summed up positions of renegade or 'dubious ' theologians and heretics. The four year course was divided into 'tracts' which were covered in their entirety in a four year cycle. We began with fundamental dogmatic theology which was concerned with methodology and sources. The other areas covered the existence of God, the Trinity, the Incarnation, and the sacraments, the four last things – death, judgement, hell and heaven – and there was also an important section on apologetics. Topics were approached from a Thomistic point of view in which priority was given to the writings of the Angelic Doctor. The subject was taught in an uncritical way, evacuating it of any kind of theological passion or excitement. One can understand why many priests who went through seminaries in this era never wanted to open a theological book for the rest of their lives.

*Moral Theology*
This subject was also taught from a Latin textbook, written by a man called Genicot in a four year cycle. It did not necessarily follow that one began with fundamental moral theology. It might come later in the cycle for a particular group of students. In fundamental moral we covered topics such as freedom, conscience, law and sin.

In what was called special moral theology we covered particular moral problems following the framework of the Ten Commandments, sacraments and the precepts of the Church. In the area of moral theology it was possible to grapple with some of the genuine moral problems of the day . In the teaching of the subject, we missed out on an historical perspective. This was not the fault of our lecturers. It was only towards the end of the 1950s that the Alphonsianum Institute for the study of Moral Theology was set up. One of the watch cries of Vatican II a few years later was that moral theology should be renewed through a return to scriptural and patristic sources and through the transcending of legalism and casuistry.

*Church History*
This subject was taught by a very elderly missioner who had returned from China. He used Philip Hughes' *Church History* – the short paperback version – as his textbook.

He had strong views on 'the evils that Luther had inflicted on the church' as well as an antipathy towards anything that appeared in *The Irish Times* on the Catholic Church. His constant refrain was, 'Do not be surprised at human nature.' This man's anecdotes from his experiences in China certainly put us in touch with the tragic history of the Catholic Church in that country but these sessions did very little to deepen our horizons about twenty centuries of Church history.

## Liturgy

The great liturgical reforms were still in the making, in France, Belgium and Germany, in the 1950s. Our formation in this area was 'pre-Vatican II' in every sense of the expression. The Latin High Mass celebrated every feastday and every Sunday with as much attention as we could muster. Twelve students would make up the schola and the rest of us were either on the ceremonies or making up the small congregation. These were the high points of our liturgical life in Glenart. The only innovation I can remember is a form of the Mass known as Fr Fennelly's People's Mass, pioneered by a parish priest in Greystones nearby in north Wicklow . We were quite excited when Fr Fennelly himself came to talk to us about the differences these small moves were making in his congregation's participation in the Eucharist. We had no idea what was to come from the Vatican Council some five years later.

## Canon Law

We were introduced to the Code of Canon Law, its overall framework, and certain specific canons, especially those that dealt with marriage. We were also introduced to a cross-section of canons dealing with suspensions and excommunications, penalties one could incur as a member of the church and what one would have to do to have them 'lifted'.

## Pastoral Theology

Pastoral theology included homiletics, catechetics and the occasional lecture on some aspect of social justice. In my time there was no practical component of catechetics or pastoral practice. We all took it in turns to preach a homily to the student congregation and over my four years I probably did this on three or four occasions. There would be a discussion of the homily afterwards. Our early efforts to preach must have shown how out of touch we were with the man or woman in the pew.

At the end of every term we had house exams preceded by a few days revision time. Before the reception of Minor and Major Orders, we had what was known as the 'vicariate' examinations which took place in Clonliffe College. We also had a special exam in the area of confessional practice to obtain the approval needed to be authorised to hear confessions in the Dublin Archdiocese. We were issued with our 'faculties' document after appearing before one of the Vicars General of the diocese in Westland Row church sacristy where we made a profession of faith and undertook to abide by the instructions of the Roman Catholic Church in regard to confessional practice.

Classes ran from about nine o'clock to one o'clock, which allowed four class periods. Sometimes these were double classes, especially in the case of dogmatic and moral theology. We operated on a five day week for seven or eight months of the year. We did have an occasional outside lecturer. The lecture that remains in my mind is one by Sir David Kelly, former British Ambassador to the Soviet Union who lived in the Wicklow or Wexford area. He spoke to us about his experiences as British Ambassador to the Soviet Union and he had a number of critical comments to make about American foreign policy and the limitations of the United Nations as a watchdog of the intentional order. Other visiting lecturers covered topics such as Modern Art, Church Architecture, Alcoholics Anonymous, Trade Unionism and the Legion of Mary.

*World Events and Local Happenings*
I have very little memory of world events during the years 1958 to 1962 and the only one that impacted very much on me and other students was the death of Pope Pius XII and the election of Pope John XXIII in the autumn of 1958. Pius XII at that time had the reputation of being one of the great Popes, scholarly, ascetic and maintaining control at the centre – he was his own Secretary of State. The election of Pope John XXIII was initially seen as a

great disappointment and at the beginning people saw him as a stopgap until someone younger took over. I remember the Director of Students, in a conference shortly after the Pope's election, encouraging us to see all this as providential. Even in 1959, when Pope John XXIII indicated that he was going to call a Council, I cannot recall any great excitement being generated by this announcement. In the climate of the times I think it would have been interpreted as a possible non-event that would take place into the future, or the dreaming of a somewhat unhinged senile Pope. We certainly had no idea what was coming next and it would be well into the first or second sessions in 1963 or 1964 before people began to realise that momentous changes were in the offing.

I cannot recall any political events of these years at international or national level that impacted on me, which indicates how far removed we were from political events of our time. We did not see the implications of a fertiliser factory being built opposite us which was going to devastate the valley right up to Woodenbridge. Internationally the cold war dominated everything and very little would trickle through about what was happening behind the Iron Curtain. The winds of change had blown all over Africa and particularly around the 1960s many African countries were moving towards political independence. The Irish economy was still in a very depressed state. Thousands of people were emigrating each year for Britain, the United States, Australia and elsewhere. We were coming near the end of Éamon De Valera's inward looking and protectionist economic policies, and Lemass, under the influence of Whittaker, was about to launch a period of economic development. I have no memory of voting in any of the elections during this four year period. I do remember voting on a referendum to change our system of proportional representation which our own student group had formally debated a few days beforehand. The traditional method or position on proportional representation was maintained by the electorate.

Various events in our domestic setting in Glenart made far more impact on me – the building of a new silage pit in the farmyard during one of the August holiday periods, a big wind through one of the winters which removed tiles from our roof and felled a number of our mature trees, the celebration of the tercentenary of the death of St Vincent de Paul in 1960, which included a visit of Fr William Slattery from Paris, the planting of Douglas firs all over our property as part of a government re-afforestation scheme, and the launching of our Nigerian Mission in 1960. Domestic and Vincentian happenings predominate in my consciousness. I remember being woken up around 5.00 am one summer's morning by a burly student who came into my room – it was one of the 'condemned cells' near the garden area – with a gun in one hand and a fox which he had just killed over his shoulder. The smell of the slain animal remained on in my room for days. This student had decided to stalk this fox through the night because it had ravaged our young chickens a few nights previously. I felt privileged in that I was the first student this man wanted to share his moment of glory with. He became our game-hunter for the next few years, keeping foxes and other preying animals at bay.

The nature lovers among our students loved Glenart. It was a paradise for our bird watchers, our fishermen and our connoisseurs of trees and plants. The sound of electric saws, piercing the air all around us, kept us aware that the forestry industry was a mainstay of local employment.

*A Monastic Lifestyle*
Apart from the first year novitiate spent in Blackrock, this four year period, 1958 to 1962, was the most monastic period in all my life. Isolated in the Wicklow Hills, living a regimented order of day, conditions were ideal to develop a life of prayer and contemplation. We had ones hour's prayer each morning from six thirty to seven thirty followed by Mass, with short periods of prayer throughout the day including Vespers. After Night Prayer, called Compline, we had 'solemn silence' until after breakfast the next morning. We began the academic year with an eight day retreat in September, which was followed up by a one day retreat each month through the academic year. Retreats also preceded the conferring of Minor and Major Orders. We had long periods of silence each day and spent the afternoons working on the grounds and on the farm, very often in silence. All of this certainly nurtured an 'interior life'. We were cut off

from family, friends and contact with ordinary people. There was no access to news outlets, such as newspapers or radio, and all recreation periods were spent together in the company of the other 20/25 students whom we got to know very well. After supper each evening we walked, three by three, back and forth on one of the walks at the foot of the tiered garden for about thirty or forty minutes.

Throughout the year we had a conference every Monday evening, given by the Director of Students, on various spiritual topics – scriptural themes, Vincentian saints, especially events in the life of St Vincent, virtues like humility, compunction of heart, faith, hope and charity, Our Lady and saints whose feast days were coming up in the church calendar. The Students' Director would slip in some admonitions about various aspects of student behaviour from time to time such as the observance or non-observance of the rule of silence, which made me think later that there was an element of 'spiritual blackmail' at work somewhere in all this. On the other hand, we never doubted that our priest formators in Glenart had our real interests at heart and when we did have legitimate complaints we could voice them directly to the authorities or through the Dean of Students. During retreats we had two or three conferences a day. We were also encouraged to read a portion of a spiritual book for about half an hour each day. This meant that over the four years we covered quite a lot of classical and contemporary spiritual writings. We also listened to books being read during dinner . These tended to be books of a historical, biographical or autobiographical nature. All meals took place in silence. We were allowed to talk at dinner on feastdays. Two students wearing white aprons over their soutanes would serve the meals, which we gulped down at red-hot speed.

Our spiritual progress was monitored from month to month through contact with the Director of Students and with retreatgivers during annual retreats. The constant emphasis was on finding and doing the will of God and making spiritual progress from month to month and from year to year. The theme of conversion and ascending the mountain of holiness was constantly put before us. Three students left the seminary from my year during my four years in Glenart. Looking back now, I see that some students found outlets for their energy by engaging in various projects on the grounds or on the farm. Sometimes one would see students looking at the trains passing nearby on the way from Arklow to Dublin. This resulted in their having to endure a certain amount of friendly banter about getting ready for 'take off'! The three students in my year who left after six or seven years in Blackrock and Glenart told none of us they were leaving. In fact it was only when we were returning by train from Dublin after being ordained to the sub-diaconate at the end of our third year in Glenart that we discovered one of our members had not come to Clonliffe to receive Major Orders. I slowly realised that he had 'departed'. This threw a blanket of sadness over our whole group as we pondered on the way back by train to Glenart that evening why we were the ones remaining on board.

*Holidays*

On Sundays, feastdays and during the holiday periods of Christmas, Easter and summer, we had considerable amounts of free time. During the Christmas period we gathered around a big log fire in the student common room and guzzled down sweets and Christmas cakes which were sent to us by our families. At Easter a number of us would do a little mountaineering and I remember cycling to Aughavanna and climbing Lugnaquilla with relative ease. I did this on three occasions during my time in Glenart. In the summer we spent the month of July with the students from Blackrock in Castleknock and the high point of that holiday was a number of football matches between the Blackrock and Glenart students. There was always some needle between the two groups on the football pitch. Matches were nearly always Gaelic football but we also played some soccer. When the new swimming pool was built in Castleknock, sometime around the late 1950s, that provided another source of recreation which meant we didn't have to go down to the Liffey to swim there.

In Glenart we played football once or twice a week but with our numbers being quite small it was difficult to muster up two sides, especially as we were carrying a number of non-footballers who togged out with us but took little part in the proceedings. Towards the end of my time in Glenart we began to play teams around about in Arklow and elsewhere. This certainly was something to look forward to.

Throughout my time in Glenart I was keen on running, running through the open fields, especially in the Rustigah area where there were marvellous views of the countryside in the direction of Croghan mountain and the rolling fields towards the sea some five miles away. I did this sometimes on Sunday afternoons or on other days and took a cold shower immediately afterwards – warm water was not available except on one day each week. When eventually I saw the movie *The Loneliness of the Long Distant Runner* I could sympathise very much with the main character in the movie and his feeling of euphoria running through open spaces. There was something exhilarating in running, in all weather, through the open countryside, jumping over ditches and crossing streams, the spring of forest pathways underneath, and emerging from an icy cold shower at the end of the run.

Another source of recreation for me was reading. I discovered a number of translations of French novels: François Mauriac's *A Woman of the Pharisees* and *Thérèse*; as well as the writings of Claudel and Bernanos. I also got my hands on most of the novels of Graham Greene and Evelyn Waugh which I devoured. The debates about whether or not there was such a thing as 'A Catholic Novel' intrigued me. My cousin Martin Rafferty kept me supplied with articles about all this.

There was a fairly primitive gramophone and about twenty or thirty records available in one particular room in Glenart, and from time to time I spent an hour or so listening to one or other piece of classical music – Beethoven's Pastoral Symphony, or Victoria de los Angeles singing some arias from a Puccini or Verdi opera would open up romantic worlds we were starved of. Glenart students were invited to the musical performances in the Mercy Convent in Arklow each year, under the leadership of a very gifted musical director from amongst the Mercy sisters. It took a few days to recover from seeing the talented young ladies performing one or other musical in vogue at that time.

*'An Even Keel'*

Towards the end of my first year in Glenart I wrote a five page article for *Evangelizare* with the title *An Even Keel*. Drawing on some imagery from Hilaire Belloc's *The Cruise of the Nona* about navigating cross currents, avoiding shipwreck on sandbanks and making the most of prevailing winds, I outlined a number of points about the unity of knowledge which I suggested would help a student navigate his way through his years of study. My main contention was that there should be no divide or tension between heart and head, between intellect and will, between the intellectual life and the spiritual life and I drew on some classical sources, St Thomas Aquinas, Cardinal Newman and some contemporary writers such as Etienne Gilson and Ronald Knox to sustain my thesis. There was nothing very original in what I had written but unfortunately a few of my sub-themes got me into trouble. My text was referred to the authorities in the house for comment. Among my sub-themes was the suggestion that truth could be found outside the Catholic Church, that textbook theology took the passion and excitement out of the subject and that there were some anti-intellectual currents knocking about in Vincentian circles.

My article ruffled some feathers and I believe that its contents were referred to the Provincial who was doing a visitation of the Glenart community around that time. The superior of the house wrote a three foolscap page commentary on the article, rubbishing some parts of it, indicating that he could not see where the article was leading, and criticising a number of specific points, such as pushing philosophy too far and not having enough faith in the authority of the church as a sure guide.

Unfortunately my essay was seen as an attack on the whole Glenart system and my use of a phrase taken directly from Belloc's book about 'intolerable tediums' gave the impression that I was bored stiff with theological courses in Glenart. As I look back now I can see why the authorities in Glenart must have thought that I was getting too big for my philosophical boots and that I needed to be pulled down a peg or two. Over the following few weeks I thought long and hard about the superior's critique of what I had written. I kept my own counsel and eventually wrote a four page reply which I never submitted.

Why? I am not sure but I suspect now, some forty four years later, that I was caught in a tangle between submitting to the charge that I was not submissive to the authority of the church and some well-founded convictions about weaknesses in the theological system that we Vincentians and students in many other seminaries were being subjected to in this pre-Vatican II era. Despite displaying some early convictions of mine about the nature and limitations of philosophy, my article in fact was badly written and it was just as well for my own sake that it was never published. My final remark in my text was to thank the superior for his patience in reading the original text and admitting that another superior might have assigned it to the waste-paper basket by now.

*Ascending the Ladder – Minor and Major Orders*
Through the fours years in Glenart we were conferred with Minor and Major Orders step by step. At the end of year one we were tonsured and took the First Minor Orders of Porter and Lector. Porter was the person who opened the door of the church and the Lector was the reader. At the end of the second year we were conferred with Second Minor Orders of Acolyte and Exorcist; Acolyte to assist at the altar and Exorcist to cast out devils and evil spirits. At the end of the third year we were or-dained to the Sub-Diaconate, which at that time was regarded as the major step towards ordination. It was generally regarded as the time to make up one's mind finally about whether or not one was going to go forward to priesthood. In the autumn of the final year we were ordained to the Diaconate and in the late spring or summer to Priesthood. All these Minor and Major Orders were revised in a decree that came out around 1972 in-troducing various reforms. Sub-Diaconate was eliminated, as were the Minor Orders of Porter and Exorcist.

I have very little memory of being conferred with Minor Orders. The ceremony took place in one of the oratories in Clonliffe College. I was conferred with Tonsure and Minor Orders by Archbishop John McQuaid. The ceremonies themselves were always very tense and I can remember the Archbishop asking a seminarian from some other congregation to close the door properly, which was part of the rite of being named Porter.

Major Orders of Sub-Diaconate, Diaconate and Priesthood took place in Clonliffe Chapel with even greater solemnity. The only thing I can remember about Diaconate was lining up with a large group of seminarians from various religious orders and one tall man trying to ease the tension by saying to a few of us, 'Let's get into line now lads; it's time to throw in the ball.' In the manner in which he conducted these ceremonies, there is no doubt that Archbishop McQuaid communicated to us that we were taking momentous steps. The ceremonies themselves were conducted in Latin. Our names were called out solemnly to come forward to receive orders to which call we would respond 'adsum'.

## Ordination to the Priesthood

I was ordained to the priesthood on 7 April, Passion Sunday, 1962 with three other Vincentian students – Eamon Raftery, Donal Gallagher and Bill Murphy. Perry Gildea was held up for a few weeks because of his youthfulness – he had not reached the canonical age of 24. Of the fourteen students who had entered Blackrock with me in 1954, six survived, four of whom were ordained in 1961 and Eamon Raftery and myself in 1962. At the end of the ceremony I remember giving my blessing to my brothers and sisters and a number of friends outside Clonliffe Chapel.

The next day I said my first Mass in St Raphael's Stillorgan, an orphanage run at that time by the Daughters of Charity. It had quite a small chapel which easily accommodated my brothers, sisters, aunts and uncles, cousins and some friends. I celebrated this first Mass with my back to the people, wearing purple fiddle-back vestments following the ancient Tridentine rubrics with great intensity. I was assisted by my brother, Jim, who had been ordained in 1960 . With the assistance of my sister Mary, who was an Aer Lingus air hostess at the time, he had got a cheap flight from Rome where he was studying at the time. I said a few brief words afterwards. My overall impression is that I was quite ill at ease to find myself the focal point of attention throughout these few days.

I returned to Glenart that evening and spent the following three months, the rest of April, May and June, as a student priest. We sat at the end of the priests' table in the dining room and I think we joined the priests for coffee after lunch. Otherwise it was back to student life for the last few months of our final year in Glenart. One distinguishing mark was that we now wore the cape with the soutane. Most mornings we celebrated private Masses in the oratories on the first floor, served by one of the students. I have very few memories of these last few months in Glenart. Probably most of the time was spent preparing for the faculties examination which took place sometime in June.

## Summer 1962: Phibsboro and Glenamaddy

Sometime towards the middle or end of June 1962, the five of us who had been ordained to the priesthood took up residence in St Peter's, Phibsboro. A programme of lectures had been organised for us to complete what was known as the pastoral year requirements which in our case had been whittled down to two months. This was in fact our induction into various aspects of pastoral ministry. It included preaching at Sunday and weekday Masses, as well as the 15th of August, and also doing a rota of confessions during the week and at the weekend. The church was packed for the Sunday Masses and I remember distributing communion practically non-stop through Sunday morning. Only priests distributed communion at that time and there was a rota of priests available during, before and after the Masses which were more or less on the hour. Preaching for the first time to a full church in St Peter's was quite a daunting experience. We preached from the pulpit at that time. Marilyn Monroe died in August 1962 and I made some allusion to her death in a homily I preached at the Monday evening Novena devotions. My few months in the confessional were a 'baptism of fire'. I was forced to grow up quickly in regard to what was happening in the world around me. At the same time, I could measure the sense of relief when a penitent acknowledged his or her sins. One was conscious of their sense of liberation after absolution had been given and they were told to go in peace. James Joyce describes this sense of relief perfectly in *Portrait of the Artist as a Young Man* when Stephen Daedalus goes to confession in the Capuchin Friary in Church Street. Other lecturers during these two months were Father Tom Cleary on confessional practise, Father John McNamara on psychology and Father Dermot O'Dowd on educational topics. It is also likely that one or two of the parish missioners spoke to us, too, about the challenges of their particular ministry.

There must have been about sixteen or eighteen Vincentian priests living in St Peter's, Phibsboro at this time. A number of them were quite elderly but overall they were very kind to us. We sat at the end of the long table in the dining room and any time we left the church or the community house we were always wearing our clerical collars, black chesterfield suits and black hats. I do not know of any priests who travelled at this time without being dressed like this.

My memories of St Peter's Phibsboro were of a large church where Masses were very well attended on Sundays and weekdays. There was a multiplicity of devotional exercises: Miraculous Medal on Monday nights, the Archconfraternity of the Sacred Heart, and many other devotions. The pre-Vatican II church was in full spate – who would have guessed that its days were numbered? The Catholic Church was at a high point of its political power in Ireland. Its seminaries were overflowing, its missions overseas were thriving and church attendance was at an all-time high. In September 1959 there were 268 students in All Hallows missionary college. Fifty-nine first year students had entered the college in that particular year. The attitudes of the Vincentians living in St Peter's at this time reflected this – 'there was not much to be worried about'. With more than the usual number of Vincentian priests being ordained in these years, the Vincentian future must also have looked secure.

During my time in Phibsboro in the summer of 1962, I spent a week in Glenamaddy. Over the few days I was there I celebrated Mass in the parish church. I stayed with Eamon and Jo Phelan who had bought our business in Glenamaddy a year or so previously. I had not been in Glenamaddy since my parents' deaths four years previously. Over the week I visited practically all the people in the town, calling from door to door. I received a very kind and friendly reception everywhere except in one house where I was 'cold shouldered' at the door. I learned afterwards that my father and this gentleman had fallen out over some particular issue, probably failure to pay rent. This was quite a shock to me at the time because I could hardly imagine someone harbouring a grudge of this kind. Many of my own contemporaries had moved from Glenamaddy: the Shannons, the Hynes, the Flynns and so on. Visiting the graves of my parents in the Lough cemetery, or what was then known as the new cemetery, I felt quite sad that they had not lived long enough to see me return as an ordained priest.

GLENART EXPERIENCE IN PERSPECTIVE

### The Last of an Old Generation

It comes as quite a shock to realise that I belong to the last generation of pre-Vatican II priests – that is, priests formed in the last 8 years before the Vatican Council began. At the time in Ireland we felt quite proud of the great accomplishments of the Irish church at home and abroad – at home, in the powerful influence it had on Irish society, abroad, in the extraordinary numbers of missionaries we had sent to both the old and the new worlds. We were held in high esteem in Rome, untainted by some of those 'radical movements' that had been developing in France and Germany in the 1950s. The Irish church was a model of orthodoxy. Under the steady hands of Cardinal D'Alton and Archbishop John Charles McQuaid, there was a great sense of security. As far as I know, there were no groups advocating any radical reform. If there were, my guess is that they were banished to the islands around Ireland or to a mission overseas. Vatican II was just about to begin its first session in September in 1962 but the preparations so far did not seem to ruffle anybody's feathers. It would be a few years yet, when Vatican II was well into its second and third session, before cracks began to appear in our church structures and in our systems of formation in seminaries and religious houses.

### The Priest as a Public Figure

If I felt ill at ease in the summer of 1962 at the end of my four years formation in Glenart and my four years formation in Blackrock, it was not because I sensed that Catholic tradition was at a turning point in its history. It was because from a personal point of view I felt ill at ease in my public role as a priest. Through my years of formation I had not overcome a shy and retiring disposition and having now to be a public person, to preach and to interact with people did not come easy to me. The monastic thrust of my formation had not prepared me for mixing easily with people. Secondly and with hindsight, I wonder now how much theology and scripture I had personally absorbed. Yes, I could confidently say that I had a good idea what the teaching of the church was but I doubt if I could say I had internalised the New Testament writings or areas of systematic and moral theology in a personal way. In some ways I would have been far more at home with Aristotle's *Nicomachean Ethics* or Thomas Aquinas' *Quinque Viae*.

## A distant God

Although I could not have admitted it to myself at the time, I am reasonably sure that the God I believed in was a distant God, a God of nature, a God of the philosophers , a God whom I could not say I knew in a personal way despite all the hours of prayer, silence and contemplation during my eight years in Glenart and Blackrock. I certainly loved the things of the Spirit, truth, beauty and goodness, but the God revealed in Jesus Christ was still a long distance away from me in the summer of 1962 at the end of my period of formation. I was still struggling to pray and to believe. I certainly had the desire to do both.

## An alien from home

My visit to Glenamaddy in July 1962 confirmed my status as an alien from home. This alienation had begun a long time before 1962. Indeed one could say that it began the September I went to Castleknock College in 1949. Of course, the fact that I had not been in Glenamaddy for eight years, apart from attending the funerals of both my parents, meant that I was increasingly out of touch with all that was happening there. The sale of the family home and business to one of our employees, a man who was quite close to our family, meant that we could no longer regard Glenamaddy as our home. My brothers and sisters at this stage were all living in Dublin and many of my own contemporaries had left the town too. With the deaths of my parents, my family had broken up and each of my brothers and sisters had gone their own separate ways, all of them in the direction of Dublin.

Glenart had provided a different kind of home for me over the previous four years, but now I was on my way to a new Vincentian community which I knew very little about and indeed it was not until the latter part of July that I was to find out what community I was going to be appointed to. I did not see all of this in negative terms. A new life I had been preparing for over eight years was about to begin. Subconsciously I knew that I was more and more out of touch with Glenamaddy and the people I had grown up with. I was not sufficiently mature at the time to be aware of what was happening or aware of the implications of losing touch with my roots in the West of Ireland.

CHAPTER 5

## *Back to School*
## *1962-1963*

*'Appointment to your* Alma Mater'

In mid-July 1962 the five newly ordained priests were invited to the Provincial's residence in Blackrock to receive their first appointments from Fr Christopher O'Leary. As we made our way across the city of Dublin on that particular afternoon, I was reasonably sure that I knew my appointment in advance. My brother Jim, who had been studying in Rome over the previous two years, wrote to me a few weeks previously to say that I was expected there the following September to begin studying either philosophy or theology in one of the Roman universities. Not mentioning this to anybody, I felt reasonably sure that I was destined for Rome to begin postgraduate studies there. Eamon Raftery was the first person interviewed and he was appointed to the teaching staff of St Paul's College, Raheny. I followed next and Father O'Leary stated straight away that I would be very happy with my new assignment. He was appointing me to the teaching staff of my *alma mater*. It was one of the biggest shocks of my life and it probably registered on my face. Fr O'Leary said a few more things to me which I cannot remember. He probably reassured me that I would feel at home in the Castleknock community. It did not dawn on me to say that I did not have a teaching subject as such because my UCD degree was in philosophy and logic. Anyway I had been called in not to be consulted but to be informed of what the Provincial and his Council had decided for me.

When I left the Provincial's office I was met outside by Father Jerome Twomey, superior of the house in Blackrock at that time. He probably read the shock on my face as he kindly took me aside for a few minutes, giving me time to recover my composure. Knowing that I was keen to continue studying philosophy he hinted that my appointment to Castleknock was likely to be for a year or two. From my point of view it appeared to be a death sentence. I had no enthusiasm for returning to my *alma mater*. Nevertheless I realised very quickly that I had no choice but to knuckle down to this assignment. There had been no dialogue or consultation with me about where I thought my gifts or talents might lie. This was par for the course at the time. My eight years of Vincentian formation was to prepare me to see such an appointment as an expression of the will of God for me.

The other three newly ordained priests had their interviews with Father O'Leary in turn. Perry Gildea was appointed to Rome to study moral theology in the Alphonsianum Institute; Donal Gallagher to the parish in Sheffield to join the parish team there; and Bill Murphy was appointed to work with the deaf community in St Peter's, Phibsboro. As we travelled back by bus to Phibsboro that evening I ruminated about what life was likely to be like in Castleknock on the other side of the desk with seven years of philosophy and theology under my belt. The more I thought about it the less attractive it appeared to me. I immersed myself in pastoral work in St Peter's, Phibsboro for the rest of the summer.

*Castleknock – eight years on*
When I moved from St Peter's, Phibsboro to Castleknock College in late August I was assigned a tiny room in what was known as the 'Priests' Corridor'. With the building of the new wing, to be known as Cregan House, there was an increase in the number of pupils to around the three hundred mark. The reputation of the college was at its peak. Before leaving for St Patrick's College of Education in 1958, Father Donal F. Cregan had built up the prestige of the school. He developed the curriculum, introducing Spanish, German and art and craft classes. He was responsible for the new building, which was later to be called after him, refurbishing many of the older buildings and also building a new swimming pool and reordering and levelling the sports pitches. There was a very long waiting list to get into the school and parents had to register their children many years in advance. In the 1960s there was very little development west of the Phoenix Park. The pressure to take in day boys was to come later.

There were sixteen Vincentians on the school staff, most of them in their twenties and thirties. The day was spent either in the classroom teaching one's subjects, training football teams in the afternoon, or running societies such as the debating societies, music societies, etc in the evening. The dean at the time encouraged me to mix as much as possible with the younger pupils so as to get to know them and befriend them. There were about fifteen lay teachers on the staff. Many of them had taught me as a pupil in the school eight years earlier.

At this time Castleknock was living through a golden age of its history. A Catholic culture pervaded Irish society and there was a community of values between the home, the parish and the school. Ireland was a drug-free society and school boy alcoholism was a problem well into the future. However, through the 1960s immense changes were to take place in Ireland in both church and society which would have profound implications for the future of the college. We were coming near the end of an era in which the Vincentian congregation could afford to have sixteen relatively young Vincentians on the staff of the college. The sun was beginning to set on this golden age but, of course, I did not know that at the time.

### 'Let him begin at the bottom'

There was no consultation with me about what subjects I might like to teach. Shortly after arriving I was informed by the Prefect of Studies that I was being assigned 3B for Latin, 2B for Religion and Latin, 1A for English and 1B for Mathematics. I gathered there was discussion between the Prefect of Studies and the President of the College at the time about assigning me to a religion class up the school. But the result of these conversations appears to have been: 'Well, as he is a young Vincentian, he should begin at the bottom.' I was given no suggestions from anyone about how to teach. The textbooks I needed for each of my classes were put into my hands and it was assumed I would get on with it. The one bit of advice that I was given was that I should come down on the boys 'like a ton of bricks' right from the very beginning, to establish my authority in the classroom. After I got the measure of the boys I could afford to relax a little later on. That was certainly good advice in relation to one class I had to deal with.

Overall I think I had a schedule of twenty-six to twenty-eight classes per week and in addition I was asked to take a few classes each week with a few boys who had come from England, in order to teach them the basics of the Irish language. The Provincial had asked me to sign up for the Higher Diploma in Education in University College, Dublin which would have meant commuting into Earlsfort Terrace on two or three evenings a week. Because this conflicted with my two or three classes with the boys who needed to learn the basics of Irish, the president of the college ruled that I should forget about doing the postgraduate Certificate in Education for a year or two. I was given no choice in the matter.

Teaching elementary Latin to the 3B and 2B classes was the most difficult teaching assignment that I had been given. Latin was my poorest subject in the Leaving Certificate and also in First Arts in UCD. I had very little enthusiasm for the subject but the task was made more difficult in having a number of weak and difficult pupils in these classes, especially in the 3B group. Three or four of the most difficult boys stretched me to my limits in keeping control in the classroom. Because there was more flexibility with what I could do in the 2B religion class, this class moved along more smoothly.

1A English was the most interesting class I taught during this year in Castleknock. There were a number of very bright youngsters in it, many of whom I got to know on the rugby pitch as the trainer of the Under Thirteens. Teaching this class was an enjoyable experience. These boys were keen to learn. Because of my lack of experience and training, I doubt if I stretched them sufficiently. IB was a small class of ten and eleven year olds. Mathematics was a subject I enjoyed teaching. I have pleasant memories of teaching this subject and observing these boys struggling with geometrical or other problems. I was intrigued by the fact that some boys saw the solutions to some mathematical problems so quickly and others took a good deal of time to break through.

A normal part of teaching these classes was to assign homework and to correct it. Examinations took place at the end of each term and the results had to be sent in to the Prefect of Studies by a certain date. As one of the priests on the staff, I took my turn in supervising study in the large study-hall. Here again you had to communicate to the boys, especially the older ones, that you meant business, which meant sending one or two of them to see the Prefect of Studies early on.

Teaching these classes absorbed all of my time and energies and gave me a realisation of how demanding the teaching profession is. Subsequently I could understand very easily how the Vincentians in the school just wanted to relax during the Christmas, Easter and Summer holidays to recover from their heavy schedule of teaching and supervision of pupils. Our commitment to the boys started with a round of Masses early in the morning and ended at 10.00 at night. For the dean it was a 24 hour commitment. Very often he would snatch a few hours sleep during the day when boys were in class.

*Vincentian Life from the Inside*
After the monastic regime of student life in Blackrock and Glenart, the structures of Vincentian life in Castleknock College did not appear to be very demanding. We had community prayer six mornings of the week beginning around seven fifteen. This was followed by Mass at a quarter to eight. If one was not on any of the Masses in the three chaplaincies we looked after, or the Mass for the boys in the college chapel, one celebrated Mass privately on one of the side-altars in or near the chapel with two boys serving the Mass. As none of the priests in the community, other than the President, was allowed to drive the college car, Brother Peter drove us to either Clonsilla, Glenmaroon or St Joseph of Cluny Convents. One had to be on the road quite early to be there on time. Even in 1962/63 Brother Peter's driving was a little erratic and he took no prisoners on the road. Our meal times followed the same pattern as the boys.

I have very good memories of community meals, especially during the holiday periods. The Christmas dinner was quite late in the day which gave many of the priests from Dublin a good deal of time to spend with their families. The superior of the community at the time loved to prolong feastday dinners or meals during holidays. Sometimes this caused some frustration among the younger members of the community who were straining at the leash to get away to Legion of Mary meetings or some other kind of pastoral commitment. This was their way of compensating for the lack of pastoral involvement with adults as priest-teachers in a boys' boarding school. Most of them had scooters which enabled them to get quickly to various destinations in Dublin as soon as a day's class was over. They looked quite a sight scurrying up the avenue on their Heinkels or mopeds a few minutes after the bell for the end of the last class had rung out. Not having a scooter, I used a bike to get in and out of town. A commitment to training the under thirteen rugby team, and taking remedial Irish classes to a few boys from England during study time, meant that my visits to town were much less frequent.

I have very few recollections of visiting other Vincentian communities in Dublin during the academic year 1962/63. The Castleknock community was quite self-sufficient as were other Vincentian communities in the Dublin area. We had some contact with St Patrick's College of Education, Drumcondra but this I think was because of the Fr Donal Cregan connection. I was to learn later that it was a feature of many Vincentian communities in the Irish Province to work in watertight compartments, independently of other communities, even though some of them may have been quite close by.

We took our turns on High Mass as celebrant, deacon or subdeacon, on feast days throughout the year and presiding at Solemn Vespers when richly adorned gold vestments were on display. In a few years' time Vatican II was going to make some inroads into all this solemnity. Nearly all the priests heard the confessions of the boys on Saturday nights during study time. Going to confession once or twice a month was a normal part of growing up in Ireland in those years. We also took our turns in giving sermons to the boys; there were no sermons at Masses in these pre-Vatican II years. Holding the attention of the different age groups in the college chapel was quite a challenge and one usually preached without notes.

When I was in the college about four weeks or so, the superior invited me into his office for a chat. My recollection is that he was looking for something to pull me up on. It was a nagging conversation that left me with a strong sense of disappointment and also with a sense of being unappreciated and unaffirmed despite making my best efforts to pull my weight as a member of the community.

I was asked to do the Stations of the Cross in St Joseph of Cluny Convent during Holy Week. Rather than relying on any booklet in use at the time, I decided to compose my own Stations of the Cross, putting quite a lot of work into this. I wondered afterwards whose needs were being met. It probably pointed up that there was a strong need in me at this time for some pastoral outlet.

For recreation I sometimes went to the Astor Cinema where there were quality continental films on offer. Renais and Antonini were just coming on stream. I can remember one day hearing some munching a seat or two behind me. When I turned around I discovered that it was Fr Stan Brindley, one of my fellow members of the Castleknock community. Though Stan and myself had responsibility for selecting movies for the boys during that year, I doubt if we could have offered them a diet of Renais or Antonini.

I found the members of the Vincentian community supportive and affirming. There was a strong *esprit de corps* about the work we were doing in the college and there was also a strong sense of commitment to community values. In retrospect, I can see that it was lacking in terms of spiritual vision and an absence of creativity in promoting Vincentian values in relation to social justice.

### Various Events at Home and Abroad

The Vatican Council began in the autumn of 1962. It got a good deal of coverage in the Irish media but because I was so busy throughout the year I have no memories of absorbing any of the information coming through from Rome. This also highlighted the fact that I had no great expectations that it was going to lead to very much anyway. I would not be surprised if many Irish people at the time felt the same way about it. There was no sense in Ireland at that time of needing a Council to take the Catholic Church in new directions. We were quite content with the *status quo*. We had the highest Sunday Mass attendance of any country in Western Europe; our seminaries were overflowing with seminarians; our houses of formation of men and women were teeming with novices; hundreds of priests, brothers and sisters were leaving the country each year to found new missions in Africa, Asia and S. America and so on. 'Why change a winning formula?' is what many people must have been thinking in the Irish church. As we look back now we can see that there were forces operating in continental post-war Europe that we were oblivious to – secularising forces that would eventually rock the church to its foundations.

On an autumn day in 1962 I met with my brother Mal before he took off for the United States. It really was the parting of the ways for the two of us. I had cycled into town to meet him in some restaurant and the journey back to Castleknock through an autumnal Phoenix Park was a very lonely one for me. Like many an Irishman before him, my brother was stepping out into the unknown. As he saw it, there were better prospects of making a livelihood in the United States. T. K. Whittaker's economic miracle was in gestation in the Department of Finance during these years but the evidence of any change in the Irish economy had yet to materialise.

I remember two 'uncomfortable' events taking place for me through this year in Castleknock. One of them was Union Night and the other was called Union Day. Union Night was a dinner which took place in the college when pastmen turned up in formal attire. For whatever reason I felt quite uncomfortable. It was more than likely that I linked up with a few pastmen of my own vintage. I think I was reacting against the 'old school tie brigade'. I also felt uncomfortable during Union Day and was very relieved when it was all over. Walking about meeting parents for the first time made me aware of how much I still had to learn about basic social skills. However, Union Day appeared to me to be an upper-crust event mainly for the parents of the boys so that they could feel proud of their offspring. Taking pride in their children getting a good education was of course a healthy pride and God knows many parents had made great financial sacrifices to send their children to the college. Maybe there were too many Jaguars in the car park that day for me to feel comfortable about the whole enterprise.

During the academic year 1962/63 I attended some of the Sunday Concilium meetings of the office holders of the Legion of Mary in the Mansion House. The vibrancy of this group at that time really made an impact on me. The movement was in full spate, spreading all over the world. At some of those meetings there were reports coming in from various places in Africa, S. America and Asia about the spread of the Legion of Mary to remote areas in these continents. The dedication of laymen and laywomen to basic forms of evangelisation was impressive by any standards. Hearing articulate reports that were being sent back from special envoys to the Headquarters in Dublin was spellbinding. In 1962 the Legion of Mary must have been at the high point of its development. The biography of Edel Quinn by Bishop Leo Joseph Suenens, Auxiliary Bishop of Malines-Brussels as he was at this time, highlighted the role a lay person could play in the church and the Legion itself offered a model of evangelisation that gave hope to many people. The waning of the Legion of Mary in the post-Vatican II church in Ireland and elsewhere as new lay movements were developing elsewhere, especially in Continental Europe, is a subject well worth investigating

During the summer of 1963 I went to work in Christ the King parish in Coventry. This was the first extended period for me of two or three weeks of working in a parish context. It was a lively and busy place and I got a good deal of encouragement from one of the curates there. I linked up with the confrères in Ullathorne School and also managed to get in a quick visit to Wimbledon using Strawberry Hill as my base. Seeing Rod Laver and Lew Hoad in the flesh gave me quite a thrill. I ended up in Dunstable for a few days in mid-July and I can remember walking around the foundations of the new circular church that Fr Maurice Regis O'Neill was building in that town.

*Reflections on my Castleknock teaching experience*
The easy relationship between boys and priests when I was a pupil in Castleknock is also a memory of the one year I spent teaching there in 1962/63. This indeed was one of the strengths of the school. The natural goodness of the boys, and their potential as young Christians, is a vivid memory I have of that one year. At the same time, even before the end of that first year I became very much aware of how inward-looking the school was.

It was living on the capital of a tradition built up over a hundred and twenty five years. During that time a powerful network of pastmen had been set up in a variety of professions – medicine, law, engineering, architecture, accountancy, and so on. However, I had an inkling in 1962/63 that there was a very limited vision of the future of the school amongst many of the priests and lay staff. This was a vision of the college 'continuing on as before', ignoring many of the changes just beginning to take place in Irish society. Donagh O'Malley's provision of state-funded education for all secondary school pupils was just around the corner.

My one year's teaching experience made me aware of how difficult the teaching profession is and this experience was sharpened later when I taught in a college of education in London. How to prepare a class properly and to structure it with a beginning, a middle and an end, how to engage the interests of a variety of pupils from the weakest to the most intelligent, how to maintain discipline, etc. were skills I only became fully aware of later on when I supervised student teachers in London schools. I certainly would have needed some help to acquire and develop these skills myself if I had continued teaching in Castleknock and I have my doubts about whether the Higher Diploma in Education, as it was set up at that time in UCD, would have provided me with this expertise.

It was often said that a school is a good place for a young priest to begin his ministry. He has to learn habits of discipline and how to structure and order his day and meet the various commitments in the classroom and outside it. My memories of my one year teaching in Castleknock are positive ones. I had to learn fast how to maintain control in the classroom, produce the goods in twenty-eight class periods each week and pull my weight in the overall running of the school. I have no recollection of reading theology or philosophy books during the year 1962/63, or attending any courses during that time. Responding to the needs of the boys and mixing with them as much as possible, getting to know them and encouraging them were my chief priorities. I can sense how easily it would have been for me to be completely absorbed in Castleknock, its myths, its traditions and its developments into the future. From the point of view of being inducted into priestly ministry, it was not very challenging. I was not interacting with adults, their problems and concerns, and there were limited outlets for pastoral ministry in the three convents where we acted as chaplains.

What I did not know during this year was that 1962/63 was to mark the end of an era. A new president was appointed in September 1963 who opened up new possibilities for the development of the school. As for myself that summer, I received a new appointment. I was asked to do postgraduate studies in philosophy in Louvain University and that meant a whole new life of study and research opened up for me. In three years' time I was to find myself back in the world of education, in a Catholic college of education, lecturing at undergraduate level. To some extent I too was taking the emigrant ship, to study first of all in a continental university where many Irish priests had studied before me and then to lecture the sons and daughters of emigrant Irish parents who had gone to London, Birmingham, Liverpool, Manchester, Luton, and other English and Welsh cities and towns in search of work, leaving economically depressed postwar Ireland. In retrospect, I can see now that my one year teaching in Castleknock College provided me with an experience of one kind of privileged education which I was to reflect a lot on later on.

# CHAPTER 6

# *Louvain at a Turning Point*
# *1963-1966*

*First Stop – Paris*

On 19 July 1963, the traditional feast of St Vincent De Paul, I was back in Castleknock to receive my official letter appointing me to Louvain to begin postgraduate studies in philosophy. I was delighted with this news as it opened up the possibility of pursuing my interest in philosophy. My UCD honours degree gave me confidence that I was capable of pursuing postgraduate studies. The biggest drawback at this stage was not having any knowledge of the French language. Unfortunately I had not taken it as a subject in secondary school and it meant getting down to business to learn the basics of the language as quickly as possible. I made arrangements to spend five weeks in Paris at the Alliance Française learning the rudiments of French. Before leaving Dublin, I linked up with Paddy Masterson, who had completed his postgraduate studies in Louvain two years previously and was now on the philosophy staff in UCD. Paddy gave me a brief run down on some of the lecturers I was likely to meet and the kind of philosophy on offer. Towards the end of August I flew to Paris and took up residence in the Vincentian Maison-Mère for the following five weeks. There was a very large group of Vincentians living there at that time, including the Superior General and his Curia. I went over to the Rue du Bac most mornings to celebrate Mass at a small altar in one of the tribunes circling the main chapel. There was a constant flow of people coming and going from the Rue Du Bac throughout the day. Next to Lourdes it was one of the most popular Marian shrines in Europe. I joined the community in the Maison Mère for morning prayer at an unearthly hour in a very austere prayer room. I sat in the visitors' section of the large dining room, which was fairly full at that time with priests sitting in rows right up to the table where the Superior General presided. The long table near the windows on the right was known as 'Montparnasse'. Some of the French Vincentians told me that the next stop after you fell off the end of this table was into the cemetery nearby, Montparnasse. The wine at meals was a real bonus for me.

A day or two after arriving in Paris I signed up in the Alliance Française and began learning the basics of French. Classes took place every morning of the week from Monday to Friday. There was also a conversation class on most afternoons. After a few weeks, when asked to speak on a particular topic, I chose to describe Leprechauns, maintaining that they were the little people who really ran Ireland. At the end of my exposition one or two people asked me very seriously if these little people really existed!

Five weeks language preparation for Louvain was quite in-adequate. If I were doing my studies all over again I certainly would have begun with learning French and German for the whole of the first year, living in both French and German speaking environments. Not having fluent French was quite a handi-cap to me in Louvain although I didn't fully realise it at the time. This would certainly have meant continuing my studies for at least four years and I knew at that time that I would be very lucky to get three years.

### Getting to know the city

Having acquired a Michelin guide to Paris, I very quickly visited all the key sights: Notre Dame Cathedral, the Royal Chapel, the Arc de Triomphe, the Louvre, the Eiffel Tower, Les Invalides, the Panthéon, the Luxembourg Gardens, Versailles, Chartres and many other places of interest. During these beautiful September days in 1963 I fell in love with Paris, enjoying very much exploring the narrow streets on the Left Bank. Memories of the strong smell of fresh coffee escaping from the cafés has al-ways stayed with me. I was impressed by the elegance and poise of the Parisians, their carefree café life and at the same time I de-tected a certain disdain for the foreigner. Later on I learned that French people appeared to be friendlier in other parts of France, especially the south. The Maison-Mère offered me a good base while pursuing my elementary French course and for exploring Paris. It was still the official residence for the students of the

Paris province and I got to know a number of the seminarians and the priests, including Fr Gunth, a Chinese missionary, Fr Cantinat, a scripture scholar, Fr Dodin, an expert on St Vincent and his times, Fr Chalumeau, the provincial archivist, and many others. I became aware of the extensive missionary endeavours of the Paris province in Madagascar, China and the Middle East. At the same time there were plenty of signs in post-Second World War France that a great missionary period was coming to an end and that many new challenges were opening up for the church in post-war France.

These were exciting weeks for me. A whole new world was opening up before me: the world of contemporary French philosophy – philosophers such as Sartre and Marcel; French theology – theologians such as de Lubac and Congar; French Literature – writers such as François Mauriac, Georges Bernanos and Paul Claudel. For the next few years I was going to become enthralled by France's liturgical developments and the Catholic Church's pastoral efforts to counter de-Christianisation in post-War France. The controversial suppression of the worker priest movement in the 1950s was still a hot topic … Although I did not realise it at the time, I was now beginning a process of re-education in both philosophy and theology. This was to open up windows for me in what was going to be a major turning point in the church's tradition. Even then I had no idea of the intense struggles that had taken place in Rome during the first session of Vatican II or the great turnabout that was about to take place in the second session, beginning at the end of this month of September. Through living in Louvain during the next three years, and with frequent visits to Paris and other places in France, I was going to be put in touch with some of the key ideas that fed into the Second Vatican Council and to get involved in discussions on both theoretical and practical levels about the renewal of the church.

*First Impressions of Louvain*
Arriving in Louvain on a beautiful autumn day in the first week of October 1963, I took a taxi from the railway station to the Vincentian house in Vaartstraat at the western end of the town. A short distance away was the Benedictine Monastery of Mont

César – also known as Klosterberg – where Abbot Marmion had lived for a number of years. Also in the neighbourhood was the Béguinage St Gertrude where many of the small houses were now quite dilapidated. Around the corner was the Stella Artois brewery which made one of Belgium's most popular beers. Being the first Irish Vincentian priest to stay in this house, the five Flemish priests and one brother in the community gave me a warm welcome. I was assigned a simple room on the upper floor of the school building. Over the next few days I was introduced to four student priests – two Vincentians from the Eastern province of the United States and two members of the Congregation of St Viator from Chicago. At this time the Flemish confrères ran an apostolic school in this house with about thirty boys boarding, around the ages of twelve to fourteen. Still living in the aftermath of the Second World War, this community had a very simple lifestyle. On most Friday nights the student priests would repair to a local restaurant to have a meal of steak and pommes frites. As winter set in we always needed to protect ourselves against the damp atmosphere of Louvain and the cold winds that frequently blew across the flat Belgian countryside from the north and the east.

On the first day I arrived in Louvain I visited the Irish College where an Irish Franciscan community had flourished for over three centuries. There were five Franciscan priests living there and about thirty students studying philosophy. I met P. J. McGrath, a diocesan priest, who later lectured in St Patrick's College Maynooth and University College Cork. He offered to show me where the Institute of Philosophy was located and also the library and some other buildings in Naamsestraat. I saw very little of P. J. for the rest of the year. He was commuting back and forth to Oxford where he was researching a doctoral thesis on contemporary English analytic philosophy. Our paths never crossed again.

Louvain at that time was a university town with a population of around 40,000 people. It was situated twenty kilometres east of Brussels, on the main railway line running west from Brussels to Liège, Aachen and Cologne. The main library was burnt down during the 1st World War and many of its precious manuscripts were destroyed. This library was rebuilt with a lot of funds from American Universities – the names of these universities are inscribed on the walls at the front of the building in gratitude to the university's American benefactors. During the 2nd World War a good deal of damage was done to the town once again by both German and Allied bombing raids. In 1963 one could still see the scars of some wartime bombing in various places around the town. A number of stories were still circulating about war-time collaborators and the punishment meted out to them at the end of the war.

The Catholic University of Louvain was founded in 1425 and was modelled on universities in Paris, Cologne and Vienna. Today it makes the claim to be the oldest surviving Catholic University in the world. Like Oxford University, most of the faculties were scattered throughout the town and some of them were located in buildings going back to the 15th century. The streets were cobblestoned and of course these cobblestones provided students with readymade ammunition when riots took place. This happened on a number of occasions over the next three years. I remember one incident when I came up a side street onto the Avenue des Alliés to see students coming from the centre of the town, armed with cobblestones and the riot police coming from the railway station, in full battle gear. I got out of town very quickly on that day. The conflict between the Flemings and Walloons was at its height in the 1960s and came to a head in 1968. The University was divided in two: Louvain became known by its Flemish name – Leuven. All teaching took place in Flemish. The French-speaking Catholic University of Louvain was built on a green site on the other side of the linguistic border at Ottignies about twenty kilometres south of Louvain. Knowing that they were very unlikely to continue to attract students from other countries, the Flemish faculties of philosophy and theology very quickly set up English speaking programmes. In 1972 the separation was completed. The process of separation was very painful. It was said that the great library was divided in two: all the books from A to L remained in Leuven. The books from M to Z were transported to the newly built French University in Ottignies. The story was somewhat exaggerated but it was in common currency to convey how painful the division of the university was to many of the professors, especially those in the philosophy and theology departments. All this was some nine years away when I arrived in the town in the autumn of 1963. As foreign students in Belgium we could not help noticing the contradictions between the claims of the Belgians to be at the centre of the Common Market, as it was known in those days, and all kinds of tribal warfare going on between Flemings and Walloons in Louvain and elsewhere.

With a student population of twenty thousand, the Catholic University of Louvain was the largest of the four universities in Belgium. There were a number of student residences in the town run by priests or religious sisters. The majority of students stayed in flats or apartments or commuted to the university from nearby towns and villages. There was a hectic student life with a lot of beer drinking at all hours of the day and night. Student power was just beginning to find its voice and from time to time there were 'high jinks' with students letting off steam over one issue or another. One of the requirements of being in a Catholic University was that each student had to take two theology courses in their first and second years. The student Masses in both the Flemish- and French-speaking chaplaincies were well attended and the chaplains did their best to adapt liturgies to their student groups. Each had its own church or chapel and they were fairly well frequented at that time. Daily Masses took place in many of the religious run houses all over the town and again small groups of students participated in these Masses. There was no shortage of priests. In the theology and philosophy departments alone there must have been more than twenty priest professors. A number of them would have looked after some of the student residences.

During my three years in Louvain I had no doubt that I was living in a Catholic country. Catholic political parties, Catholic trade unions and many other Catholic groups were very much in evidence. I was to learn very quickly that there was great interest in what was happening at the Vatican Council, now moving into its second session in the autumn of 1963, and the role Belgian bishops and Louvain theologians were playing in this and subsequent sessions. The quip that surfaced some years later that Vatican II was a meeting of the Belgian bishops and their theological advisers – most of them from Louvain of course

– which bishops and theologians from other parts of the world could tune into – was passed around for some time in the immediate aftermath of the Council. Of more substance was Yves Congar's tribute to Louvain theology published in his Vatican II diary in the year 2000: 'It is being said that this is the First Council of Louvain, taking place in Rome – *Primum Concilium Lovaniense, Romae habitum*, and this is largely true, at least as far as theology is concerned. And at the centre of this theology we find Monsignor Gerard Philips who is the primary architect of the theological input at the Council' (Congar's Diary, March 1964).

Through its 480 year history the university of Louvain has survived all kinds of vicissitudes and political upheavals in the lowlands. It was closed on a number of occasions around the time of the French Revolution and the two World Wars but managed to re-open very quickly when peace returned. The Catholic Bishops of Belgium are the trustees of the university and the funding comes from the state. In 1963 the Rector was a bishop. In recent years laymen have held that post. Towards the end of the war Cardinal Suenens was one of the Vice-Rectors of the University. He went on from there to become an Auxiliary Bishop to Cardinal Van Roey, and eventually he became Cardinal Archbishop of Malines/Brussels, the largest of the seven dioceses in Belgium.

At the end of the first week of term, there was an official opening of the university year which took the form of a procession of professors in their academic gowns from the central administration building in Naamsestraat to St Peter's Church, some hundred yards away at the centre of the town. The opening Mass of the year was celebrated in Flemish and French. Quite a large group of professors, lecturers and students attended that Mass in October 1963. This was the traditional way of beginning the university year going back to the origins of the university in the 15th century. I was impressed by the rich ceremonial occasion. The procession of the professors in their colourful gowns and headgear straight out of the middle ages and the High Mass in St Peter's Church incorporating all the triumphalist trappings of our pre-Vatican II liturgy.

During my first two years in Louvain the students who were

priests wore their clerical attire attending lectures. Priests were restricted by local church law from going to the cinema but before the end of my time there both these regulations had fallen away. Not that there was any formal declaration that they were no longer in force, but I think students, particularly in the light of what was coming through from the Vatican Council, began to make up their own minds about the rightness or wrongness of these matters. I felt no compunction about going to a number of movies in Brussels before the end of my time in Louvain. Were these developments the first tangible signs of a clerical culture beginning to break up, which would gather quite a momentum before the end of the 1960s ?

### The Institute of Philosophy

The Institute of Philosophy was founded in 1889 by Monsignor Mercier, who later became Cardinal Archbishop of Malines/ Brussels. This institute was set up to counter various philosophies, especially positivism, then beginning to dominate intellectual life in many universities in Europe. The Institute of Philosophy was a direct response to Pope Leo XIII's appeal to Catholics around the world to make St Thomas Aquinas the centre of philosophical studies for all those preparing for priesthood. From the very beginning Mercier wanted to set up a programme of lectures with Thomism as the central core of the curriculum. Nevertheless, he wanted it to be an enlightened form of Thomism that would be in dialogue with contemporary philosophies and with the findings of the empirical sciences. This would be in contrast to 'Thomism of the strict observance' taught in some of the Roman colleges. During the first half of the twentieth century, the Institute of Philosophy acquired an international reputation and attracted students from all over the world, especially from the United States.

### The Philosophy Curriculum

Over the years the curriculum has evolved. Today the Institute follows a variety of contemporary philosophical interests: phenomenology, an American brand of the philosophy of language and the philosophical status of psycho-analytic discourse and so on. Thomism is dealt with as one of the important currents of thought in the course on the history of philosophy of the Middle Ages.

In the 1960s students could get a baccalaureat in philosophy in two years and a licentiate in two further years by taking about ten to twelve courses each year. At baccalaureat level courses included: history of philosophy divided into ancient, medieval, modern and contemporary periods, and general introductions to key areas of philosophy: general metaphysics, special metaphysics – which included natural theology, epistemology, philosophical anthropology, philosophy of nature and ethics. A number of electives were also on offer, which could be taken in other departments. These included: psychology of religion, philosophy of art, philosophy of law, introduction to sociology and so on. The possibility of building bridges to other disciplines was a key element in the curriculum. The courses at licentiate level over a two year period were studies of texts from each of the four great periods of philosophy. Students also took a number of electives to make up the required eleven or twelve courses. Very often lecturers offered courses on areas of research they were currently engaged in.

The methodology in place was mainly a lecture system. Examinations at the end of the year were oral – exams in which you had 15 to 20 minutes to prove that you had absorbed the contents of the course. The three week exam period each summer was exhausting for both students and professors alike. I had one written examination at the end of my second year, a comprehensive exam, which was the gateway to doctoral studies. One had to attain a certain grade to be allowed to proceed to doctoral research. There were no tutorials of any kind during my three years in Louvain. The oral examinations had added difficulties for students who didn't have fluency in French. However, I found that overall the lecturers were fair in the way they operated the system. It was not uncommon for a number of the students, even at postgraduate level, to return early in the autumn to take repeat examinations. The lecture system was built on the assumption that the lecturers themselves were the authorities in the areas they lectured in and in which they had specialised over many years. It was only when students reached licentiate level that they were required to begin writing themselves. A one hundred page thesis was one of the requirements of the final licentiate examination.

*Albert Dondeyne*

Dondeyne was one of the most interesting and inspiring lecturers I had in Louvain. His area of expertise was on various aspects of the existence of God. His lectures were very much alive because of the impression he gave of 'philosophising on his feet'. He would walk back and forth on the lecture podium, drawing little squiggles on the board, or screwing up his face in a tortured expression when trying to work something out. One got the impression that he was struggling to find a way to speak metaphysically about God or indeed to find a way to affirm the existence of God.

His doctoral thesis was on the agnosticism of Immanuel Kant and one got the impression that he spent most of his earlier life trying to break through the idealism of Neo-Kantians such as Leon Brunschvicg and other Idealist philosophers of the early 20th century. He did so by bringing Aquinas' doctrine of abstraction into dialogue with these philosophers.

From his course on Kant one certainly picked up that he was sympathetic towards Kant's negative critique of the traditional arguments for the existence of God. Dondeyne was searching for a way to speak metaphysically about God. At the same time a good deal of his 1964/1965 licentiate course concentrated on Kant's *Critique of Practical Reason*, outlining Kant's idea on the existence of God being a postulate of the practical reason. The existence of God is invoked to give coherence to our moral life. All of Dondeyne's lectures in my two years were an effort to formulate a way to God with morality as its starting point.

In my second year he introduced us to texts from Emmanuel Levinas' *Totalité et Infini*, which had just been published. Though I did not fully realise it at the time, the publication of this book marked an important turning point for continental European philosophy. Lévinas was distancing himself from Heidegger and was taking phenomenology down a new road. Lévinas claims that there is a transcendent element in our encounter with the other, especially with 'the widow, the orphan and the poor'. At one level one could say that there were many Vincentian echoes of finding God in the poor running through Lévinas' writings. I can still remember Dondeyne's enthusiasm as he outlined some of Lévinas' themes in this book. These themes were a vindication for Dondeyne that one could link phenomenology and metaphysics and that metaphysical statements about God were possible. In the last twenty years Lévinas has come to be regarded as one of the great phenomenologists of the twentieth century. Because of his religious background – he was an expert on a variety of Talmudic texts – he related easily to philosophers working out of a religious background. He visited Louvain a number of times before 1963 to give a series of public lectures and to consult the Husserl archives.

The search for a moral proof or way to God has always intrigued me and led me eventually to concentrate on this area in selecting a topic for doctoral research. Attending Dondeyne's lectures over these two years stimulated my interest in this area. Later on I studied Henri Bergson's *Two Sources of Morality and Religion*. It is a way to God with the experience of the 'mystics' as a starting point. When I studied Bergson's writings I came to the conclusion that his way to God starting from the experience of the mystics was more a matter of testimony than philosophical argument and that it had limited philosophical value. I also looked at Newman's argument from conscience. There is, I believe, a convergence between a number of these philosophers and religious thinkers about taking our moral experience as a starting point for a 'way to God' and Dondeyne in his day made some significant contributions to that discussion.

Dondeyne's *European Thought and Christian Faith*, published in 1958, was widely read. The contents of this book were in marked contrast to the inward looking tendencies of the papal encyclical, *Humani Generis*. Dondeyne argued that Thomism should enter into dialogue with contemporary European philosophy, especially with various phenomenological and existential movements in post-war Europe. Dialogue with atheists rather than condemnation of them was one of the underlying themes in this book and this approach was to bear fruit some seven years later in the way the Second Vatican Council dealt with the notion of atheism in *Gaudium et Spes, The Church in the Modern World*. Through the 1950s Dondeyne took the view that Thomists needed to enter into dialogue with phenomenology and existentialism. This did not stop him pointing out in his writings that there were traces of Cartesianism and also traces of a new kind of empiricism in these currents of thought.

Dondeyne made an enormous contribution to Catholic intellectual life in Belgium in the post-war years. Through this period he gave lectures on a variety of topics about various aspects of Christian life - the role of lay men and women in the church, the church in dialogue with the world, tolerance in church and society. He exercised the same kind of influence in intellectual circles in Belgium that Cardinal Cardijn exercised in working class circles in the JOC movement. Many of Dondeyne's talks and articles in various Belgian journals were 20th century expositions of *fides quaerens intellectum*.

The division of the university in 1972 was a very sad day for Dondeyne. In his role as President of the council of the Institute of Philosophy, he presided at the united council of Flemish and Frankophone professors for the last time. The Institute of Philosophy, like all the other departments in Louvain, had to yield to the political pressures splitting the country into two linguistic regions. For Dondeyne, the man of dialogue, this scission was profoundly disappointing. It is Dondeyne – the philosophical and theological bridge-builder – the man of hope and optimism who lingers on in my mind. He died in 1985.

### Georges van Riet – Theory of Knowledge

Van Riet lectured us on Hegel's *Phenomenology of Mind* and in particular on ten or twelve pages in this text, which deals with the master/slave relationship. This was one of the most demanding courses I had to take during my time in Louvain, partly because of the difficulty of Hegel's text and getting inside Hegel's philosophy. It was also because Van Riet himself was very demanding in his expectations of one's understanding of the text and one's capacity to take a critical stance towards it. Van Riet certainly inculcated in his students the importance of accurate interpretation of philosophical texts and a critical attitude towards philosophers of all persuasions.

*Jacques Etienne* – Aristotle's *Nicomachean Ethics*
Professor Etienne gave us a commentary on Aristotle's *Nico-machean Ethics*. The course itself was a comprehensive examination on 'the final end of man', 'the concept of virtue', 'action and contemplation', and 'the nature of friendship'. Etienne drew a good deal from the marvellous commentary on the *Nicomachean Ethics* by *Jolif and Gauthier*, which had just been published in France. On a number of occasions later on when I lectured on philosophy in Strawberry Hill I chose the *Nicomachean Ethics* as a basic text. It is a great starting point for discussion of some of the key questions in moral philosophy.

*Fernard van Steenberghen* – History of Medieval Philosophy/ Metaphysics/Is there a Christian Philosophy?
Professor van Steenberghen was an expert in medieval philosophy. Many students opted to do doctoral theses under his guidance. He introduced them to a methodology for elucidating unpublished medieval philosophical texts. He was an expert on the various philosophical movements of the thirteenth century and pointed up the diversity of philosophical viewpoints through this period. He also wrote a marvellous little book entitled *Aristotle in the West*, which told the exciting story of how some of Aristotle's writings reached the west through Islamic scholars in north Africa and Spain.

In one of his courses, he brought us through the famous debate of the 1930s, 'Is there any such thing as Christian Philosophy'?' and in this he was reacting mainly against Etienne Gilson. This debate flared up in the 1930s and became quite a talking point, certainly in Catholic circles, before the Second World War. Gilson used the word 'Christian' in the titles of nearly all his books: *A Christian Philosophy of the Middle Ages*, his great work, *A Christian Philosophy of St Thomas Aquinas*, *A Christian Philosophy of St Augustine*, *A Christian Philosophy of St Bonavenure* and so on. The young Fernard van Steenberghen of the 1930s must have seen all this as 'selling the past'. He certainly got very worked up on a number of occasions as he outlined his own position in this debate. He was not in favour of any facile concordism between philosophy and Christianity. He advocated a healthy separation between philosophy and theology. I think van Steenberghen was right. To follow Gilson's way of thinking was to leave oneself open to the charge that Bertrand Russell brought against philosophers of the Middle Ages, even Aquinas, that most of this philosophy was theology in disguise.

Professor van Steenbergen had very little time for the sliding of some of his fellow philosophy lecturers towards phenomenology. Did he see this as a betrayal of Thomism? This movement was already well under way in my time. Van Steenberghen inculcated an enlightened brand of Thomism which, according to him, provided the right framework for genuine philosophical investigation. He communicated his 'metaphysical system' to us with great enthusiasm and forthrightness. On one particular day when questioned about his approach, he stated that he was 'ontologically secure'. One certainly felt that he was going to maintain rigorous standards in examinations for the sake of the reputation of the Institute. Some ten years later, he retired at the statutory age of sixty-five. He continued on with his research in medieval philosophy and produced articles from time to time.

*Jean Ladrière* – Philosophy of Nature
Professor Ladrière lectured in the traditional area of cosmology or what became known as the philosophy of nature. He was proficient in various branches of scientific knowledge, and his knowledge of contemporary science poured out of him in a torrent of words from the beginning to the end of his lectures. Very few students could keep up with him. After a few lectures, I opted to study a particular text which dealt with Heisenberg's 'Uncertainty Principle'. I remember taking the oral examination in his apartment looking out on the roundabout at the centre of the town near St Peter's Church. One got the impression that you were doing him a favour in coming along to be examined on an area of philosophy. I doubt very much if he ever failed students. In his writings and lectures he came across as a convinced Christian. He had been a student for the priesthood in the Leo XIII Seminary for a number of years but decided to leave and to concentrate on a career in philosophy.

*Gerard Montpellier* – Empirical Psychology
The philosophy department in Louvain took seriously the findings

of the empirical sciences, the natural sciences and later sociology, psychology, biology etc. It appears to have been a trend in the department right from the beginning of the twentieth century. It dealt with various experiments to do with vision. Professor Montpellier was nearing emeritus status in 1964/65. He was quietly spoken, and very courteous to students in lectures and in examinations at the end of the year.

*Other Professors*

There were a number of other professors in the faculty of philosophy with whom I had little contact – Verbeke, de Waelhens, Wenin and Van der Wiele. They concentrated on lecturing in the Flemish speaking section of the Institute. Professor Wylleman was the secretary of the Institute. He was a friendly and approachable man and a chain-smoker. I remember when I did my final comprehensive licentiate examination he called me in and looked at my text and suggested that I sign all the pages of my exam paper, take it home and type it up for him. This I was glad to do and felt relieved that whoever was reading my exam paper would have a legible text in front of him. Professor Joseph Dopp lectured in contemporary philosophy – logic and contemporary Anglo-Saxon philosophy, logical positivism and linguistic analysis. I was exempt from having to study logic because of what I had covered in my UCD degree and I was very relieved for that. Dopp's *Truth Tables* were the *bête noire* of many philosophy students in Louvain. Professor Wenin lectured in philosophical anthropology to the Flemish students as did a Capuchin priest, Fr Herman Leo van Breda who was reputed to have acquired Husserl's philosophical papers from Husserl's widow on the outbreak of the Second World War. It was said that, as a reward for doing this, he was offered a lectureship in the Philosophy Department . Professor Tamineux was the youngest lecturer in the Institute. He lectured on philosophy of art. When I returned to Louvain in the autumn of 1994 for a few months, Professor Tamineux's name was the only one I recognised on the list of current lecturers in the Institute in that year. *Sic transit gloria …* Professor De Waelhens was an expert on contemporary phenomenology with a number of publications to his name including a book on the writings of Merleau-Ponty. He was the professor most out of tune with the Thomistic tradition in the Institute. The President of the Institute of Philosophy in my first year in Louvain, 1963/1964 was Professor de Raeymacker, a tall stately figure. He had written a book on the *Philosophy of Being*, which was regarded as a classic in its day in Thomistic circles. I went to one of his lectures and came away dazed at this airy world of Thomistic metaphysics. Mountaineering at 10,000 feet is the best example I can think of to describe this experience.

*Visits to Trier, Paris, Toulouse ...*

At the Halloween break, near the end of October 1963, I visited an American Vincentian in Trier, staying in the Vincentian house there for a night or two. John McKenna was studying liturgy under Balthazer Fischer, one of the great German liturgists in the Liturgy Institute in Trier. I remember vividly on Halloween night going out for a meal with him in a restaurant in the centre of Trier and rediscovering the restaurant over forty years later. My outstanding memories of that visit are of passing through Bastoigne on the way to Trier and learning something about the famous Second World War battle that took place there. During my Castleknock schooldays this battle had been graphically portrayed in a movie called *The Battle of the Bulge* which coloured my views of what I saw in Bastoigne that afternoon. I also have memories of seeing crowds of people visiting the cemeteries in Trier on All Souls Day. A number of the churches I visited had long lists of Germans on war memorials – soldiers who had died in Flanders Fields during the 1st World War and soldiers who had died in Hitler's lunatic campaigns on both the Eastern and Western fronts during the 2nd World War. Ireland had escaped all these World War massacres. This kind of experience and visits to some of the war cemeteries started to bring home to me the carnage of these wars and the suffering it had brought on some many people across Europe, including Germans.

During the Easter break in 1964, I returned to Paris to try and improve my French over the holidays. I was enthralled by the Holy Saturday night liturgy in St Séverin. In subsequent years I was always impressed by the simplicity of the liturgies in French churches. While I was in Paris I explored what was being taught in the philosophy department of the Institut Catholique. I certainly got the impression that it was predominantly versions of Thomistic philosophy and theology that were taught there. A number of prominent Dominicans of the day were lecturing in the Institut Catholique at this time.

I arrived in Paris on the morning of Palm Sunday, in time to hear one of the Lenten sermons of Père Carré – a famous Jesuit preacher – in Notre Dame Cathedral. Notre Dame was packed on that Sunday afternoon. I began to realise the impact Lacordaire must have had when he did something similar in the previous century. The only difference was that Lacordaire did not have the benefit of French radio to spread his message around France. Reading French newspapers over this period made me realise how much coverage was given to the Catholic Church in the quality newspapers: *Le Monde* and *Le Figaro*. I spent some of that Easter holiday period in Toulouse, the period after Easter trying to improve my French and where I would have to make an effort to communicate in the language. One of my memories of these few weeks in Toulouse was attending a rugby match. I came to realise that in this part of the south of France I was in the heartland of French rugby.

Over my three years in Louvain, I saw very little of Belgium. It was only in the mid-1970s that I visited Bruges and Ghent for the first time. I visited the Abbey of Maredsous on one occasion. It happened to be a Sunday. Vast crowds of people were milling around the shops near the entrance. The monastery had all kinds of gift shops which attracted a large variety of people. I was so shocked by all this that after a brief visit to the monastery chapel I left a short time later. I also visited Mont César, the Benedictine Abbey on the western side of Louvain. I was very unimpressed by the Benedictine liturgy on the Sundays or feast days when I went there to join the congregation for Sunday High Mass or Sunday evening vespers. While I was in Louvain I was not aware that Mont César was the monastery where Abbot Marmion had spent many years of his monastic life as student director and spiritual father to his Benedictine brethren. When he was here he was asked to sit on a committee to examine the teachings of one of the theologians in the theology faculty in the University of Louvain. Dom Columba Marmion, as he was known then, encouraged moderation in the church's handling of the case. He advocated that the theologian in question should be asked quietly to pull in his horns a bit.

At Easter during my third year in Louvain I visited a number of American army bases and missile sites in Germany. All I had to do was to celebrate Mass and hear confessions. This work was well rewarded financially but, because there were so many American student priests in Louvain, there were no openings for me to do this on a regular basis. A few carloads of priests would take off from Louvain every weekend to cover the American bases all over western Germany along the Rhine and down into the Black Forest.

Overall I lived a very spartan and studious life in Louvain during my three years there. The studies were demanding, the exam periods stressful, and my limited French did not make things any easier. I regret very much not learning Flemish at that time. It would have been easy for me to have learnt the basics and to have been able to communicate with the Flemish Vincentians in the house. This would also have been very useful to me later in visiting the University of Nijmegen in Holland. During my three years in Louvain I did visit the Netherlands on a few occasions. One of these occasions was to experience a very dynamic liturgy in the Augustinian Church in Nijmegen where liturgical developments had taken off. In retrospect I realise that it was a mistake for me to have lived in the Flemish house. The Flemish confrères spoke Flemish, and myself and the five or six American priests who were living there spoke English. I should have opted to join a French-speaking religious community in Louvain.

LECTURERS IN OTHER DEPARTMENTS

In my second and third year I had more time to take up the option of attending lectures in some other departments out of personal interest. Among the lecturers I got to know were the following:

*Louis Janssens* – Moral Theology
Over two years I attended quite a few lectures of Louis Janssens. He was one of the best lecturers in the theology department. He

lectured to undergraduate students in a large amphitheatre, using a microphone clipped to his lapel, and was able to put a summary of the whole of his lecture on the board, while continuing to engage in a dialogue with students. This group included quite a few students from the American College and seminarians from a variety of religious orders, as well as seminarians from some of the Belgium dioceses resident in the Leo XIII Seminary.

Born in 1908 in the village of Olin in Flanders, Louis Janssens completed his doctoral studies in Louvain in 1937. Under the direction of Cardinal van Roey he researched a Christian response to fascism and communism which at this time were spreading all over Europe. This research led to the publication of his first book entitled *Person and Society*. He became a fulltime lecturer in the theology department in Louvain in the early forties. In 1964 Janssens was 56 years old and at the height of his intellectual powers. He lectured on themes in fundamental moral theology, on key areas in sexual morality and on areas of justice and human rights. He was in fact setting the groundwork for what came to be known later as a teleological approach to ethics as opposed to a deontological approach. Janssens claimed to derive some of his key ideas from texts of Aquinas. I often wondered whether or not he was reading some of his own personalist approach in moral theology into these texts. His course on natural law to postgraduate students in 1964/65 was very much a personalist understanding of natural law and a move away from a biologically orientated understanding which had predominated in the Catholic tradition for many years. He was moving from an understanding of natural law based on a static understanding of human nature to a dynamic understanding of natural law based on a philosophy of the person.

Janssens concentrated on his lecturing and took very little part in department or faculty meetings. He lived near a community of the Daughters of Charity in Heverlee and was chaplain to them for most of his life. During Vatican II he gave them lectures on what was taking place at the Council in Rome. Although he was not a *peritus* in Rome during the Council, Janssens made a major contribution to one of the first drafts of the decree on religious liberty. Some people believe that the draft that was discussed at one of the intermission meetings in Switzerland before the Third Session was put together by Janssens at the invitation of Bishop De Smedt of Bruges. His views on religious liberty were published in Flemish in 1964, to be followed by French and English language translations a few months later. The title of the English translation was *Liberty of Conscience and Religious Liberty*.

In the autumn of 1963 he wrote an article, in collaboration with Professor J. Ferin from the medical faculty, on the contraceptive pill, making a case for its use in certain circumstances. This article, entitled *Progestogenes et morale conjugale*, was published in a prestigious theological journal, *Ephemerides Theologicae Lovanienses*, and word spread very quickly amongst Catholic moral theologians that one of their number was breaking away from the traditional ban against contraception. Until Pope Paul VI published *Humanae Vitae* in 1968, Louis Janssens' authority was often invoked by those who claimed that in certain circumstances the use of contraceptives was morally justifiable. Louis Janssens was not a member of the Papal Commission set up by Paul VI to examine the question of contraception. His position would have been reflected in the papal commission's Majority Report advocating the development of the Catholic position and also in the accompanying pastoral document giving arguments as to why this development could be justified. At the heart of Janssens' position is his well worked out personalist moral theology and it is at the level of fundamental moral theology and understanding of the nature of the human act, the object of the act, the intention and the consequences – that the real debate was taking place. From 1965 to 1980 Janssens continued to develop his personalist approach to ethical questions in a number of articles published in *Louvain Studies*, including a famous article entitle *The Distinction between Moral and Ontic Evil*. In typical Louvain fashion, he carried on a dialogue with various Roman authorities on various issues in sexual morality through this period. It was said that the Holy Office had Louis Janssens in their sights and this I could well understand. Janssens was one of the key exponents of a teleological approach to ethics which was 'put outside the pale' in Pope John Paul II's encyclical *Splendor Veritatis* published in 1993.

As I became more familiar with Louis Janssens' ideas

through attending his lectures, and reading the notes of his courses during the years 1963 to 1966, I became more and more interested in moral theology. Louis Janssens communicated an enthusiasm for living the Christian moral life and I think it was this inspirational approach that awakened my interest in the subject. Living the Christian moral life was demanding and exciting and this enthusiasm he communicated to his students. For me he represented all that was best in the Louvain approach to theology and philosophy. He was a dedicated scholar but at the same time he had strong pastoral interests, sharing in the anxieties and cares of people of his day, drawing their attention to Christian ideals and encouraging them to keep moving forward in their efforts to live the Christian moral life. It was said that he kept very much in touch with his Flemish farming background and he made himself available to speak to groups of priests in Flanders and elsewhere on various moral and pastoral issues. Louis Janssens died in December 2000 at the age of 92.

*Jean Giblet*

Jean Giblet was a lecturer in New Testament studies. Apart from reading his lecture notes, I attended a number of lectures he gave in the theology department and also an evening course he gave in the Catholic student chaplaincy – in the spring of 1964/65 – a Lenten series of lectures on the Sermon on the Mount. He communicated easily in simple French and he gave me an idea of some of the developments in New Testament studies. Overall his approach was a pastoral one, how to read the scriptures critically and at the same time in a way that nourished one's Christian life. When the university split in two in 1972, Giblet went on to lecture in Louvain la Neuve.

*Antoine Vergote*

I had read books and articles by Victor White, Raymond Hostie, Joseph Nuttin, and others on the relationship of psychology to religion. I was aware that holiness and wholeness go together and that there was much to learn from Freud, Jung and other psychologists about various aspects of human development. In 1963, the year I arrived in Louvain, a new chair in psychology of religion was set up in the psychology department and the person appointed was Antoine Vergote. He had qualifications in philosophy and theology and he had spent a number of years studying psychoanalysis. The lectures of Vergote, which I attended in Louvain, certainly made me aware how important it is to investigate the relationship between psychology and religion in our contemporary world. In the latter half of the twentieth century, religion was often dismissed on flimsy psychological grounds or random quotations from Freud or some other psychologists of the twentieth century. This sharpened my interest in the subject and later on I had an opportunity to lecture on some of Freud's writings, especially his book *The Future of an Illusion*. The fact that Louvain University took seriously psychology of religion brought home to me how important this subject was in any analysis of religion in the twentieth century.

Getting some depth in examining the nature of psychological discourse is very important in any contemporary discussion of religious belief or of atheism. While I was in Louvain, Vergote brought out a book which was translated into English with the title *The Religious Man*. In this book he goes to great pains to establish the methodological neutrality of the psychologist and he takes Freud and Jung and other psychologists to task for transgressing this neutrality and for making statements about the existence or non-existence of God which lay outside the province of the science of psychology. There is an interesting chapter in this book outlining a psychological profile of both believers and non-believers, theists and atheists. Vergote brings out in a striking way how a careful study of the science of psychology can help to purify religious faith.

Under the auspices of Louvain's psychology department, Carl Rogers, the famous American psychologist, gave a public lecture on non-directive counselling. I attended the session and was enthralled at what Rogers had to say. He was one of the pioneers of non-directive counselling. A friendly and attractive lecturer he created quite an impact on his audience. He showed a video of an interview with a client which highlighted how much skill was needed if the needs of the person being counselled were to be attended to. It also awakened my interest in the exchange going on between the psychotherapist and his/her patient – an area that Vergote also devoted a good deal of attention to.

*Professor Guelley* – the Theology of Religious Life

Professor Guelley gave a number of lectures in the autumn of my first or second year in Louvain on aspects of religious life. It was probably a series of six lectures, which took place in one of the large amphitheatres, probably in Pope Adrian College. Lectures were very well attended and this would not have been surprising considering the number of religious houses of men and women that were dotted all around Louvain. Many religious orders had houses of formation in or near the town. There was quite a range of religious present from different age groups. This series would have corresponded to any similar series of lectures in Milltown Park, run by a group of religious who had maintained their vitality and sense of purpose, believing that they had an important role to play in the church and in society into the future. Books were beginning to appear at this time about the future of religious life. There was an awareness among religious that things had to change or were about to change. It would be a few years yet before this debate got fully underway. The numbers who began to leave religious orders and congregations of course sharpened the debate. Among the issues dealt with in this particular series of lectures was the question of the relationship between religious life and the world and questions about the predominantly monastic understanding of religious life that prevailed at this time.

In the autumn of 1994 I visited Louvain-la-Neuve and I had a meal in a restaurant in the centre of the university campus which was frequented by professors and lecturers. I was amazed to see the same Professor Guelley sitting at a nearby table, who had lectured us on religious life in Louvain some thirty years previously. He was dressed in a smart suit, collar and tie, and although now well on in years, seemed to be in quite good health. I thought about approaching him and asking him what he thought of the state of religious life in Belgium and in the western world today, knowing that many orders were dying out with very little hope of surviving into the future. I hesitated, thinking this would probably put the poor man on the spot but I regret that I did not pluck up my courage and initiate a conversation with him.

## *Roger Aubert* – Church History

During my time in Louvain I heard a lot about the lectures of Roger Aubert in the history department. He was in the process of editing a five volume work on church history which was to become a classic. I went to two or three of his lectures in my third year in Louvain during which he brought church history alive for me. The few lectures I attended were clear, inspiring and comprehensive regarding the topic he was dealing with.

In 1975 when I attended a Colloquium in Louvain to mark the 450th anniversary of the setting up of the university, I went to a lecture by Aubert on the history of the theology faculty and again I was struck very forcefully by the brilliance of this man. It was said in Louvain in my student days that he had written a doctoral thesis on the act of faith, which was later published. Students also said to me at the time that the post-modernist church of the 1930s and 40s cast all kinds of shadows on theologians exploring traditional themes such as the act of faith and that Roger Aubert was 'encouraged' to move into the less hazardous waters of church history.

## *Professor Gérard Philips*

Finally, I will mention one other Louvain professor whose lectures I did not have an opportunity to attend but who had a profound influence on students in Louvain in the 1960s. Professor Gérard Philips had pursued doctoral studies at the Gregorian University in Rome. He lectured for many years at the diocesan seminary in Liège and became a Professor of Dogmatic Theology in Louvain University in 1942. Over the years he specialised in the area of ecclesiology. Even before the Council began he had published a book on the role of the laity in the church which was later translated into English under the title *Achieving Christian Maturity*. This was a remarkable book in that it anticipated many of the themes of the Council on the role of lay men and women in the church. It also anticipated some of the tensions that would arise after the Council between clergy and lay people as efforts were made to provide theological education and ministerial training for lay men and women.

Philips played a key role on the central Theological Commission of the Vatican Council, eventually becoming a co-chairman. It was said that his skills in finding a formula to bring conservative and progressive groups together were honed as a member of the Belgian senate when he had to find formula to satisfy both the Walloon and Flemish politicians in the Belgian parliament.

During the fourth session of the Council, Philips suffered a severe heart attack from which he never fully recovered. Working in the boiler room of the Council as co-chairman of the Theological Commission took a toll on his health. When the Council was over he returned to Louvain where he wrote a commentary on *Lumen Gentium*. Of all the theologians in the theology faculty in Louvain in the 1960s Philips, I think, was the theologian students admired most. He had a profound knowledge of the church's tradition and at the same time he wanted to bring this tradition into dialogue with new questions and new challenges arising for the church in the second half of the 20th century. Gerard Philips died in 1971.

*Visit to Taizé*

Shortly after Easter in the late spring of 1965 I visited Taizé in the south-east of France for the first time. I was travelling to a meeting of Vincentians at a retreat centre at Prime-Combe, near Montpellier and on the way we called in to Taizé. I was in the company of three Belgian Vincentians. On a beautiful Saturday we travelled down through Belgium and north east France, spending Saturday night in a hostelry on the outskirts of Macon. We had a lovely meal in a village near Macon with plenty of the local burgundy to keep the conversation rolling.

The next day we arrived in Taizé in time for the Sunday morning Eucharist. This was a great liturgical eye-opener for me. Word was beginning to filter through from the second session of Vatican II about the discussion of the new Constitution on the Liturgy. Up to this point I, and others, were saying Mass with our backs to the people and I was also saying private Masses rather than concelebrating. All I would have known was the traditional Latin Mass with its stiffness and formality. As an ecumenical community, Taizé was already moving forward very much with a beautiful and creative Sunday morning liturgy. The Chapel of the Resurrection had been opened just a few years previously. The church itself was quite full on that Sunday morning but not crowded, as was to happen some years later. I remember the simple procession of the Taizé brothers in their simple white tunics into the church, taking their places around the altar, and the Eucharist being led in a very simple way by one main celebrant facing the people. I was also very impressed by the music which in the years ahead was going to develop into the famous Taizé chants that were going to become known worldwide. Already a number of Catholic priests were members of the Taizé community. It was only on my next visit some ten years later that I learned about the arrangements made in regard to a distribution of a 'Catholic ' and 'Protestant' Eucharist during the communion of the Mass. This certainly highlighted the scandal of our divided churches.

Taizé has always intrigued me. The simplicity of its liturgy, the spirit of hospitality, the idealism and enthusiasm of the young people drawn there, the beauty of the Burgundian countryside, the Romanesque churches in the villages nearby, lingered on in my mind after this first visit . The Taizé Community was rooted in traditional monastic values and at the same time there was a freshness and openness about their way of living the Christian life. Through the 1970s I returned four times searching for some answers to questions raised for me on this first visit in 1965.

*Doctoral Thesis on Maurice Nedoncelle's* Personalist Way to God
In searching around for a topic for a doctoral thesis, my interests lay in Continental European philosophers such as Karl Jaspers, Emmanuel Mounier, Gabriel Marcel, Henri Bergson, Maurice Blondel, and others whom I would love to have pursued further, but my inadequate knowledge of French and German placed linguistic obstacles in the way. Through conversations with a fellow student, Vincent Liddle, who was writing a doctoral thesis on the moral philosophy of Maurice Nédoncelle, I learned that Nédoncelle had in fact interesting material on 'a personalist way to God'. After studying this material, I came to the conclusion that, even though it was in French, it could be mastered in a relatively short space of time and I decided to take the risk of studying a topic that had always interested me – exploring a way to God with moral experience as its starting point.

In September of 1965 I approached Albert Dondeyne to discuss the possibility of researching a doctoral thesis on Nédoncelle's 'Personalist Way to God'. He encouraged me to go ahead and agreed to be my director. I knew I was taking a great risk in choosing this subject – all the source materials being in French – but I decided that as my interests really were in this area, my enthusiasm for the subject matter would sustain me through the long hours of study that lay ahead. Before I approached Dondeyne I knew that he would have an interest in this area. Nédoncelle had in fact been awarded an honorary doctorate from Louvain University some years previously and it is more than likely that Dondeyne had encouraged the university authorities to make this move.

From September right through to Christmas 1965, I worked hard on Nedoncelle's books and articles in Louvain. Nédoncelle could not easily be classified as a phenomenologist or an existentialist or Thomist. It could be said that he had philosophical themes in common with Martin Buber, Gabriel Marcel, and Maurice Blondel. At this time Nédoncelle was a Professor of Theology in the University of Strasburg. I made contact with him by letter in November 1965 and he encouraged me to come to meet him. In the spring of 1966 I made arrangements to stay in the international seminary in Strasburg – at one time under the direction of French Vincentians – and met Nédoncelle on a number of occasions during the following two months. Nédoncelle gave me an unpublished manuscript outlining the essentials of his philosophy which he had written when he was quite a young man. It was very useful to me in trying to discern where the essential lines of his philosophy lay.

Having contact with Nédoncelle himself was a great support in trying to make clear the fundamental lines of his personalist way to God. As I look back on it, he gave me great support and encouragement and, in fact, when I had completed the first draft of my thesis, he looked it over and communicated to me that I had got a good grasp of the main lines of his philosophy. He drew my attention to a number of points that needed to be further developed or clarified.

I worked hard right through the year 1965/1966 but it was obvious at this stage that I was not going to meet the summer deadline of defending the thesis. I went to Paris for most of July and August of that year, staying in the Maison Mère, and put together the final draft. I arranged to meet Dondeyne before I left Louvain at the end of August 1966. Having read my thesis, he instructed me to go ahead and have it printed up in order to defend it. However, I was due in Strawberry Hill in September 1966 to join the staff there and to begin lecturing in the theology and philosophy departments. At this stage I had decided to put the finishing touches to the thesis in London through the year 1966/1967 and to prepare to defend it in the summer of 1967.

One of the most unsatisfactory parts of writing my thesis was the lack of direction I got from Dondeyne. He had become the head of the Institute of Philosophy in September 1965. It was very hard to make arrangements to see him and even when I did so I did not feel that he had mastered the material I had given him. My lack of fluency in French did not make things any easier. It was my contact with Nédoncelle himself and the awareness that overall I had made a reasonably good fist of outlining his way to God that gave me the confidence to proceed with defending the thesis. In my first year in Strawberry Hill, I made arrangements to complete my lecturing at Easter which gave me the time to produce my final version with footnotes etc and arrange for the printing of twenty copies. I sent the requisite number of copies, and an abstract of the thesis, to Professor Wylleman, the secretary of the Institute, by a date in May 1967 and he informed me that the date set for the defence of the thesis was 12 July, a month later.

The following quotation from the introduction to my thesis locates Nédoncelle at the centre of mid-20th century Continental European philosophy in dialogue with a number of his contemporaries.

A good deal of discussion about the existence of God among contemporary continental philosophers centres on one's understanding of the person that precedes the affirmation or denial of such a being. The starting point is the person-centred world of the phenomenologists and the personalists and not the cosmological centred universe of the medieval world. It is one's view of the person and what one considers to be most profound in the person, that leads some philosophers to affirm the existence of God today and which leads others to deny his existence. More specifically it is their views on inter-subjectivity, that is on the relationship between persons, that marks the parting of the ways between these two groups. Sartre's impoverished notion of a human relationship and his reduction of all forms of human love to inverted forms of it, rule out for him the development of a way to God with inter-subjectivity as its starting point. The fact that Merleau-Ponty cannot reconcile the 'contingent freedom of the subject' with the existence of an Absolute and Necessary Being raises similar difficulties in his case. For both these philosophers, the exclusion of God is closely related to their conception of inter-subjectivity.

For Buber, Marcel and Levinas on the other hand, inter-subjectivity serves as a starting point for a way to God. Buber was one of the first philosophers to draw attention to inter-subjectivity as a possible starting point. For him it is along the lines of an I/Thou relationship rather than an I/It relationship that one searches for a way to a personal God. Marcel's way to God is along similar lines. For Marcel inter-subjectivity is the interior dimension of the mystery of being and it is to the extent that I enter into communion with other persons that I gain access to the most fundamental order of existence where God manifests himself as an Absolute Thou. Another contemporary philosopher, Emmanuel Levinas, acknowledges that he approaches God along the same lines as Buber and Marcel. He concentrates, however, on the ethical dimension of intersubjectivity, that is on the absolute demand the other makes on me. It is here that the Transcendent Other makes himself known to me.' It is '*à partir du visage d'autrui*', that is in the demands of the widow, of the stranger and of the orphan, that the Infinite Other manifests himself. God is not accessible for Levinas in the 'grasping of the intellect', which he thinks compromises the divine transcendence. It is in an 'ethical optique', where I experience the exigencies of justice, truth, and of goodness, that God reveals himself ...

Maurice Nédoncelle has affinities with Buber, Marcel and Levinas in that he, too, takes intersubjectivity as a starting point for his way to God. In recent years, he refers to this approach as a 'personalist' way. It is worth noting, however, that we find the essentials of this approach to God in a work published in 1942 called *La Réciprocité des Consciences*, a few months before Sartre's *L'Être et le Néant* appeared. For Nedoncelle it is by reflection on, and by analysis of the 'origin and destiny of persons', that one builds a way to God.'

*Defence of the Thesis*

I arrived in Louvain from London a day or two before 12 July 1967. Attending the defence of the thesis itself were the two Readers, one of whom was Professor van der Wiele, the secretary of the Institute, Professor Wylleman, and the President of the Institute, Albert Dondeyne. The two Readers were lecturers unknown to me. I made my presentation in French from a prepared script, outlining the contents of the thesis and some conclusions I had drawn at the end. Dondeyne and the two Readers proceeded to ask me a number of questions. I was very conscious of my lack of fluency in French and I certainly dropped into English here and there during the course of the defence. The main critique of my thesis was that I had not distanced myself sufficiently from Nédoncelle's philosophy to take on a more critical stance towards him. It would have been obvious from reading the thesis that I had access to a number of unpublished manuscripts, acknowledged in footnotes, and that I had consulted Nédoncelle about my interpretation of his ideas. In so far as I had a defence against this criticism, it was that in the course of researching the thesis I discovered that Nédoncelle was influenced by Leon Brunschvicg, Maurice Blondel and Henri Bergson, all three being heavyweight philosophers. I did not have time to investigate sufficiently how dependent or otherwise Nédoncelle was on these three philosophers. I am not too sure that this reply cut much ice with my examiners.

Subsequently I became aware that one of Professor Dondeyne's concerns was my inability to establish the point of contact between phenomenology and metaphysics in Nédoncelle's way to God. I had asserted that there was such a point of contact but I failed to convince him that Nédoncelle had made this move in a convincing way. After about forty minutes the examiners withdrew for fifteen to twenty minutes, returning to announce that I had been awarded a distinction, the equivalent of a second class honours. I was very relieved that I had got through and I could now turn the page and get on with my life. Writing and completing this doctoral thesis had hung over me for the previous three years and I felt very lucky to have it behind me.

With two American Vincentians and the Flemish Vincentians in the house in Vaartstraat, I had a small celebration that evening. My three years in Louvain had been difficult and stressful ones attending lectures, taking examinations and completing this thesis. A day or two later, I said goodbye to the Vincentians in Vaartstraat to go on a long holiday to France and Spain. I let Father Kevin Cronin, Principal in Strawberry Hill, know that I had got through and he sent me a telegram of congratulations.

### The Pyrénées

A day or two later I departed by train for the south of France. A great weight had lifted off my shoulders and I was looking forward very much to what indeed was my first real break for a number of years. Through my contact with the Daughters of Charity near Toulouse, I had made arrangements to act as chaplain to a *'colonie des vacances'* in a place called Marignac near Luchon-du-Bain in the Pyrénées, about one hundred kilometres from Lourdes. I spent a three week period there, staying with the local curé, saying Mass on a number of days each week for the Daughters of Charity, the children they were looking after from various poor areas in Toulouse and the young university students who had been taken on as helpers and guides. Apart from saying Mass on certain days of the week, I had very little else to do and the curé invited me on about five occasions to climb some of the highest mountains in the Pyrénées.

I remember one of those climbs very vividly. There was one particular mountain about seven or eight thousand feet high, or maybe higher. The curé fitted me out with good strong boots and some climbing equipment. He also brought ropes because we passed over a glacier at one particular stage in the climb. We set out very early in the morning before sunrise and by the time we got to the foot of the mountain dawn was beginning to break. We climbed strenuously for five or six hours and around midday we had reached the summit. The view of the mountain peaks all around us was stunning. This was the highest mountain I had ever climbed and I lived on the experience for many years afterwards, hoping very much to repeat it. The opportunity did not occur until twenty years later when I was staying in Courmayear near Mont Blanc where there were plenty of high mountains to climb. Unfortunately for me my limbs were beginning to stiffen up a little bit and I restricted my climbs to mountains about three thousand feet high. I also became aware of how fit I would need to be, and safety precautions I would need to take, if I was to climb some of the really high mountains in the Alps. At this stage I was much less prepared to take risks.

When we reached the top of this particular mountain in the Pyrénées I felt quite faint and nearly passed out. This was due to lack of oxygen. After resting for ten minutes or so, we had a little snack and I fully revived. It was then that I really began to enjoy the glorious panorama all around me. There were high mountains on every side. We were right on the border between France and Spain and could see down into both countries but not very far because on each side were mountains very nearly as high as the one we were on. The return to ground level was uneventful. We got back to the curé's house in Marignac quite early in the afternoon. He pointed out that the dangerous time would often be in the afternoon when clouds could come down very quickly. I felt a great sense of achievement and satisfaction after this day's climb and my hunger for mountaineering was whetted.

The curé was a very prayerful man and he reminded me of all that was best in the curé of Bernanos' novel *The Diary of a Country Priest,* without the neurotic hang-ups of that particular character. He was a member of one of the groups of priests who had bonded together in a prayerful and supportive way. He brought me on five climbs in all through my three weeks in Marignac and it helped me to put aside all the troubles and cares of my previous three years in Louvain and the extra year preparing for my doctoral defence.

*Critique of Louvain's Philosophy and Theology Departments*
Both the philosophy and theology departments were very
strong on the historical method – situating schools of philosophy and theology in their historical setting. Individual theologians and philosophers would also have been treated in the
same way. The assumption was that both philosophy and theology developed from one century to the next and it was vitally
important to know the context of a particular teaching or idea
and to be able to trace the development of a doctrine over a period
of time. One lived easily with the development of doctrine in
Newman's sense of this expression.

Around the time of Jansenius, the theological faculty was divided – some professors were strongly opposed to Jansenius,
others were sympathetic to some of his positions. In previous
centuries the faculty was also divided into supporters and oppo-
nents of Erasmus who had lectured in the theology faculty for a
short period. On the other hand, the faculty as a whole was
strongly opposed to Luther's 95 theses and took the initiative
with the universities of Paris and Cologne in condemning
Luther's views on many issues. The French theologian Chenu
has remarked that Louvain appears to have navigated calmly
through the modernist crisis. Some attribute this to the importance given in the theology faculty to knowledge of the biblical
languages.

A second strength of the Louvain faculties of theology and
philosophy was their willingness to engage in dialogue with the
empirical and social sciences of the 20th century. Louvain
philosophers and theologians had the opportunity to consult
with experts in all these areas. All the different branches of theology and philosophy benefited from this exchange. Louis
Janssens' ground-breaking article about the use of contraceptives in the *Ephemerides Theologicae Lovanienses* in 1963 is partly a
result of dialogue with Professor Ferin, in the medical faculty,
about the medical aspects of the use of these drugs. Louvain was
not afraid to let the experts in different branches of scientific
knowledge set the agenda for theological deliberations.

In both faculties students were required to take lectures in all
the key areas in both theology and philosophy right up to the
end of their licentiate studies, the second year of postgraduate

work. Louvain required a good grounding in each area of these two disciplines before a person proceeded to a specialisation in their own area of doctoral research. The consequence of this was that students had a good overall grasp of key areas of theology and philosophy before they started to specialise.

In both the philosophy and theology departments, one was encouraged to take elective programmes in a number of other faculties – psychology, sociology, law and anthropology. Even though one might not be able to take very many of these elective programmes over the two years of postgraduate work, nevertheless there was an opportunity to step outside one's own field to acquire a basic understanding of the key concepts in the above areas. This was another way in which Louvain encouraged its students to engage in dialogue with other key disciplines and also to come to appreciate the methodology of another non-theological or non-philosophical discipline. Although I wasn't aware of it at the time, now with hindsight and with more knowledge of what was going on in various universities in other countries, I would have a number of negative points to make about the teaching of theology and philosophy in Louvain in the 1960s.

A serious drawback in my time in the 1960s was lack of library facilities in both philosophy and theology. There is now a well-equipped theological library in place and also a philosophy library on a smaller scale. It is one of my regrets that both of these facilities were not available during my time in Louvain. There was, of course, a central library where philosophical and theological books could be consulted. However, getting access to books was complicated and required a good deal of patience.

To a large extent the teaching in Louvain at baccalaureate and licentiate levels centred on a lecture system. The lecture system did not encourage sufficient critical thinking on the part of students. I know that efforts had been made to supplement the lecture courses with seminars and tutorials. To do this would have required the expanding of the teaching staff in both faculties and this would have been a costly operation. Nevertheless, many universities in the United States and in England had learning systems in place that encouraged students to be much less passive in their responses and to be personally more active in the learning process.

Because most of the students in the philosophy and theology faculties were seminarians in the 1960s, it is not surprising that most of the lecturers were priest professors in both faculties. With the participation of more male and female lay students, more lay theologians and philosophers have taken up positions on the teaching staff in both these faculties. However, from recent visits, I wonder if gender balance, particularly in the theological faculty, has yet reached the desired level.

The Louvain theological faculty of my time concentrated on providing good academic foundations for professional theologians. I never got the impression that the pastoral department was very strong in the sense of being linked closely to parish life. I doubt if we can keep apart now good academic theology and good pastoral practice. One might well argue that all good theology is pastoral and *vice versa*. However, one must provide a lot more theology that is linked to Christian life and pastoral practice. I have not seen this reflected in the Louvain I visited in the 1970s, 80s and 90s. There has been a decline in the institutional church in Belgium, in terms of the participation of people in any kind of regular Sunday practice. The decline in the number of seminarians has reached alarming levels. The dramatic rise in the average age of priests has increased to crisis proportions, putting intolerable burdens on elderly men. A whole new challenge awaits Louvain in regard to its links to church life in Belgium today in both the French and Flemish speaking Catholic universities. I do not sense that the theological department in Louvain has done any pioneering work on how we are going to call people – men and woman, married and celibate – to ministry into the future and how the church is going to prepare these people for ministry.

It will be interesting to see what kinds of topics are chosen for doctoral theses in the years ahead. If links between the theology department and church life continue to weaken, there will be the danger of theology getting caught up with esoteric areas of theology far removed from the lives of people in today's world .

*Walking a path between philosophy and theology*

Though I did not realise it at the time, my interest started to move from philosophy to theology during my three years in Louvain. This was due in part to being at home on the border-line between philosophy and theology. The philosophers I had studied in Louvain for my doctoral thesis, Maurice Nèdoncelle and others, lived on the borderline between philosophy and theology and travelled easily from one to the other, as did Albert Dondeyne, the most inspiring lecturer I had in Louvain. His book, published in the late 1950s, *Contemporary European Thought and Christian Faith* was a good example of a philosopher moving back and forth between the two disciplines. Through attending lectures of Louis Janssens in moral theology, Jean Giblet in New Testament studies, and Roger Aubert in church history, and through reading the lecture notes of courses given in the theology department at both baccalaureate and licentiate levels, my interest in theology was re-awakened. A third reason is that reading the text of some of the heavyweight philosophers such as Hegel and Kant in particular was very hard going and I began to question whether I wanted to do this for the rest of my life. A fourth reason is that I discovered gradually that I did not want to stay inside the confines of just one discipline. In Louvain I discovered gradually that I was more at home in moving from philosophy to theology, to psychology, to literature, and later on I was going to be drawn into management studies as I became more and more involved in administration.

So when I was offered a position in both the theology and philosophy departments in Strawberry Hill, I had no difficulty in accepting this invitation to lecture in both. As time went on my interest became more and more focused on moral theology but I did retain an interest in philosophy and continued to lecture in philosophy of religion and moral philosophy.

*Three Difficult Years*

I pointed out earlier that my three years in Louvain were very difficult and stressful years for me. Attending lectures in French without a proper grounding in the French language, and enduring a passive lecturing system where there was very little give and take between the lecturers and the students, was not easy to take. There were many boring sections to the course and boring lecturers too, but I have always maintained that only 50% of the lectures one is supposed to attend in any university are worth going to. I had to take sixteen oral examinations at the end of my first year in what was quite a stressful atmosphere. One also had to live with the tension of waiting for examination results to know whether or not one could proceed to the next stage. Completing a doctoral thesis with uncertainties about the final outcome also added a good deal of stress to life in Louvain. However, I would not have exchanged my position with any other Vincentian in the Irish Province. I felt quite privileged in having been chosen to pursue postgraduate studies in Louvain. There was a great sense of achievement in getting through the various hurdles and tremendous elation when I completed the doctoral programme.

My living conditions were not ideal. As I said earlier, I would have been better off living in a French-speaking community with more contact with the university. I had no great health issues during my time in Louvain although I did pick up quite a few colds and this I put down to the cold weather in quite a damp atmosphere. I remember the town of Louvain often being covered in fog, which was probably due in part to the factories on the perimeter of the town belching out smoke and fumes. EU environmental laws restricting such practices were still a long way away into the future.

*Sources of Spiritual Inspiration*
Community life with the Flemish and American Vincentians and the three members of the Congregation of St Viator was very limited. Community prayer took place in a cold, poorly decorated chapel. We said private Masses in cell-like rooms in another part of the house. We had very few pastoral outlets. Some of the American priests went back and forth to American army bases in Germany at weekends on a rota basis. Whatever breaks I got came through contacts I had made in France during holiday periods over the three years. I was impressed by a number of the priest professors who provided good models of being

dedicated scholars, with a strong commitment to Christianity and pastoral life coming through at various points in their lectures. Dondeyne, Giblet and Louis Janssens were outstanding in this regard.

From time to time I attended Sunday Mass in the French-speaking chaplaincy church. I was impressed by the efforts the chaplains made to make the celebration come alive and the efforts made to provide a sense of welcome. If I was a bit more adventuresome I could have discovered the theological riches in museums, art galleries and churches in Brussels, Bruges, Ghent, Antwerp and other Belgium cities. Pressure of work and scarcity of funds kept me rooted to my desk in Vaarstraat.

*Vatican II and after ...*

Because of the presence of a number of Louvain theologians at the deliberations of Vatican II, especially Gerard Philips, students in Louvain got a privileged insight into the deliberations of the Council as they were proceeding. Gerard Philips and others were missing from Louvain through most of the autumn term through the four years of the Council, 1962-1965, but when they returned in the springtime they took up their lectures again and many of their courses were commentaries on some of the documents coming together in the second, third and fourth sessions, especially *Lumen Gentium* on the church, *Sacrosanctum Concilium*, the Constitution on the Liturgy and *Gaudium et Spes*, the Church in the Modern World. Through contact with the theologians and philosophers involved, we began to pick up on some of the excitement of what was happening in Rome from 1962 to 1965. We believed that there was a new church in the making that was going to pull out all the stops in responding to the needs of people in our time. As news seeped out about the various battles being fought and won by the progressive groups in Rome, an enthusiasm and euphoria was created. We heard about Georges De Smedt, the Bishop of Bruges' famous speech in support of the right to religious liberty which later was reflected in the *Declaration on Religious Freedom*. There was the promise of a new spring in the air for the Catholic Church in Europe and around the world. Needless to say the contribution of Cardinal Suenens as one of the key players did not go unnoticed by the Belgian press, both religious and secular. In the intervals between the four sessions of the Council, Suenens called together his own theological advisers from Belgium, particularly from Louvain University, and from other European countries, to discuss the issues brought up in each session and to prepare for the sessions to come.

One very dark cloud on the horizon in Belgium through these years was a massacre of a number of missionaries in the Congo, raising questions about the effectiveness of the missionary activity of the Belgian church in this area over the previous hundred years. All of this was tragic news for many Belgian families. I remember seeing notices and photographs of murdered missionaries in shop windows in one or two towns I passed through in Belgium at this time.

Through the 1970s, the euphoria generated by Vatican II through the Council years evaporated very quickly. Cardinal Suenens was caught in the crossfire between the extreme Flemish and Walloon groups, creating tribal warfare in Belgium on the linguistic question, as to where and when French and Flemish should be spoken. As is often the case, the linguistic war was a cover for an economic war as Flanders gradually gained economic superiority over Wallonia at a time of considerable economic expansion in Flanders and considerable economic decline in Wallonia with the closing of coal mines and the shutting down of factories. This tribal warfare was to lead to the splitting of Louvain University in the early 1970s. The University of Leuven was set up as the Flemish-speaking Catholic University and a new French-speaking Catholic Louvain University was built on a green field site in Ottignies just over the linguistic border fifteen kilometres south of Leuven, which became known as Louvain-la-Neuve. Cardinal Suenens' reputation as the religious leader of the Catholic Church in Belgium was tarnished by all this as he had stated in the mid-1960s that he would never agree to the splitting of the university in two. The theology and philosophy departments were the last to agree to this division but they too had to acquiesce with the overall decision. For students from outside Belgium, this appeared to be a sorry day for the Catholic University of Louvain. It was part of the strength of Louvain that it was a crossroads between French and German cultures. The Flemish-speaking Catholic University in Leuven moved quickly to set up an English-speaking department in the hope of continuing to attract students from English-speaking countries and this it has continued to do.

On my visits to Louvain in the 1970s, 80s and 90s I was continually taken aback by the decline of the church in this one-time Catholic country. By the early 1990s seminaries were virtually empty. The median age of priests was well into the 60s. Many priests left the priesthood in the 1970s – men who would have been leaders now if they had persevered in the priesthood. The decline in any kind of regular church participation was also striking. Had Vatican II come too late for the Belgian church? Had the implementation of its decrees been badly organised? Had a wave of materialism and consumerism overwhelmed the people of Belgium? Had the enlightenment gathered new force, leading to the marginalisation of the church in society? Those of us who shared in the euphoria and enthusiasm for what had been accomplished in Vatican II and shared in the hopes it generated, had no idea what was going to happen in this little country called Belgium. But of course the struggles of the Catholic Church in Belgium to move forward and indeed to survive were going to be played out in other European countries too, even if there was a time-lag of ten or twenty years from one country to another.

*Can One be a Christian Today?*
Throughout my time in Louvain, and for a number of years afterwards, one of my chief interests was affirming the existence of God, in the face of various forms of atheism, which had sprung up in Europe over the 19th and 20th centuries. My chief Louvain mentor in all this was Albert Dondeyne. For over twenty years Dondeyne had attempted to enter into dialogue with contemporary philosophy, especially with phenomenology. His efforts to build a way to God with morality as a starting point was the positive side of that enterprise. The section on atheism in the *Pastoral Constitution on the Church in the Modern World* owes something to Albert Dondeyne. He was certainly consulted on the content of this section. Being a true philosopher, he was a man of dialogue with contemporary atheism rather than a man

who condemns or rejects without trying to discern what is true in his opponent's position. It was not until some years later that questions about the nature of the church or about religious life became more acute for me. In Louvain I was trying to work out the grounds for affirming the existence of God and the grounds for being a Christian. Some years later, Hans Küng published his book *On Being a Christian*. This book is a brilliant exposition of the concerns of any thinking Christian in the latter part of the 20th century in trying to sustain his or her belief in the God of Christianity, confronted with the various intellectual movements in the 20th century.

Through my three years in Louvain I began to understand the great intellectual challenge the Enlightenment posed for Christians and the importance of taking seriously thinkers such as Feuerbach, Marx, Nietzsche, Freud, Sartre and others.

*The Excitement of Living the Christian Moral Life*
The other debt I owe to Louvain is a rekindling in me of the excitement of trying to live the moral life – of doing the good, of finding the balance between action and contemplation, of living a virtuous life. Professor Conor Martin's introduction to Aristotle's *Nicomachean Ethics* in University College Dublin had already introduced me to all of this. But here in Louvain it was played out in a new register by the genius of Professor Louis Janssens. His commitment to presenting moral theology in a positive and attractive way resonated with me at every level of my being. It was only later when I started to teach moral theology myself that I began to realise the full implications of the personalist moral theology he was outlining during my years in Louvain. Studying in some depth the ethical teaching of both Old and New Testaments, and wrestling with Louis Janssens' version of *Fundamental Choice*, added to that excitement.

*Methodology – Tools to Handle Philosophical and Theological Questions*
It was only in retrospect that I realised what I had acquired in Louvain. It had given me a framework, in both philosophy and theology, from which to view the world and everything in it. I acquired a confidence in placing philosophical or theological ideas or themes in their historical setting and mastering the tools

to begin looking critically at one or other philosophical or theological teaching. What I had been given would mature into a number of philosophical and theological convictions and, at the same time, I became quite sceptical of bodies of knowledge in both areas that could not be grounded and sustained inside each discipline. Rather than any kind of facile adapting of Christianity to the modern world, Vatican II was really 'ressourcement' – a return to more authentic Christian teachings in our understanding of the church, in the practice of our worship and in our presentation of the 'two sources of revelation' – scripture and tradition.

One effect of all this was to help me to distinguish what was essential in the Christian tradition and what was accidental. My theological and philosophical education in Louvain helped me to cope with the changes that occurred in our post Vatican II world and in our post-modern and indeed, some would say, post-Christian world of the present day.

*Louvain – a Gateway to Continental Europe*
Louvain from 1963 to 1966 was my gateway to Continental Europe. During those three years I learnt to be at home on the Continent and subsequently through holiday periods loved to explore some new part of Europe that I had never visited before. At first the riches of its traditions lured me away from the USA. Through many visits to the United States from 1974, I began to appreciate the vitality and youthfulness of that country too. Nevertheless, intellectually, I am at home in Europe. Its many cultures can be endlessly explored, revealing new facets of the biblical Greek and Roman cultures that have come together in so many different ways. My visit to St Séverin during Holy week of 1964, my visit to Taizé around Easter 1965, and a visit to the Augustinian church in Nijmegen, where I experienced a Mass for young people, opened my eyes to the possibilities of reverent, prayerful and simple liturgy. My three years in Louvain had opened the door for me to these and other rich experiences. I felt at home in continental Europe and at ease in moving around from one country to another.

# CHAPTER 7

# Strawberry Hill:
# The World of Education,
# 1966-1982

*Appointment to Strawberry Hill and First Impressions*
I was appointed to the staff of St Mary's College, Strawberry Hill, London in July 1966 to lecture in both the philosophy and theology departments. A whole new world was to open up for me over the next sixteen years as a member of the Vincentian community and as a lecturer on the college staff. I was initiated into the world of third level education, which meant acquiring the skills of lecturing in both philosophy and theology in a relatively short time. I had opportunities to engage in priestly ministry with staff and students in the college itself and with parishioners in neighbouring parishes. In time, I was going to be involved in administering a large department of Religious Studies and in exercising the role of Superior in the Vincentian community. These 16 years in London were to be very enjoyable and satisfying years for me.

At Heathrow Airport I was met by one of the members of the Vincentian community and brought the 20 minute journey to Strawberry Hill on a late summer afternoon. I got a very warm welcome from Fr Kevin Cronin, the Superior of the Vincentian community and Principal of the college. For the next few days I explored the college campus with great interest. I was installed that day as one of the first occupants of an apartment beside three new student hostels. That evening I joined the 10 members of the Vincentian community for the evening meal, in what was known as the Walpole House Dining Room, with a beautiful view across the lawn.

Over the next few days I discovered that the river Thames was about 3 minutes walk from the college grounds; a local Mercy convent was 10 minutes away alongside the river in a house formerly occupied by Alexander Pope; the towns of

Twickenham, Richmond and Kingston were a short distance away on the banks of the river Thames as was the Tudor palace of Hampton Court, a mile or two upstream. Nearby was the little village of Strawberry Hill, the local Catholic church, a few shops, the village post-office and a small railway station where one could get the train into Waterloo, 30 minutes away.

As the students were not due back for two weeks, I had plenty of time to explore the college buildings and the college campus of about 30 acres, some of which was used for rugby, soccer and hockey pitches. The historic part of the building was known as Walpole House and attached to it was the Waldegrave Ballroom, now used for staff meetings and the occasional staff and student functions at Christmas. At the end of the year, what was known as the Going Down Ball, took place in these beautiful rooms. Because the college had just expanded to over 1000 students – the first intake of girls was due in a week or two in September 1966 – there was a recently built dining room and gymnasium at one end of the campus near what is known as the 'Chapel in the Woods' built in Horace Walpole's lifetime. (Some years later, when only one tree remained alongside this chapel, one of the students renamed it 'The Chapel of the Lonesome Pine'.) Three years previously an imposing college chapel, modelled on the cathedral of Albi in France, had been constructed. The architect was Sir Albert Richardson, a well known architect of his day. One of the most beautiful features of this new chapel was fifteen stained glass windows by Gabriel Loire, made at his workshop in Chartres. Some years later, I started to bring first year students on a tour of this chapel, dialoguing with them about church architecture and having great fun with them trying to identify each of the Loire windows illustrating in a symbolic way the fifteen mysteries of the rosary.

I remember vividly the first staff meeting of the year, presided over by the Principal, Fr Kevin Cronin. At the beginning of this meeting Fr Cronin welcomed the 15 or more new lecturers who had just been appointed to the staff and we were named, each of us rose to our feet to take a bow and a polite clap from the older hands.

The college campus came alive when the students arrived and it was a busy few days while they were settling in to their accommodation and finding out their lecture schedule. I was to learn very quickly that there were students in Strawberry Hill from all over England, Wales and Northern Ireland. There was an interesting variety of accents to get used to – from London cockney to West Country to valleys in Wales, to Liverpool, to Manchester, to Newcastle and also to Belfast, Derry, Armagh and other towns in the North of Ireland. Over the next few weeks I was to learn that there were also students attending the college from Malta and Gibraltar. Very quickly I got immersed in the busy life of the college, with lectures beginning in the morning at 9.00 am and ending about 5.00 in the evening. Dinner followed with the Vincentian community in Walpole House. These first few weeks in Strawberry Hill were intriguing ones for me. Apart from getting involved academically and pastorally, I had the opportunity to start playing tennis with staff and students as well as exploring some of the sights of London. I was adapting to being an Irish priest lecturing in one of the best known Catholic third level colleges in England.

## St Mary's College of Education

St Mary's College was founded in 1850 by the recently restored Catholic hierarchy. It was one of the oldest Catholic Colleges of Education in England. The original Teacher Training College was situated in Brook Green, Hammersmith. The property there was sold in 1923 and with the proceeds, the Principal, Fr James Doyle CM, acquired Horace Walpole's 30-acre property in Strawberry Hill including his 'Gothic Castle'. Over a ten year period, Walpole had constructed a villa which was partly a castle and partly a cloister with artefacts of all kinds. The whimsical style of doors, windows and staircases came to be know as 'Strawberry Hill Gothic'. Horace Walpole had bought the original property in 1747 and lived there until his death in 1797. Son of a former PM, Horace Walpole recorded the social and political events of the 18th century in the 10,000 letters he wrote to all kinds of friends and acquaintances. A grand-niece, Lady Frances Waldegrave, inherited the property in the 19th century and the place became an important meeting point for politicians and socialites in the reign of Queen Victoria. When the Catholic Education Council acquired the property in 1923 it was put to a much different use – providing a centre for training teachers for the Catholic emigrant communities all over the realm. I imagine that Walpole would have turned a few times in his grave if he could have foreseen to what purpose his lawns, fields and villa were going to be used for in the 20th century. One thing is certain: the move from Brook Green to Strawberry Hill gave the college of education a new lease of life, enabling it to expand its student intake to 300 students and providing it with much needed sporting facilities which it had lacked in Hammersmith.

In 1913 the college was linked to the University of London which awarded the college external degrees. In the 1950s London University set up the Institute of Education and from then on it took responsibility for the supervision of degrees in external colleges. In 1968 a new four-year B Ed degree was introduced which ran side by side with a three-year certificate. A few years later the college began to offer three year BA and BSc degrees for students preparing for other professions. A whole new future opened up for the college to prepare people for a variety of professions, with teaching degrees still at the centre of the curriculum. The Catholic Church in Britain now had an opportunity to make its presence felt in third level education in a new way.

The 1950s and the 1960s was a period of expansion for the Catholic Church in education at all levels. The burgeoning Catholic community required more and more elementary and secondary schools. By the early 1960s there were 9 Catholic Colleges of Education scattered around the country preparing Catholic teachers for these schools. In 1982 St Mary's negotiated a link with the University of Surrey for degree validation. This arrangement has continued right up to the present day. New courses have been put in place and at present the college has just under 4000 in all years.

From 1899 onwards, St Mary's was administered by the Vincentian Fathers on behalf of the bishops of England and Wales. The college had run into some difficulty in the latter part of the 19th century and it was felt that more stability would be provided if a religious order or congregation administered the training college. Good reports had reached the authorities in England about the Vincentian administration of a similar college in Dublin, St Patrick's College. The Irish Province of the Congregation of the Mission maintained 5/6 priests on the staff through the first half of the 20th century. The expansion of the Vincentians on the staff increased to 10 priests by the mid-1960s when the student population went above the 1000 mark. The Vincentians held the positions of Principal, Executive Vice-Principal, and Dean of Students. They also maintained a presence in the theology and education departments. As time went on, I began to realise, more and more, that there was a very large number of Irish priests and Irish religious sisters involved in parishes and schools all around England and Wales and this diminished somewhat the anomalous nature of Irish Vincentian priests administering Strawberry Hill. A certain measure of inculturation was called for. To have administered Strawberry Hill for nearly 100 years is a great tribute to the Irish Province of the Congregation of the Mission, especially to the priests who held the post of Principal.

### PHILOSOPHY COURSES TAUGHT IN STRAWBERRY HILL

*Philosophy of Religion*
Over my 16 years in Strawberry Hill I taught philosophy of religion at a number of different levels to students in both the theology and philosophy departments. I taught an introductory course in philosophy of religion under the title The Basis of Belief to 1st Year students in 1969/1970 and through the following three years, covered the following topics:

- *Asking Ultimate Questions.* Using sources such as the *Dutch Catechism* and Karl Jasper's *Ways to Wisdom* illustrated how people ask ultimate questions about our origin and our destiny in both philosophical and non-philosophical terms.
- *Novelists, Poets, Film Directors.* I then went on to illustrate how ultimate questions are posed explicitly and implicitly by our own contemporaries in the spheres of literature, drama, and cinema. I drew on the writings of Waugh, Greene, Bernanos, Mauriac, Solzhenitsyn, Frost, Pasternak, Camus, Salinger , Joyce, Merton and Dag Hammarskjold. Although I felt less sure of myself in the world of cinema I touched briefly on one or two of the movies of Ingmar Bergman or on a current movie or piece of TV drama.

- *Variety and different levels of questioning.* To put order into the different levels of questioning I used Bede Griffiths' *The Golden String*. His conversion story conveys brilliantly that he was searching passionately for the truth with both his heart and his head and it also conveyed the message that a degree of asceticism was needed if we were to touch base with the deepest levels of our searching.
- *The Option for Atheism.* I then went on to show that the option for atheism was a path that had been taken by a number of influential thinkers in the 19th and 20th centuries – Marx, Freud, Sartre, Camus. My aim was not to turn these students into atheists but to communicate to them that they had certain intellectual challenges to face up to in our contemporary world.
- *Philosophical Ways to God.* I then outlined very briefly some of the traditional and contemporary ways to God using simple formulations of St Thomas Aquinas' *Quinque Viae* and also outlining some contemporary formulations of the moral argument.
- The final part of the course distinguished between the *Way of the Philosophers* and the *Way of Revelation* and looked at various ways of relating faith and reason so as to avoid the notion of faith as a bold leap in the dark on the one hand and the reduction of faith to a kind of rationalism on the other hand.

DEGREE COURSE IN PHILOSOPHY OF RELIGION

Over the years I taught philosophy of religion as one of the 4th Year BEd options. At this level students had already had a reasonably good background in both philosophy and theology and I was able to address issues at the level of introducing students to key texts of philosophers of the past and the present. Because I was on the Board of Examiners for this course I was in a position to select topics I was interested in myself as well as having input into the examination papers that were set. The following is a brief outline of the topics I covered:

*A Atheism*
The course begins by outlining a number of atheistic positions. This is done through a careful study of a number of philosophical

texts, putting these in the context of the writers' own works and in their historical context. The overall approach was to present these positions as coherently as I could. My aim was to let students see a representative example of a variety of ways our contemporaries argued that God's existence could be rejected. Some students were looking into the void for the first time in their lives.

I chose *Jean Paul Sartre* as representative of atheistic existentialism. He was very popular in post-war France. His perception of the 'other' as a threat popularised in the famous phrase 'Hell is other people' from *No Exit* ruled out the affirmation of God as the Other in Sartre philosophy. After outlining the key principles of Being and Nothingness, I would have shown that for him God is a contradiction in terms. In the threatening atmosphere of post-war France, in which the communist and capitalist worlds were squaring up to one another, Sartre certainly reflected a lot of the apprehension and pessimism of the day.

*Albert Camus* I used the writings of Albert Camus, especially some extracts from *The Plague*, to illustrate the difficulties of a very good man confronted with the problem of evil in the world and especially the suffering of innocent people. Many efforts have been made to reconcile the existence of evil in the world with the existence of a creator God who is benevolent and omnipotent. Camus outlines the problem in a dramatic way. I would have used philosophy to distinguish between different kinds of evil and to look at the various attempts of philosophers to reconcile free will with the way it is used by many people to inflict so many terrible evils on their fellow human beings. How does one reconcile this with the existence of a creator God? I pointed out that only the tortured Christ on the Cross in the little Chapel of Reparation at the centre of Dachau would have offered a way forward. This was not so much a philosophical solution as a way of putting the reality of evil in a theological context in which one could live with the mystery of evil. In doing so I had, of course, transcended philosophy.

*Sigmund Freud* In presenting Freud's atheism I used his book *The Future of an Illusion* and key texts from some of his other writings to outline his overall position. 'Fear made the gods.' Freud outlined brilliantly the psychological need to project a

God into existence. One is forced to examine very carefully the meaning of the word 'need' and to draw up carefully demarcation lines between philosophy and psychology. Every so often Freud makes philosophical statements which go beyond the empirical findings of the discipline of psychology he contributed so much to. Facing Freud was a daunting challenge for many of the young people I was teaching.

*Karl Marx* 'Religion alienates', 'Religion is the opium of the People.' I tried to take students from these popular perceptions of Marx' atheism into some of his key texts against the background of the influence of Hegel, Engels and Feuerbach and the industrial world of the 19th century. In this case, I drew the boundary lines between sociology and philosophy, pointing out the need to preserve the demarcation lines between these two disciplines.

*Frederick Nietzsche* I always found it hard to grapple with Nietzsche. His aphorisms and pithy sayings captivated many people of his day and still captivate many people in our day too. Some philosophers say that Freud, Marx and Nietzsche were the three great atheistic thinkers of the 19th and 20th centuries. Some would say that we have come to terms with Marx and Freud but that we are still grappling with Nietzsche.

These are the main atheistic positions I dealt with. I would have made forays into the English empirical traditions as represented by Hume, Russell and Ayer. I tried to contextualise the thinkers I dealt with and grappled with some of their key texts on the existence of God, pointing out what I thought was true in their overall critique and at the same time I tried to show that the conclusion that God does not exist did not necessarily follow from their premises or arguments. In 20th century Britain agnosticism and atheism were in the air we breathed. I maintained that some hard philosophical thinking was needed to get to the bottom of the mountain, to begin exploring possible paths to the top in which one could affirm the existence of God.

*B Ways to God*
*The Ontological Argument*
From Anselm in the 12th century to philosophers of the present day, the ontological argument has had a good innings. Asking

students to grapple with it was a good way of sharpening up their ability to think logically. Many people think that the ontological argument is like the magician pulling a rabbit out of a hat. However, to pinpoint the logical fallacy takes some clear thinking and in the process one clarifies one's understanding of one's concept of God as 'a being than which no greater can be thought' .

## The Five Ways of Aquinas

I outlined the cosmological argument, the argument from degrees of truth, beauty and goodness and the argument from finality. From time to time I would couple these 13th century texts with contemporary expressions of the same arguments. One moves eventually from the world of science of the 13th century, or even the 20th century, to the level of metaphysics and begins to ask questions such as why is there something rather than nothing? Making this metaphysical jump was always difficult for students, especially those who may have had little background in philosophy.

The fourth way and fifth way offer two other interesting starting points – from degrees of truth, beauty and goodness in the fourth way and from finality or the final cause in the fifth way.

## The Moral Way

Because of my own studies in Leuven and the influence of Albert Dondeyne, I explored the various moral starting points as a way to God. Immanuel Kant's affirmation of God as a postulate of the moral order offered an interesting path to God. God gives coherence to my moral experience. Martin Buber's probings in his famous book *I and Thou*, leading to the statement 'It is between man and man that we meet God', has always intrigued me. Gabriel Marcel's analysis of hope in *Homo Viator* 'to say that you love someone means that you shall never die' develops further some of Buber's insights. In the case of all three, one was walking a tightrope between philosophy and theology.

I have never been sure if it is right to include Henri Bergson's 'Way of the Mystics' under the title 'A Moral Way to God'. In his *Two Sources of Morality and Religion*, Bergson writes beautifully about the mystical experience of John of the Cross and Teresa of Avila and puts it into a philosophical framework, which is very appealing. There is an echo of religious mystical experience in all of us, he says. And even though we may not be able to climb the mountain of the mystics, he gives us a sympathetic 'reading' of their writings and experiences, of the barriers they went through to arrive in the presence of God. At the end of the day, however, I think this is an argument from testimony rather than a philosophical argument and strictly speaking it is not philosophy. From a philosophical point of view there can only be an extrinsic relationship between the quality of their lives and their claims to have had an experience of God.

When I was giving these lectures in the 1970s I would have touched very briefly on some of the writings of Emmanuel Levinas, in particular, *Totalité et Infin*. The way he had turned metaphysics on its head, challenging Heidegger and other contemporary phenomenologists, was very interesting. His rooting of metaphysical experience in our encounter with the other, 'the orphan', the 'widow' and the 'poor' has opened up a very rich seam of philosophy in the latter part of the 20th century. The demand that the other makes of me, particularly in certain circumstances, takes precedence over all other kinds of thinking. He has opened up paths to God, especially over the last twenty five years of his life, that are well worth exploring. At the same time he has drawn attention to the limitations of Heidegger's philosophy in which the possibility of the affirmation of a transcendent God disappears.

## C Other Topics
In some of the philosophy of religion courses I taught in the 1970s in Strawberry Hill, I would have dealt with a number of other topics, such as the immortality of the soul and miracles. However, the content of most of the philosophy of religion courses I taught were confrontations with contemporary atheism and explorations of ways to God.

## D The Way of Revelation
Many of the students I taught would have known there was another approach to God – the way of revelation – and indeed this

is the way adopted by most believing Christians. Sometimes I would explore with them Karl Barth's 'No' to philosophy of religion. Does one get down on one's knees and listen to the Word of God? In my view this amounted to philosophical suicide and the denial of a place for reason in relation to revelation. A lot of work had to be done before one got down on one's knees to listen to the Word. The obstacles that atheists place in our path have to be removed and one has to struggle to see how far reason can go in affirming the existence of God. Not to do this is to short circuit the process and to fall into some kind of fideism. The Catholic tradition has always maintained the importance of philosophical reasoning in relation to theology and it was interesting to see this position stated so strongly in Pope John Paul II's 1996 encyclical *Fides et Ratio* on the relationship between faith and reason. It is important to live with the tension that exists between the God of philosophical reasoning and the God of Christianity. One has to use all one's philosophical resources to start moving up the mountain and to discover the limitations of human reasoning. A moment comes when God begins to reveal himself in his Word and in his church. One may then leave one's philosophical strivings to one side at least for the moment. It is through the use of our reason that we are able to remove the obstacles that atheists put in the way of exploring the philosophical ways to God.

### MORAL PHILOSOPHY

Over the years in Strawberry Hill, I covered quite a few courses under the heading of moral philosophy and of course it was a background to a lot of the moral theology I did at the same time. Among the philosophers I dealt with under this heading are the following:

*Aristotle:* I brought students through the *Nicomachaen Ethics*, especially through Book 1. Having covered courses in both University College, Dublin and in Leuven University, which analysed the *Nicomachaen Ethics* I did not have to spend that much time working on the text. I would have continued to read a number of commentaries and articles on the 'final good', on the virtues, on friendship and on action and contemplation. The extraordinary insights of Aristotle are still so relevant to any analysis of the moral life or moral action today. Alistair McIntyre returned to Aristotelian themes in his book, *On Virtue*, a very healthy reaction to the hair-splitting that has gone on in 20th century English analytic moral philosophy circles.

*The Stoics:* Because of the influence Stoicism has had at various periods in the church's history, I found it very interesting to probe the writings of Stoic philosophers. A very good summary of their position is to be found in the Open University Introductory Course on Moral Philosophy. It is interesting how frequently in the history of Christianity the influence of the Stoics, in terms of enduring one's sufferings, fatalistically keeps on recurring from one generation to the next. Joy evaporates and living the Christian life becomes a hard uphill slog.

*Thomas Aquinas:* Natural Law

Professor Bertie Crowe, University College, Dublin had given me a good introduction to the historical antecedents of Aquinas' natural law theory. In Leuven I had followed Professor Louis Janssen's personalist interpretation of some of Aquinas' natural law texts. I came to realise that, although we may have quite a lot of difficulty in determining the secondary and tertiary principles of natural law, for me the theory always guaranteed the objectivity of right and wrong. Louis Janssen highlighted the fact that we sometimes give the theory of natural law a physicalist or biological foundation. I've never been too sure how much Janssens himself read into Aquinas' texts in his personalist interpretation of natural law. When the English and American jurists formulated the notion of 'crimes against humanity' to try the Nazi war criminals in Nuremberg after the Second World War, one could sense that natural law theory was not dead. Our judiciary and lawyers have to invoke something deeper than positive law of the state to provide a basis for right and wrong.

*Jean Jacques Rousseau:* Freedom

Rousseau's pre-French revolution writings on freedom introduced new thinking on the nature of freedom in relation to nature and education.

*John Stuart Mill:* Liberty and Equality
A good deal of our discussions today about the nature of freedom in society were anticipated by John Stuart Mill.

*Immanuel Kant:* The foundations of the Metaphysics of Morals
The clarity of Kant's writings only struck home to me as I started to read this text. One can sense the strong humanist basis of his ethical theory and his profound respect for the person.

*Contemporary Ethics:* A whole variety of theories have been put forward in the 20th century about the nature of ethics from Sartre's existentialist ethic – one creates one's own morality – to English moral philosophers espousing intuitionism, utilitarianism, etc – and the hair-splitting of the Oxford and Cambridge moral philosophers. To my mind, Iris Murdoch, a rebel in the English context, struck a nail on the head when she said that the proper background to morality is some kind of mysticism. When I am bound up with an ideal of human flourishing, a myth – a religion – or a philosophical one, it is necessary to motivate people who want to do good and avoid evil as well as engaging them passionately in the exercise of virtuous deeds. Her commitment to the Idea of the Good and her sympathy towards Continental European philosophy marked her off from most of her English contemporaries in Oxford and Cambridge philosophical circles.

### HISTORY OF PHILOSOPHY

During my first 3 years in Strawberry Hill I taught a history of philosophy course to first year students in the philosophy department and modelled this more or less on the four history of philosophy courses offered at Baccalaureate level in the University of Leuven. I cut my teeth as a lecturer in philosophy in preparing and delivering this course.

In the very first lecture I indicated that the course would be a search for a definition of philosophy. There was only one way to do that. We had to jump in at the deep end and see how philosophers of different periods in the history of philosophy had engaged in this task. I had a good deal of fun in interacting with the class on the notion of philosophy as a 'way to wisdom', 'philosophy is to be on the way rather than having arrived', 'every person is a philosopher' and so on.

In ancient or Greek philosophy I concentrated on the Sophists, Heraclitus, and Parmenides, culminating in Plato and Aristotle. The main theme I was trying to address was the beginning of philosophical reasoning as these early philosophers began to break away from myth. Philosophy was a search for order and rationality. Philosophy was a search for the ultimate nature of things, a search for the essence of things. With Plato and Aristotle two contrasting views about the great philosophical problems in regard to the nature of knowledge and the nature of ethics began to open out before these students. There was also the contrast between philosophy as a speculative science and philosophy as a practical science opening up before them.

The second part of the course dealt with medieval philosophy, running from Augustine to Anselm, Bonaventure, Aquinas, Scotus, etc. In this period I was trying to show how philosophy was disengaging from religion. I would also have shown how Gilson's use of the terminology, 'Christian philosophy' was playing into the critique of Bertrand Russell, of Aquinas, and other medieval philosophers. 'There is little of the true philosophical spirit in Aquinas ... through his religious beliefs he already knows his conclusions in advance.' I tried to show that this statement of Russell's did not do justice to the genuine philosophical awakening in the medieval period. The history of philosophy showed that philosophy and theology could have multiple influences on one another, some positive and some negative, and that it behoved both philosophers and theologians to draw up clear demarcation lines between the two kinds of knowledge. No philosopher can escape completely the cultural milieu he belongs to. Part of a philosopher's task is to bring a critical attitude to bear on these influences and this includes Christianity for those who claim to be Christian.

The period of modern philosophy ranged from Descartes, Malebranche, Kant and Spinoza – of the idealist camp to the empiricist tradition exemplified by Hobbes, Berkeley and Hume. It was easy to see how philosophers were bewitched once either by a rationalist or idealist tendency, on the one hand, or an empiricist tendency, on the other. Through this period I would have been trying to show how philosophy was measuring up against the Enlightenment and the development of mathematics and the physical sciences.

Students would slowly begin to realise how important it was to distinguish between philosophic method and the methods of particular sciences. Again one can see how philosophy and science can have mutual influences on one another – some positive and some negative. The philosopher's task is not to cut himself off from the findings of particular sciences but to draw clear demarcation lines between the two.

And in the fourth and final section I would have been trying to show how contemporary philosophy was related to life, especially in what we have come to call existential phenomenology – Kierkegaard, Husserl, Sartre, Heidegger, Jaspers and Marcel. I would have also touched very briefly on logical positivism and linguistic analysis, especially Wittgenstein. At the same time, I wanted students to know that there were many divergent currents of thought in the 20th century. In this last section of this history of philosophy course I concentrated on existentialist phenomenology, showing how Kierkegaard had provided a number of the themes and Husserl had provided the method to reflect on these themes. I also pointed up the divergence between atheistic existentialists such as Sartre and theistic existentialists such as Marcel. As to the claim that existentialism was a 'philosophy of lived experience' often expressed in novels and plays, arising out of the angst about the human condition in post-war continental Europe, I went on to critique this description and tried to show, for example, that Sartre in *Being and Nothingness* was trying to come to terms with key philosophical problems in post-Cartesian modern philosophy. At the same time, I argued that if philosophy is to be truly philosophy there has to be a certain disengagement from life. Philosophers want to begin with the real and with our individual experience but the whole thrust of philosophy is to get to the essence of things, to get to what is universal , to get to what is ultimate and to do this there is a sense in which philosophy has to be a systematic and scientific reflection on reality.

The aim of the course was to provide an overall historical framework for students beginning to dip into philosophy and get them to face up to the 'scandal' of philosophy – diversity and contradictions – and at the same time to realise that there was such a thing as 'unity of philosophical experience' or what we used to call a *philosophia perennis*. I have always been impressed by Etienne Gilson's thesis in regard to Descartes – in rejecting the medieval or scholastical philosophy that he retained far more of the philosophy than he realised. We see this repeated many times in every period of philosophical endeavour. A philosopher tries to break away from his predecessors and begin again. In doing so, a philosopher takes away with him from his mentors more than he thinks he is leaving behind. I would have drawn out examples of this in all the four periods of the history of philosophy I had covered in this course.

At the end of the course, students could see the difficulty of trying to give a definition of philosophy . We had come across a whole variety of definitions and descriptions in the course of this introduction. There is a sense in which each of the great philosophers begins anew. The efforts of philosophers to engage in the great questions of their day, their efforts to give a comprehensive account of the world and human experience, their efforts to ground philosophy in an initial and for them a profound experience or insight (Dondeyne's 'primitive fact'), their efforts to safeguard the independence of philosophy and not to be taken over by theology or religion or any of the particular sciences, the constant effort to begin radical reflection with the assumption that none of their predecessors quite got it right – all this amounts to the adventure of philosophy which is always with us. It is fascinating to watch young, and not so young, minds opening up to the great questions about the world and human experience.

I have always found Karl Jaspers' Introduction to Philosophy – *Ways to Wisdom* – one of the best books to recommend to young students. He touches on the roots of philosophical thinking and he articulates the great questions asked by many people who begin to reflect on life's experiences. The book is based on a series of radio talks he gave on a Swiss radio station shortly after the Second World War when people were beginning to recover from the horrors of that period, and asked fundamental and radical questions anew. One of my regrets is that I never had time to really keep up with continental European philosophy. I was fascinated by Merleau-Ponty, Paul Ricoeur and Emmanuel Levinas and the multiplicity of thinkers that branched off in various directions in both France and Germany in the latter half of the 20th century. From time to time I would dip into Richard Kearney's introduction to these thinkers and this would leave me with a tinge of regret about not keeping up with philosophical developments in continental Europe. I came to admire those people engaged in philosophical teaching or research all their lives. At the same time I became absorbed at what was going on in the world of theology. I don't think the pursuit of philosophy on its own would have completely satisfied me and secondly I doubt if I had the enthusiasm and willpower to devote all my energies mastering philosophical texts of the contemporary or any other era. I have discovered key choices we make in our lives are dictated by circumstances beyond our control and the opening up of opportunities we had not foreseen. When I left Leuven I did not realise that over the following ten years I would be moving gradually into the world of post-Vatican II theology, especially moral theology.

## IMPLEMENTING VATICAN II'S LITURGICAL REFORMS

By the time I arrived in Strawberry Hill in September 1966 the first significant changes implementing Vatican II's constitution on the Liturgy, *Sacrosanctum Concilium*, were starting to come on stream. Using the vernacular, saying Mass facing the people, concelebration rather than private Masses, were all under way. Our youthful group of students and most of the staff took all these changes in their stride. Only minor changes were required in reordering the sanctuary in the recently built college chapel. The lightly built high altar was brought forward about 15 feet to the centre of the large sanctuary. A new wrought iron lectern, built by the Handicraft Department, was put in place. The college crypt had been fitted out with 10 small altars for private Masses. Over these next few years these small altars were removed from the central area of the crypt and a free-standing altar was put in the centre. With the college chaplain we took it in turns to say a morning Mass at 8.30 am and evening Mass at 5.30 pm in this crypt, which was attended by a small number of students. The crypt itself could hold comfortably about 30 people. On Sundays there were two Masses, one at 10.30 in the morning, where the college choir sang, under the direction of the Head of the Music Department, and one at 6 pm.

One of the most interesting developments I got involved in was in giving shape to the Sunday Evening Mass. This Mass was poorly attended. In 1966/67 and 1967/68 there was no music. The college chaplain usually presided at the 10.30 Sunday Morning Mass and the other priests on the staff took it in turns to preside at the 6.00 Sunday Evening Mass. None of us looked forward to this, as it was quite lifeless and often difficult to hold students' attention. In the autumn of 1968/69 three priests on the staff, including myself, were given responsibility for this Evening Mass and we took it in turns to say it, all three of us attending from week to week. At this stage all three of us had experienced Masses for young people in Germany, Holland and France, using contemporary forms of music and adapting the liturgy to this age group. Over a number of months the three of us, with a small group of students, had attended a similar kind of Mass run by the White Fathers in Totteridge, Mill Hill. We talked to Fr Fitzgerald, the Rector in Totteridge, who had also worked with Father Domerson to develop a good Sunday Morning Liturgy in St Margaret's near Richmond. He agreed to allow one of the students to come down to Strawberry Hill each Sunday evening for the following six months to help us to get this Mass underway. So with the help of a number of students, one of them being Frank McConnell, a very good guitarist, we launched this folk Mass on a particular Sunday in the academic year 1969/1970. There was a very reluctant response from the students. None of them, or very few, had yet experienced the use of folk music in liturgy and many of them would continue to experience very formal liturgies in their parishes for many years to come. I will never forget the dismay on the face of the Dutch White Father student when he came into the sacristy after this first Mass. There was such a flat response to his enthusiastic approach to leading the congregation, he very nearly lost heart on that first day.

Gradually, over the next few months, things picked up. This coupled with real effort on the part of us priests to put a good homily together and to be around to chat to students before and after Mass began to have results. As new instrumentalists joined the choir, violinists, flautists and some good singers, the quality of the music deepened. We made great efforts to develop the repertoire of music sung from one Sunday to the next. By 1972 we had packed congregations at our Sunday Evening Masses including the galleries around the sides of the chapel and at the back of the church. At the end of 1972 we had a 'Going Down' Mass on the final Sunday of the year and on this occasion we had an altar right down the centre of the church with the seats facing inwards. This idea I had picked up from participating in a student pilgrimage to Chartres in the month of May of that same year – 1972.

The Mass itself had its critics amongst one or two of the priests. It was generally acknowledged that it had the capacity to attract a very large group of third level students, involving many of them in not only the music but also other aspects of the liturgy of the Mass. Readers, Eucharistic ministers, distributors of leaflets, money collectors, bidding prayers and so on. Throughout the 1970s it was said that there were more young people of this third level age group attending this Mass in Strawberry Hill than in any other university chaplaincy around the country.

One of the constant criticisms that came up in my time in Strawberry Hill was that we were going to make it very difficult for these students to return to their parish communities during the holidays and when they left Strawberry Hill. Our response was that it was our hope that parish communities would themselves get their act together and provide a Mass that would be attractive to young people. If we did not do it in Strawberry Hill, or if it was not done in the parishes, many of these young people would be lost to the church for good. Secondly, we were opening up possibilities to what these students themselves could do with a sympathetic chaplain in the schools they were going to teach in later.

*Fr Joseph Gelineau SJ.* In the summer of 1978 an international meeting of liturgical musicians known as *Universa Laus* took place in Strawberry Hill during the summer holidays. I attended a few sessions and I remember especially a lecture given by the French Jesuit, Fr Joseph Gelineau who had composed the famous chants for the psalms many years previously. During the course of that session someone suggested that we were all the poorer now having let go the Solemn Latin High Mass. Gelineau responded by saying, 'Yes, we have lost a lot.' The synthesis of words and music and action in the traditional Latin High Mass put together over the preceding centuries we had now let go. He did not advocate returning to it. He went on to say that there are now new possibilities in the revised post-Vatican II liturgy and it may very well take us a 100 years to form a new synthesis of words and music and action.

A few months later, during a midterm break, I attended a Mass in St Ignace, rue de Sevres in Paris. It happened to be on the day on which they were commemorating the setting up of a famous choir there 21 years earlier and the priest presiding that morning invited Fr Gelineau to give the sermon. I will always remember him saying, 'It has taken the choir 21 years to realise some of the potential of post-Vatican II liturgy. It will take another 21 years to teach this to the congregation at large.' For him there was all the difference in the world between an expert choir singing good music with the congregation as spectators, and the congregation actively involved in the singing itself. Some time later I heard that Gelineau had moved from St Ignace to a parish outside Paris and was concentrating on training lay people to lead a variety of liturgies. He was, of course, preparing for the situation when there would not be enough priests to preside at the Eucharist and at other liturgies. He was in charge of a few small parishes where participation in weekly Eucharist was very low. However, many people still wanted to be baptised, married and have their funeral Mass in the church. The great challenge, he believed, was to try and discover what sense of the sacred remained for people today and how to use music, movement, silence, to gain access to their notion of the sacred. Today, at the age of 85, Gelineau is living in retirement in a Jesuit house in Haute-Savoie, high up in the French Alps, enthusiastic about all that the Vatican Council's Constitution on the Liturgy opened up but also aware that so much still needs to be done to inculturate that vision in the lives of Christians in many parts of the world today at continental, national, regional and local levels.

## TWO VISITS TO EAST AFRICA

In the summer of 1972 I travelled to Kenya / Tanzania / Zambia to find out if there was a need for teachers in the secondary schools there. Over the years there had always been a number of Strawberry Hill students, usually just qualified, who had volunteered to teach for two or three years in third world countries, in Nigeria, the Cameroons, Uganda, Kenya, Zambia and Malawi – all former British colonies. We decided to explore further ourselves the need for teachers in these countries as well as exploring the possibility of a link up between St Mary's College and one or other college of education in an African country. I was given the task of exploring this further. I had established contact with an Irish Jesuit, Fr Colm O'Riordan who had been responsible for setting up a wonderful structure of Catholic secondary schools in Zambia in the previous 10 years.

In discussion with Fr O'Riordan it was agreed that I would tour a number of the secondary schools and colleges of education in Zambia. So in early June 1971 I flew out from London to Amsterdam where I joined a Raptim flight to Cairo, Nairobi and Dar es Salaam. The plane was full of missionaries. We had an overnight stop in Nairobi. I remember getting off the plane there sometime in the late afternoon and experiencing the balmy heat all around me. That night I stayed in one of the old colonial hotels on the main street of Nairobi. In the evening I walked without any difficulty through the central part of the city. Despite the Mau Mau activities of some years previously, the centre of Nairobi was safe to walk through. I had a good look at the Cathedral built by Archbishop Whelan, an Irish Holy Ghost father some years previously. The influence of the Holy Ghost Fathers in setting up the Catholic Church in Kenya started to come home to me. My main impression of Nairobi over the evening that I spent there was of wealthy Europeans and Americans arriving to visit the Safari wildlife parks or the beaches in Mombasa.

From Nairobi I flew on the next day to Dar es Salaam, arriving late in the evening. On waking up the next morning the strong rays of the morning sun were bursting into my room. When I went to the window there was a marvellous view of the Indian ocean, a hundred yards away glittering in the sunlight. Later on that day I completed the final stage of my journey, travelling on a small plane to Lusaka, the capital of Zambia. I was ferried by Fr O'Riordan to the Jesuit House in central Lusaka where I met a number of German and Irish Jesuits. The Jesuits staffed the diocese of Monza south of Lusaka where an Irish man, Bishop Corboy was Bishop. He had been appointed straight from Milltown Park to that post in the early 1960s.

Zambia is a landlocked country bounded by the Congo and Tanzania to the north, Malawi to the east, Zimbabwe and Botswana to the south and Angola to the west. It covers an area of 290,000 sq miles which means that it is about six times the size of England. Most of the country lies 5,000 ft above sea level and like the other countries on the high plateau of central Africa it enjoys a warm sunny and temperate climate. The population of 4 million is spread unevenly over the flat countryside with a heavy concentration in the ten towns strung along the one line of rail from Livingstone in the south to Kitwe in the north.

After finding my feet in Lusaka over a few days I started visiting a number of schools there. Then I began my tour of schools and colleges around the country, moving north first to Kabre Broken Hill, where there was a Teacher Training College. From there I went to Kitwe and Ndola in the middle of the copper belt. The price of copper at this time was just beginning to go down and that was to have a calamitous effect on the economy of Zambia from which I think it has never recovered.

After a few days in Kitwe I travelled with a Canadian Brother in a lorry through the Congo pedicle to Kasama, one of the larger towns in the northern part of Zambia. This Brother was an excellent singer with a beautiful tenor voice. He sang many songs on the way telling me that one of his greatest regrets was not being able to follow up his interests in singing classical music to audiences who would appreciate it. In passing through the Congo pedicle I became aware that it was here that Dag Hammarskjold's plane had crashed during the Congo war 10 years previously and all the controversy afterwards about whether his plane had been sabotaged or the crash was an accident came back to me. Conor Cruise O'Brien's *To Katanga and Back* was to add a lot of fuel to that controversy.

In Kasama I remember meeting a red-haired Scots White Father, who had many roles in the town. He was secretary to a Zambian Bishop, the Mayor of the town and the man around whom everything appeared to revolve. I met a number of White Fathers here and in other parts of Africa and my esteem for them grew rapidly when I saw them in action. It was generally accepted that they were the real professional missionaries in Africa. They spent many years learning the local languages and doing the ground work which has led to a flourishing of Christianity in many countries. One of them said that they were now moving into a second phase of missionary activity – handing over the running of the church to Africans themselves.

Their role now was to support and encourage them. And then he said graphically. 'Our task is to be the spare wheel in the car in case it breaks down.' They were there to help the car start up again and to get on with things. I was amazed at the way they were adapting to playing this secondary but crucial role in the development of the church in many parts of Africa.. The temptation of many missioners is to hold on to power and to underestimate what the Africans themselves can accomplish.

Going south from Kasama, I visited 3 very impressive schools run by Irish Sisters. One of them in a place called Lwitikila was beautifully landscaped. Of the 100 secondary schools in Zambia at this time, about 30 of them were Catholic schools and very often they were run by orders of priests, sisters or brothers. Their strength was in the numbers of core staff who were permanently committed to the schools. Many of the State schools had a quick turnover of staff and there wasn't the same stability in them. This showed in the examination results where the Catholic schools consistently held the top 20 places around the country from year to year.

When I arrived back in Lusaka I moved quickly down south to the diocese of Monza where Joseph Corboy was bishop. In 1962 he was named the first bishop of this diocese. After attending all the sessions of the Vatican Council he began developing a variety of schools and pastoral centres, inviting many religious orders of men and women from Ireland to run them. I remember visiting the famous secondary school the Jesuits were running there. As I went up the drive I saw an army unit, dressed in battle kit, going through training exercises on one of the playing pitches. It turned out to be sixth-formers led by the headmaster, also in battle gear. I believe that something similar went on in Clongowes through the post-War years, and possibly also in Stonyhurst. Depending on whether you came from Ireland or England this Zambian School was known as the Clongowes or Stonyhurst of Zambia. It had a tremendous reputation. Many of the wealthiest Zambians sent their children there. Already many of their past pupils were holding leading positions in government, medicine and law and other professions.

One thing that came home to me on my visit to these schools in Zambia is that secondary school education was modelled on the public school system, as we know it in England, or the private schools in Ireland. The aspirations of Zambians at this time were focused on joining the professions, but with the decline of the Zambian economy and its inability to provide jobs for many of its secondary school graduates, these hopes became more and more unrealisable. It struck me even then that it was important for many of these schools to have domestic science, technology and agricultural subjects on their curriculum. At this time Zambia looked as though it had a great future ahead of it even though the signs of economic decline were already evident in the mines in the copper belt. The principled stand of Zambia against the apartheid system in South Africa also meant that the gateway to imports and exports south along rail and road was closed in Rhodesia, or what later was to be called Zimbabwe.

I spent a few pleasant days with the Jesuits in this school near Monza. On a Sunday afternoon I remember meeting 3 or 4 Holy Ghost Fathers who had transferred from Nigeria having been expelled from there at the end of the Biafran war. They had spent the previous months learning the basics of a language in this area and had just returned from 3 or 4 mission posts where they had celebrated Sunday morning Mass. Their constant refrain was that here in Zambia they were looking after quite small groups of Christians, in their 10s or 20s, whereas in their former mission posts in Nigeria they would have been looking after thousands. In subsequent years I met Holy Ghost Fathers in many parts of the world, especially in the United States, men who had been part of the very large group of Spiritans who had worked in South East Nigeria where Bishop Shanahan and his followers had done such great work to build up the church. It was said that 500 Spiritans had to leave Nigeria before and during the Biafran War and were never able to return. One thing that came home to me from encountering these men in Zambia, and others that I met later on, is that it was very hard to move to a new mission, especially when the first mission was Nigeria. The vibrancy and the enthusiasm of the missioners there was hard to emulate elsewhere.

A day or two later, I got a lift south to Livingstone, stopping off for a night to stay with a few English diocesan priests from the diocese of Nottingham who were working in a mission post about 40 miles north of Livingstone. My memory is that they were finding it difficult to adapt to the tough circumstances they found themselves in. In Livingstone I stayed with the Irish Capuchin Fathers, making the acquaintance of Fr Jude, a tall, young, energetic Irishman. The Victoria Falls were nearby and I was enthralled by the cascading waters over a one mile stretch of the Zambesi river, falling hundreds of feet to the rocks below and the way the light was refracted through the roaring torrents into all the colours of the rainbow.

One day Father Jude asked me would I go with him in his jeep to collect some piece of machinery in a small town some 10 miles south into Rhodesia. Whatever he was up to was quite illegal and he told me that there was a chance we might be put in prison for the night. He joked with the border guards, asking them were they going to search him and his jeep. They smiled at him and let him pass on. When he had collected his equipment we went for a drink to a famous colonial hotel not far from the southern side of the Falls and then came back to the border post once again. He joked again with the customs men on duty and they waved him through.

I would like to have gone south of Livingstone to visit Bishop Donal Lamont in the diocese of Umtali but this was not possible because of the travel restrictions between Zambia and Zimbabwe at that time. I was to meet Bishop Lamont about eight years later when he came to preach at a Sunday evening Mass in Strawberry Hill. He preached an eloquent homily on that occasion when he left aside his prepared script to speak about the deaths of two of our young students who had been killed the previous evening in a motor accident. I also met him later in All Hallows in Dublin when he called there to meet Cardinal McCann from Capetown.

Over my six weeks in Zambia I started to form a number of convictions about the proposed linking up of Strawberry Hill with a Teacher Training College in Zambia or any other country in Africa, and also some views about the need for volunteer teachers. On the question of a link between St Mary's, Strawberry Hill and a Teacher Training College in an African country, I was beginning to realise that we were 10 to 20 years behind the times. I was beginning to have doubts whether such a linkage would really be for the benefit of the African institution. Secondly, a conviction was also forming that we had to be very careful about recommending students to teach in secondary schools in African countries. I had met a number of volunteer teachers in State schools who were quite disillusioned about the system. I also met others who were very content with their one or two years' teaching experience in these schools. But this very often was in the Catholic schools where there was much more stability and support. I felt that it was an organisation called VMM, the Volunteer Missionary Movement, set up by Edwina Gately, that we should support rather than any other group such as VSO. However, another year would elapse and there would be more visits to other African countries before these convictions started to crystalise in my mind .

This six week visit to Zambia was an extraordinary experience for me. It was my first insight into the missionary church in an African country. I began to realise how much missionaries from Europe had contributed to the setting up and development of Christianity in Africa over a 100 year period. It was quite astonishing what had been accomplished in building up parish and diocesan structures, and all that had been achieved in the worlds of education and health care by missionary congregations in many African countries. I returned to London sometime in late August quite chastened by all that I had seen in Zambia over these 6 weeks, and quite convinced that one needed to be very mature and tough to take on voluntary service in an African country in the 1970s. At the same time, I had met many volunteers who assured me that they had benefited far more from the experience than the young pupils they had taught.

Teachers go through various phases during their time in developing countries. At first there may be a honeymoon period – a period of elation – when things are new and exciting. This may be followed after a few weeks or a few months by a period of depression when one has to knuckle down to an ordinary day's teaching with sometimes more than ordinary frustrations or difficulties. The culture shock – and in my view it should not be minimised – can take some time to adapt to. One is taking a risk in various senses in going to a developing country to teach – a risk in the kind of teaching community one finds oneself in, a risk in the kind of pupil one is landed with, a risk in that one may not be sure if one has the personal resources to adapt and so on … From the point of view of human logic and of human wisdom, one may find it difficult to justify taking such a risk. One may have to appeal to a higher wisdom to do so. A White Father, with 18 years' teaching experience in busy regions in the north of Zambia, summed all this in this striking, if exaggerated way: 'One needs to have a hole in one's head to come out here, but if you are a little bit crazy it helps.' I have no doubt that it was gospel risk he had in mind.

## A Second Visit to East Africa

In the summer of 1973 I visited Malawi, Uganda and Ethiopia after spending some time in Kenya. In early June of 1973 I flew out with British Airways to Nairobi, this time staying with some of the priests working in the Catholic Teacher Training College in that city. I made contact with one or two of the priests working in the Catholic Education Office and picked up some general information about schools and the need for teachers in Kenya. From there I flew on with East African Airways to Blantyre, the capital city of Malawi, one of the most beautiful African countries I had ever visited. Small in size, it ran alongside Lake Malawi. It was ruled at this time by President Hastings Banda who had the reputation of running the country very efficiently.

Some of his dictatorship tendencies surfaced later. One could argue now that many African countries were not ready for parliamentary democracy in the 1960s. So much of what has happened in the last 40 years would bear out that conclusion. However, one could ask 'are the Africans themselves responsible for what has happened or must a lot of the blame be placed on the colonial systems of the western world?' Not enough attention has been given to the efforts of Julius Nyerere to introduce an African brand of socialism in Tanzania. Some would argue that it was economic disaster for the country but I wonder is that a superficial judgement.

I stayed for a few days with the English De Montfort Fathers in Blantyre. They had a number of missions in the southern part of Malawi. It was one of them who told me that quite recently the Malawian Archbishop of Blantyre had gone out to the airport to welcome one of his priests back after doing postgraduate studies in Rome. When he greeted the priest, the man informed the archbishop that he was not intending to return to the exercise of priestly ministry. He was leaving the priesthood. Inside a short time he had obtained a senior government post in the area. I often heard this kind of story in my travels in Africa and elsewhere. Some priests never returned from Europe because they were bewitched by the standard of living there. Perhaps this is inevitable in a young church. Very often it is left to the white missioners to help pick up the pieces. However, experiences like this certainly convinced me that all undergraduate preparation for priesthood, and many of the postgraduate courses, should be done at various centres in Africa itself. I found it interesting to learn as the years went on that this gradually became the policy of the authorities in Rome and in the funding agencies in Germany.

My travels in Malawi brought me up to the new capital city of Lilongwe, where I met Bishop Patrick, a White Father, a black bishop who later resigned from his post and has taught in an ecumenical centre, Selly Park, outside Birmingham for many years. From Lilongwe I moved up to Mzuzu, made famous by travel writer, Laurens van der Post who had written so movingly about the mountain countryside there. In Mzuzu I got a great welcome from the Kiltegan Fathers and the Medical

Missionaries of Mary, who ran a hospital nearby. The bishop at the time was Canadian and over the week I spent there this place struck me as one of the ideal missionary places I had visited. I could sense the spirit of co-operation between the missioners there and the commitment of the priests and sisters to the work in hand. Many years later, in the last years of Hastings Banda's dictatorship, the Kiltegan Father, who was Prefect Apostolic there, was one of the leaders who got the Catholic bishops in Malawi to bring out a critical statement of what was happening in the country. For a while he was a marked man and had to leave the country for some time.

I visited a number of schools in Malawi and the convictions I had already formed in Zambia the previous year were reinforced by what I saw there. Malawians too were beginning to stand on their own feet and any kind of linkage to a College of Education in London would have been a retrograde step. The Ministry of Education in Zambia was in the process of dismantling twelve Teacher Training Colleges which were going to be merged into three large colleges. This undertaking was going to be funded by the World Bank. My experiences in Uganda a few weeks later were to confirm these convictions and also the conviction that one needed to be very careful in recommending students in Strawberry Hill to go overseas for voluntary service. They needed a lot of luck to be channelled into the schools where they would be really needed and where a good support system was in place.

I made my way back to Blantyre, waiting for missioners going in my direction, and flew from Blantyre to Kampala, the capital of Uganda. It was my intention to spend three weeks in this beautiful country . I remember in particular the magnificent sunsets.

I stayed for a while near Lake Entebbe. But my visit was to be cut short dramatically after the President, Idi Amin, announced that the East African Asians were going to be expelled from the country. Many of them had English citizenship and found their way to London. I can remember walking through the main street of Kampala and seeing signs in shop doors thanking the people for their custom but regretting that they would be closing down their shops over the next few days.

While I was in Kampala I stayed in the White Fathers 'compound' on the edge of the city and had an experience on entering the compound for the first time which I will never forget. I was crossing a grass lawn to the main entrance when a large dog on a chain came rushing at me. I misjudged the length of the chain so the dog actually nipped the skin over my stomach, leaving 2 or 3 bloody marks and tearing my shirt. I was scared out of my wits, because I knew how common rabies was in some of these countries. I was lucky in that this appeared to be a rabies free area. Nevertheless, the White Fathers brought me to a clinic and I was given an injection with the re-assurance that I should be okay. I lived with a certain amount of anxiety over the following few days.

After a day or two in Kampala, I went to a large town about 50 miles south of there to visit a Teacher Training College run by the Sacred Heart Sisters, near the town of Mbarara. Some of these sisters had come from their famous Catholic College of Education in Scotland, Craiglockhart. It was while I was in conversation with a number of the sisters there that I realised finally that the plans formulated in Strawberry Hill to link up with a College of Education in an African country were at least 20 years behind the times. From now on I had no further doubt about it. The Sacred Heart sisters communicated to me over the few days I spent there that it was 'hand-over time' for them to let Ugandans run the college. Their work of founding and building up the college was nearly over.

I stayed in the major seminary in that town . When I learned from the White Fathers that Fr Jock Dalrymple was just about to begin a retreat to priests over the following 5 days, I decided to join in. This retreat was an interesting break for me in the midst of all my own concerns, giving me time to reflect on my experiences in Africa and at the same time trying to get the measure of where I was in all this. Reflecting on what I had undertaken that year and in the previous year, the idea that I might be seconded from Strawberry Hill for two or more years came to a head. Now it was fairly clear to me that this was unlikely in the light of the conclusions I had come to about a link up. I settled down to the idea that I would be continuing my lecturing in Strawberry Hill at least over the next few years.

Fr Dalrymple gave thirty-minute conferences twice a day and I appreciated very much his dry sense of humour and the skilful way he presented his ideas on priestly life in the immediate aftermath of Vatican II. He was upbeat and optimistic but with his feet on the ground. When the retreat was over he took the train from there to Mombasa. He was a railway enthusiast and loved travelling on some of the famous railroads in Africa and elsewhere.

Because of the uncertainties in Uganda at that time, especially because of Idi Amin's antics, I was encouraged by a number of White Fathers to get out as quickly as I could, especially if I wanted to be back in London in September for the beginning of the academic year. I returned to Kampala, and in the space of a few days I visited some Mill Hill Fathers in the Diocese of Jinja, including one man who had studied in Strawberry Hill. At this point I had a few weeks to spare . I found out from a travel agent that I could get a relatively cheap flight to Ethiopia and spend a few weeks there before returning to London. I flew out to Ethiopia the next day. In Addis Ababa I stayed in the Vincentian house in the centre of the city, not far away from St Mary's Secondary School for girls run by the Daughters of Charity where Sister Mary Dixon DC was in charge. I was astonished by the poverty of that city. Around the corner from the Hilton hotel on Churchill Avenue were some of the worst slums that I had ever seen. Haile Selassie was still in power but with only a few years to go.

While I was in Addis I set up the beginnings of a project, in collaboration with Sister Mary Dixon, to maintain a small primary school in a very poor area of the city supported by Strawberry Hill. The school was known as Kechenie School and it looked after the children of families who had to beg on the streets of Addis each day. In many of these families there were blind or handicapped children. The money needed to run the school was sent out from Strawberry Hill and provided a modest salary for two teachers and helped to maintained two run-down classrooms. A Strawberry Hill student came to Addis Ababa a few years later and kept an eye on this project. She sent back information to Strawberry Hill on how the school was progressing. This helped to keep the funds flowing.

On one of the days I spent in Addis Ababa I visited a very well-run school with Canadian brothers in charge. It had the reputation of being one of the best-run schools in the city and it attracted the sons of well-to-do people including government ministers. When I asked one of the brothers how he saw the role of the brothers in this school he acknowledged that most of the children came from well to do families who were able to afford the school fees. He was conscious that they were educating the elite and he told me that they were doing their best to pass on principles of justice to their pupils. The following day I was visiting a seminary some forty miles north of the city where I met a White Father. I happened to mention what the Canadian brother had said to me about passing on principles of justice to their pupils. The White Father gave me a sceptical smile and said, 'Did you ever hear of an elite group dispossessing themselves for the sake of the poor?' I never forgot his words.

From Addis I flew in a small plane to Bonga a few hundred miles west of the capital where I met the Dutch Vincentian Provincial, Fr Will Bos. From there I went on to Buba. I meet a young dynamic Dutch confrère, Jan Ermers, who was working on a special agricultural project in that area funded by the Dutch government. He was full of energy and enthusiasm. In the course of that visit he introduced me to the 'cathedral of Buba', a small little wooden building with a tiny spire that held about 12 people. The impression I got during that visit was that quite a number of the Dutch Vincentians were concentrating on development work and channelling in funds from various agencies in the Netherlands. One or two more were keen anthropologists.

One of the final memories I have of my visit to Ethiopia was visiting the Catholic cathedral in Addis on 15 August. The congregation packed the cathedral and many people who could not get inside were milling around the entrance . The Mass itself was in the Ethiopian rite, using the special liturgical language called 'geez'. The ceremony went on so long that I left before the end, exhausted by the heat and the crowd.

At some point in arranging my ticket through the summer I discovered that my cheapest way back to London was through Cairo. I decided to spend a few days there, which turned out to be a week. I never felt more afraid in any city that I have gone to.

The hotel I stayed in was a very modest one, without air-conditioning. To escape the midday heat, I used to go down for a few hours to the Hilton, some ten minutes away, and sit in the Foyer. Around midday each day I noticed a number of Muslims kneeling on a grass verge just outside the entrance and bowing profoundly in the direction of Mecca. Because I was low in funds I did not travel outside the city or explore the Nile valley, something which I regretted later. However, my week of enforced residence there gave me time to write up a report on my visit to Malawi, Uganda and Ethiopia. When eventually I did get a flight back to London I was very relieved to escape the humid heat of Cairo and the grinding poverty of that city.

## Some Final Reflections on African Visits

Later on I was to visit South Africa and West Africa but my 12-week visit to East Africa over two summers left an indelible mark on my psyche. I could sense why some people fall in love with Africa as instanced by the film *Out of Africa*. At the same time, I experienced some of the contradictions in African society. Many Africans aspire to emulate Western capitalism and at the same time to retain all that was best in their own culture. Over my two summer visits I had seen too many examples of failed projects and I knew that whatever way resources were channelled into African countries, they would have to be carefully monitored so that the project itself was going to be for the long-term benefit of African people themselves. It is so easy to perpetuate a new kind of dependency where economic gain is the real agenda for both the donor and the recipient.

I also saw how sensitive missionaries had to be in their efforts to evangelise and make the gospel come alive in African countries. God was already present in so many ways in the cultures of these people. It required extraordinary maturity on the part of European missionaries to introduce programmes of catechesis in which the values of the people are respected and the gospel is truly acculturated. One had to adapt to a process of religious development very different to what was taking place in European countries. One also had to have the patience to allow the seeds of the gospel to take root and grow at an African tempo.

I was also left with the question of whether or not I would have survived for one or two years if I had been seconded to Nigeria or Zambia or some other African country – survived physically, psychologically and spiritually. With the support of the Vincentian community, I'd settled down reasonably well in London over the six years that I had spent there. Would I have been able to make the transition to another continent and another culture? These are questions I have often asked myself.

Shortly after arriving in Strawberry Hill in September 1966 I began to move into the area of moral theology, teaching one or two courses in my first year but then moving gradually to take over the whole area – biblical ethics, fundamental moral, social and political ethics, medical ethics, sexual ethics. I was given a free hand to construct my own courses. With Professor Gordon Dunstan, a professor of Christian Ethics in King's College, London University, we drew up the syllabi for each of the above areas, and the examination papers for all the external colleges of London University. I remember going to visit Professor Dunstan in King's at an early stage of our discussions and he introduced me to lemon tea. He had a number of publications in the Christian ethics area especially in the area of medical ethics. When a number of the colleges doing theology in BA and BEd programmes decided to change the title from 'divinity' to 'religious studies' he strongly objected and in fact resigned from a number of examining boards in protest.

It took me about five years to work up my moral theology courses. The lectures I had attended in the Leuven theology department proved invaluable. In my travels in Europe in the early 1970s and later in the United States, I made a point of finding out what was being taught in other centres such as the Institut Catholique in Paris, the Gregorian University in Rome, Notre Dame in Indiana, USA and the Catholic University in Washington DC. Courses in biblical ethics and fundamental moral were fairly easy to set up and I covered these courses in first year and third year respectively. The syllabi for the other areas of special ethics / social and political and sexual and medical ethics were very open-ended. I made an agreement with Professor Dunstan that I would choose one or two issues under discussion in Britain each year in each of the above areas. I taught all these moral theology courses from 1971 right up to my final year in Strawberry Hill in 1981/82.

In 1973 I became a member of the Catholic Moral Theology Association which met once a year. Various members read research papers they were working on over the three or four day meetings and it was a very good exchange between lecturers from universities, such as Heythrop College in London, and Catholic Colleges of Education and seminaries around the country. When I moved to Dublin in the summer of 1982, I joined the Moral Theology Association in Ireland. As things worked out, because of administrative commitments, I taught very little moral theology in All Hallows. In Strawberry Hill I had the best of both worlds – teaching moral theology and philosophy of religion. It enabled me to keep a foothold in both the world of theology and the world of philosophy. So much of what I was doing was walking a tightrope between the two disciplines. I was able to look at the question of what is specific about Christian ethics from both angles. Moral theology was a popular subject with students. I've always felt that young people have an innate interest in finding out what is right and what is wrong. From specific questions in morality, one is able to move on to profound Christian themes and eventually one confronts some of the basic philosophical and theological questions about the meaning of human existence.

*Biblical Ethics*
In my four year moral theology courses in Glenart from 1958 to 1962 no course on biblical ethics was taught. So much of what we covered in our moral theology textbooks was in fact moral philosophy. Lip service was very often paid to biblical, patristic and theological themes underlying ethical decisions. It was only after the Vatican II document on priestly ministry suggested that moral teaching should be rooted in the scriptures that both scripture scholars and moral theologians started to take seriously the moral teaching of both the Old and New Testaments. Negatively we learned that one could not methodologically pull

a quotation out of any book of scripture to use it as a 'proof text' to back up a moral position. Positively scripture scholars started to highlight the rich moral themes in both Old and New Testaments. I always felt that moral teaching comes alive when it is seen in its proper context, whether that be myths or stories or historical circumstances in which the teaching has been proposed. It is then too that the inspirational dimension also comes to the fore. This culminates in the person of Jesus Christ, the 'teacher of the way'.

Over the years biblical ethics was one of the courses I enjoyed teaching most of all. From the 1950s onwards Catholic and Protestant scholars began to systematise the ethical teaching of the Old and New Testaments. Many fine articles started to appear in both scripture and theological journals about biblical ethics. On a one month's study course in Jerusalem in August 1978 I had an opportunity to check the catalogue for biblical ethics material in the library of the École Biblique and I started building up my own bibliographies. I continued to work on this material in subsequent years.

*Fundamental Moral Theology*
In this course I dealt with fundamental concepts – freedom, conscience, law and sin/guilt. In dealing with these four traditional fundamental concepts I was trying to give students a framework to see the fundamentals of our moral life philosophically and theologically. Over the years I often wondered if it would have been better to have begun the course in moral theology with specific moral questions and to have worked back to these four fundamental concepts. I made some effort to stay in touch with the students' own moral experience. All the way through my 12 years teaching moral theology in Strawberry Hill, I stayed with the traditional approach.

(a) Freedom
I usually began this first part of the course by questioning in a provocative way the whole notion of freedom. I would outline the different factors that inhibit our freedom or appear to condition us to behave in certain ways, using some of the findings of contemporary psychologists, especially the behaviourist school.

I would then suggest that there are two levels which we can reflect on in relation to our freedom. The first level is on the individual actions we perform. Secondly, I would raise the question about a more profound level at which we exercise 'fundamental choice' – a level where we make 'fundamental options'. In doing this I would ask them to reflect on some of the key decisions they had made in their lives, getting married, opting to be a teacher, leaving home, etc. I would make the claim that we all do make fundamental options or fundamental choices but that it can be quite difficult to get to the level where we become aware of what these choices and options are. We opt for values which run through a whole series of choices we make. Often I would say that we might need the help of a psychologist or psychotherapist over a period of time to discover what the fundamental choices are that we have made. Rather than doing away with freedom or diminishing responsibility, we will be trying to locate where we exercise real freedom in our lives.

I believe that in the Catholic tradition, especially because of our confessional practice – in the confession of individual sins we have often arrested people's moral development by encouraging them to stay focused on individual actions in their lives, rather than on the fundamental moral orientation of one's behaviour. A fundamental option can culminate in an individual action but more often than not we exercise our freedom through fundamental options, which run through a whole series of actions.

When I gave these lectures students would look dazed at first. Then it would start to dawn on them for the first time that there was a more profound way to reflect on the exercise of freedom in their own lives – a level which led to liberation and authenticity and moral maturity.

(b) Conscience
What is conscience? I began by outlining a number of definitions of conscience quoting Shakespeare, 'conscience does make cowards of us all', Freud, 'conscience is the relic of the super ego in all of us', Eysenck, 'conscience is a conditioned anxiety response'. I ended with the definition of Aquinas, 'conscience is a dictate of the practical intellect about the goodness or badness of

an action to be performed here and now'. At the end of the day Aquinas' definition was the most satisfying for me. In unpacking this definition, one had to introduce students to a number of key concepts in Aquinas' moral philosophy, e.g. 'practical reason' and so on.

I would move on then to the question 'Must conscience always be obeyed?' and then discussion would begin in earnest. Because of the *Humanae Vitae* debate about contraception, after the appearance of the encyclical in 1968, there was tremendous debate about the rights and duties of the individual conscience in relation to church authority. I would try to stand above the debate but nevertheless give students some clear principles about the formation of conscience, drawing their attention to our capacity for self-deception and self-delusion. At the same time I would emphasise the duty we all had to follow our conscience. I left students in no doubt that I believed in the primacy of the individual conscience. 'I will drink a toast to the Pope – yes – but to conscience first' (Newman).

(c) Natural Law

At this stage I would raise the question of the existence of an objective norm of human behaviour. I would present students with an extreme form of situation ethics and some related theories, and then I would open up Aquinas' natural law theory, introducing them to a good deal of Aquinas' moral philosophy. In this context the question of 'absolutes' in morality unfolded. I would then begin to touch on some of the debates amongst contemporary Catholic moral theologians about the principle of double effect and also about methodology in moral theology. I reviewed the arguments in favour of a deontological approach which appeared to be safeguarding absolutes and traditional positions in sexual and medical ethics. I would then outline the arguments of the teleological approach when one was faced with a genuine conflict of values and would have to work out a calculus of values in which one would have to prioritise some of these values over others .

I have always felt throughout my time teaching moral theology in Strawberry Hill that a personalist interpretation of Aquinas' natural law theory was the best basis on which to ground an objective morality. At the same time it is important to be open to all the new information coming to us from various sciences today – psychology, sociology, anthropology, etc. – and to work out ways of taking account of this new knowledge in determining what we think is right and wrong in regard to specific moral problems today.

## (d) Guilt/Sin

In this area I would introduce students to some elementary notions in the area of the psychology of guilt – different kinds of guilt. The development of the sense of guilt and various mechanisms we use to avoid a sense of guilt or to project it on to others. At the same time, I would be trying to draw attention to the sense of well-being or the feeling of satisfaction we have when we perform good actions.

I outlined the teachings about the sense of sin in both Old and New Testaments and the deepening of the notion of sin in relation to the kind of God one believed in. Many of these students would one day be teaching in Catholic schools all around Britain and would be carrying considerable responsibility for the moral education of children and adolescents. I was trying to inculcate in them a mature sense of sin and guilt, knowing that directly or indirectly they would be communicating their own sense of guilt to the pupils they taught .

Working in the area of fundamental moral theology was working in the 'engine room'. So many of our debates about specific moral problems are determined by our understanding of fundamental concepts. Many of these arguments continue today. The division between deontologists and teleologists has sharpened further in recent times after the publication of Pope John Paul's encyclical *Veritatis Splendor* in 1993.

### Moral Education

Over my years in Strawberry Hill I got more and more involved in discussions about the nature of moral education and I found myself becoming more and more critical of some of the views being put forward about moral education in philosophy circles. One of the lecturers in the education department, Tony Higgins, ran a special programme funded by a trust, looking at the implications of Laurence Stenhouse's 'components of the morally educated person'. I had grave misgivings about Stenhouse's approach and believed that he neglected many areas of our moral experience or trivialised our moral sense in certain ways .

The notion of 'autonomy' runs through a lot of moral education literature and is central in philosophy of education discussions over the last thirty years. I've always felt that it is a notion that needs to be severely critiqued, otherwise the notion can be masquerading an extreme form of relativism or subjectivism.

## Stages of Moral Development

I also took a deep interest in Kohlberg's stages of moral development which to my mind highlighted both the strength and the weakness of Catholic moral education. Kohlberg pointed up how important it is for young people to experience a phase of moral education when moral principles are taught authoritatively. This we have tended to do in the Catholic tradition and this is one of its strengths. One cannot ignore or bypass this stage of conformity. However I've always felt that many Catholics are stuck in this conformity phase of moral development and that we do little to bring them on to the next stage of acting autonomously, that is of helping them to make personal decisions of conscience. In the Catholic tradition we often pay lip service to the primacy of conscience and do not try to bring people beyond a conformity level.

## Specific Areas of Moral Theology

The syllabus I had worked out with Professor Dunstan in King's College, London in the early 1970s stated that three topics were to be covered in each of the following areas: social and political ethics, medical ethics and sexual ethics. The topics were not named. It was our understanding that we would choose topics that were under discussion in society at the time, either because of impending legislation, debate in the media or for some other reason. This meant that the topics chosen could vary from year to year.

As a lecturer my task was to develop a methodology that would enable students to tackle problems in each of these areas.

They had to acquaint themselves with knowledge from the empirical or social sciences such as biology, sociology, psychology, etc., and with legislation if it existed. Then they had to bring theological insights to bear on the issue, facing up to the fact that some of the problems which we had to deal with were being addressed for the first time.

## Theology of Education

Around 1974/75, in collaboration with Paddy Walsh in the philosophy department, and Teresa O'Donovan in the education department, a number of staff seminars were organised on aspects of 'theology of education'. We felt that the time had come to bring theology to bear on a number of philosophy of education issues. Some people thought at the time that what we wanted to deal with could have been called Christian philosophy of education. Not subscribing to the notion of Christian philosophy of anything, I believed it was better to be up front about theology as a discipline and put forward points of contact between theology and education, recognising that both subjects had their own methodologies and parameters. To some extent we were reacting against the tendency in the philosophy of education world to close the door towards any theological contacts or influences. At the same time we felt that in a Catholic college with a strong theology department there should be more interaction between theologians and educationalists/philosophers/psychologists/sociologists on a number of issues.

Among the topics we dealt with are the following:

- The nature of theology of education
- Theology and indoctrination
- Theology as one of the 'forms of knowledge'
- Theology and moral education
- A theological critique of the notion of 'autonomy' as the aim of moral education

Fr Kevin Nichols, who was the National Director of Catholic Education in the Catholic Church in England, was also writing articles along these lines and he encouraged the group in Strawberry Hill to continue their work. The interaction between the three departments of theology, philosophy and education went on for about two years. Some themes resurfaced in Paddy

Walsh's book on the philosophy of education. Paddy moved from Strawberry Hill to become a lecturer in philosophy of education in The Institute of Education, London University some years later.

As a result of visits to various Catholic universities in the United States over these years, and to other third level colleges in France and Belgium, I began to formulate my own priorities in regard to the distinctiveness of such an institution from a Christian point of view. With the development of new degree programmes, St Mary's College was now in a position to talk about a new kind of presence in higher education in Britain. I was not at all sure that the bishops of the country were aware of new possibilities of a distinctive kind of presence in third level education opening up before them. In November 1976 I circulated a four page paper to some of my colleagues on the staff of the college about this. The paper put forward a number of practical suggestions under eight headings to promote further discussion.

• An institutional commitment to Christianity

This raised questions not so much about mission statements or Board of Governors' commitment to Christian principles, but about how individual members of staff could bring their Christian beliefs to bear on the ethos and curriculum. It also raised questions about how those members of staff who held key administrative positions could promote the college as a Christian institution.

• The College Curriculum

With subjects like philosophy, history, literature, psychology, sociology, etc on the college curriculum, and practical subjects like art, music and drama, the college was in a strong position to develop a curriculum that would give considerable attention to Christian beliefs and practices in our contemporary world.

## • The Theology Department

Here I made a strong pitch that this department should be given priority in regard to the allocation of resources. It was incumbent on this department to take the lead in promoting an integrating Christian vision for the college and for this reason I advocated that more specialialisation and research take place .

## • A Chaplaincy Team

I suggested that a team of three people was needed to take responsibility for the development of the prayer and liturgical life of the college. This team had the task of challenging both staff and students to deepen their Christian commitments. In this context I would have been impressed by some of the chaplaincy centres I had visited in Catholic universities in the United States and also some Newman centres linked to Ivy League colleges where they had the power and the freedom to challenge the views of both staff and students from a Christian point of view.

## • Pastoral Care

I argued that the pastoral care of students was the responsibility of all the staff of the college including the wardens of hostels. At the same time I recognised the need for a skilled counselling service

## • Developing a Theology of Education

Over the years I had noticed that the world of philosophy of education tended to live in a world apart, dominated by a number of leading exponents from London University's Institute of Education. No serious effort was being made to bring theological themes to bear on topics being dealt with in philosophy of education such as indoctrination, moral education etc. For this reason, I was advocating with a few other colleagues in Strawberry Hill that we initiate a systematic and serious study of the bearing of theology on a number of these topics. I took the view that such a study be called a 'Theology of Education '.

## • Marketing and Recruitment

I had seen a good deal in the United States of the efforts Catholic Universities and Colleges made to attract students to their respective institutions and I realised that St Mary's would need to raise its game if it was to be successful in communicating to Catholic schools around the country the new degrees it had on offer. We were entering into a competitive market for students and we needed to make the most of our links with Strawberry Hill alumni around the country.

• Links with other Third Level Institutions

My paper also advocated that we step up our interaction with other third level colleges both inside and outside Britain. I proposed in particular that we establish links with a continental university, naming Louvain as a possibility, and also with a university or college in the United States which in fact we had already done in the early 1970s but which had fallen into abeyance. I also mentioned a link with a third level institution in the Third World but with some hesitancy, knowing that the efforts we had made to do this in 1971 and 1972 had not been successful and that there were very good reasons for moving very carefully in this regard.

I concluded this short paper by saying that St Mary's was at a turning point. It had an opportunity to become a distinctive Christian presence in third level institutions in the country. I expressed the hope that the college would go forward, making the most of these opportunities.

*New Appointment to Dublin*

By April 1982 I knew that my time in Strawberry Hill was coming to an end and that I was on my way to a new appointment. The Provincial, with the backing of the Council, strongly urged me to accept an appointment to All Hallows in Dublin. I had very little enthusiasm for the actual appointment but having spent 9 years on the Provincial Council and participated in decision-making re appointments of many other confrères who accepted difficult appointments, I felt now that I had no option but to accept. It was my intention to sort out all my books before I packed up. Returning from 4 weeks in a parish in the United States in mid-August 1982, I lost my enthusiasm for the task. So I packed all my belongings and books into a rented van and set off on the M4 across England. The date was 31 August 1982. I put off the date of my arrival in All Hallows to the last moment, which was probably another indication of my lack of enthusiasm for taking up residence in a seminary.

I left St Mary's College quietly without any great fanfare, heavy in heart leaving friends and colleagues and a place where I had felt at home for the previous 16 years. Giving myself plenty of time to absorb the English countryside on this final journey westwards I took the road from the M4 to Monmouth and spent a couple of hours in Tintern Abbey. 'The ruined choirs where sweet birds sang' reflected my mood. I was travelling into the unknown. From my point of view I was leaving my home in the Strawberry Hill Vincentian community behind, and my friends in and outside the college.

As I travelled to Holyhead I was tempted to have a last go at Snowdon. I resisted the temptation. My passage was booked on the last boat to Dún Laoghaire that evening. After an uneventful crossing I drove my rented van from Dún Laoghaire harbour, to Glenageary, up Adelaide Road some 10 minutes away, where my brother, Martin, my sister-in-law, Betty and their 5 children lived. My first words to Betty when she opened the front door were: 'Can there be life after London?' I had closed the door on one chapter of my life; a new chapter was beginning.

### STRAWBERRY HILL IN RETROSPECT

I had spent 16 years of very varied and enjoyable ministry/lecturing in St Mary's College, Strawberry Hill, in the full flush of the euphoria and disappointments of the post Vatican II church. I was at the height of my physical powers, beginning in Strawberry Hill in 1966 at the age of 30 and completing my 16 year term at the age of 46. The following are a number of points that strike me now as I look back on those 16 years, with a time perspective of 20 years in which I have been engaged in other ministries that involved a good deal of travel in various parts of the world, and with a base in Dublin, Ireland.

*'Half a Life'*
Recently I heard Vis Naipaul, one of the latest recipients of the Nobel Prize for literature, speaking about his most recent book

*Half a Life*. In the book he describes his own situation and the situation of many other people who move from one country to another, growing up as migrants in a host country. They feel that they half belong. All the time they wonder what is taking place in the country that they have left. Many of Naipaul's books are written from this perspective. As I look back now I can see that my own situation was similar. The sixteen years I lived in London was 'half a life' – I spent a good deal of energy adapting to what was virtually a new culture, living and working in a 3rd level English institution in London and at the same time keeping in touch with the first 27 years of my life, lived in the West of Ireland and being educated at 2nd and 3rd levels in Dublin.

The three years I spent in Continental Europe, studying philosophy in Louvain University, were transition years and did act as a bridge between my two lives.

As an Irishman adapting to life in England, things were made easier by the fact that I was a Catholic priest and that so many of the students I taught in Strawberry Hill had Irish backgrounds – sons or daughters of people who had emigrated to various parts of England or first or second generation Irish. It was often quite difficult to know how close the students' connection was to Ireland. Invariably their accents were the same as their peer groups in schools, which outweighed the Irish accents they were hearing in their own homes in Birmingham, Liverpool, Manchester or wherever they came from.

A large proportion of Catholic priests in dioceses all over the country, especially in the North of England, were Irish priests who had been educated in Irish seminaries. I did not have that much contact with Irish priests around England during my time in Strawberry Hill. Later on I became more aware of the contribution of Irish priests to the English Catholic Church when visiting many parishes up and down the country as President of All Hallows.

At first I did not realise how Irish my own accent was – a few comments from students or from staff that they were having difficulty understanding me would have forced me to speak more slowly and more distinctly, gradually modifying my west of Ireland accent. However, this process had begun many years before when I took up permanent residence in Dublin.

During my first seven years in Strawberry Hill I did not travel that much to Ireland, even during holiday periods. I read *The Irish Times* every day, especially the news sections. I also read the *Guardian* and the *Times*, often getting through all 3 papers through breakfast and following up any articles I was interested in later in the day. I had no contact with Irish pubs or Irish clubs in London, holding the view fairly strongly that if I was living and working in England it was important to integrate into the society there. During my 16 years at Strawberry Hill I went to one Irish music event in Kingston but felt no desire to follow it up. To a great extent I was completely out of touch with popular Irish music. I kept in touch with the young Irish poets, especially Brendan Kennelly and Seamus Heaney. I remember a lecture that Seamus Heaney gave in the Waldegrave Ballroom as a guest of the English Literature Society in Strawberry Hill to a packed audience of students and staff in 1981. Heaney was asked by one of the students how he knew he had a calling to be a poet. He gave a marvellous description of his own first moves towards writing poetry as a student in Queens University, Belfast and later as a lecturer there. Then realising that so much of his poetry was centred on the North of Ireland he moved south to Co Wicklow and gradually realised that he had this calling to be a poet. He made a great impact on me that day, not only in the way he described his youthful desire to be faithful to something deep within himself which he wasn't quite sure about at first, but also because to me he seemed to transcend Irish/English antagonism and touched on values that transcended both cultures and were truly universal.

Now I realise that there are many different ways of being Irish. A hard republican line is not the only option. Between that and slavish 'West British' attitudes there are positions in which one could come to appreciate one's own Irish background and culture and at the same time be open to all that was best in English culture of the past and the present and indeed of continental European culture too. My three years in Louvain had prepared me for all this.

Not having experienced personally the English educational system at first hand – primary and secondary schools – or having a degree qualification from an English University, made me very wary about intervening in educational or other debates or discussions in any kind of forceful way. It was only later that it dawned on me that there could have been some advantages in having been educated in Irish first, second and third level institutions and also in a continental European university. V. S. Naipaul's *Half a Life* rang many bells for me.

## Living in an Educational World

For 16 years I was exposed to a whole range of educational experiences: I visited primary and secondary schools, including State schools and private (Public) schools, grammar schools and secondary modern schools; I supervised brilliant to mediocre student teachers; I participated in discussions about moral education, religious education and ethos in schools, especially Catholic schools. I could see at first hand how a good Headmaster/ Headmistress could set the tone of a school, how a gifted teacher preparing his or her lesson conscientiously could enthral and excite his or her pupils. I also observed how pupils could very quickly find the weak links in teachers, especially in regard to maintaining discipline in the classroom. I could see how much energy and enthusiasm is required of teachers to persevere in the teaching profession. I've always been in favour of the possibility of early retirement for teachers for the sake of the teachers who have run out of steam and also because of the damage that can be done by weak and poor teachers who pass on their frustrations to their pupils. As R. S. Peters, the famous philosopher of education used to say, there is a 'sacred space' between teacher and pupil and when for one reason or another respect between teacher and pupil is damaged, irreparable harm can be done to pupils in the classroom situation. Teaching is emotionally demanding and I'm not surprised that many drop out at one point or another. In an environment in which market forces have taken over, teaching, medicine and ministry are professions that deserve the title 'vocation'. One cannot measure any of these three professions in terms of monetary reward.

The development of Catholic Colleges of Education in Britain in the 1950s and 1960s opened up new possibilities for a new kind of presence of the Catholic Church in third level education – a situation where provision was made for BEd and BA degrees funded by the state, with the possibility of theology as a strong component. I'm not sure that the Catholic Church in Britain realised the full potential of this situation. Most bishops seemed to think that the one and only purpose of a Catholic College of Education was to provide Catholic teachers for Catholic schools. This of course was one of their main purposes. With hindsight I wonder whether new possibilities for research around a whole range of subjects and issues – the nature of Catholic school, religious and moral education, liturgy and catechesis, etc., could have been set up.

The Catholic Church in England and Wales put an enormous amount of funding into their primary and secondary school systems. Was the link between school and parish life ignored? It was said in the 1970s that only 30% of pupils from Catholic schools maintained a link with church life afterwards. This percentage is now well below 20%. The danger signals were already there in the 1970s. What was called for was a new alignment of Catholic schools with Catholic parishes. One could respect the different but complementary aims of both the Catholic school as the context for religious education – religious education that respects the rights of pupils and helps them make mature decisions of conscience about the faith itself – and the aim of the parish to lead to adult commitment to the faith, involving adult conversion and appropriate catechesis to integrate people into a mature Christian community. In this latter context, Christians are called to make a radical critique of the culture of their times in order to determine what is supportive and what is opposed to the Christian faith they profess.

Another area that interested me a lot during my time in Strawberry Hill was the debate around comprehensive, grammar and secondary modern schools. I leaned very much in the direction of equality of opportunity for all children. I had quite a lot of reservations about whether money should be able to buy an elite education for children of rich parents who could afford it and drawing off the gifted teachers for these schools. At the same time I began to realise the importance of safeguarding a school tradition and of quality in education.

As time went on I became more aware of the complexity of the debate around comprehensive and grammar schools.

Striking the right balance between equality of opportunity and the quality of education could be difficult and I experienced the tensions involved in striking such a balance in relation to some of our own Vincentian schools some years later.

## Lecturing in Philosophy and Theology

When I was leaving Strawberry Hill I did not realise that my life as a lecturer in both philosophy and theology was virtually coming to an end. From 1982 onwards my life was going to be totally pre-occupied with administration. I had worked up a fair degree of competence in the areas of philosophy of religion and moral theology. I enjoyed very much lecturing in both areas and walking the boundary line between both philosophy and theology. With all that was opening up in the post-Vatican II church in regard to the relationship of faith and contemporary culture on the one hand and in regard to moral argument in a religious context on the other, these were exciting areas to be working in. I enjoyed very much the exchanges with students in lectures, in seminars and in tutorials.

Looking back at things now I regret not stretching myself a little bit more, particularly in these areas, to write and publish articles. The fact that I was stretched so much not only across these two disciplines but involved in many other things during the 1970s was my excuse at the time.

The other excuse of course that I came up with from time to time in Strawberry Hill was that it was better to keep my head down in regard to the views I held on a number of matters. I would also have excused myself by saying that I was a journeyman between the theological and philosophical experts and the people I was lecturing to.

## Travels on Three Continents

It is only on reflection that I realise how much travelling I did, particularly during the summer months, over the 16 years I was in Strawberry Hill. All this travelling was on my own initiative. Meeting strangers belonging to different cultures, being challenged to see the world through other people's eyes in continental Europe, in a number of African countries and in the United States, broadened my horizons. There was, I felt, no better way to leave aside the fatigue and wear and tear of an academic year in Strawberry Hill and be refreshed in mind, body and spirit, than by putting on my knapsack and 'taking to the road', and coming back to the beginning of a new year, two or three months later, refreshed and renewed and appreciative of both the Vincentian community and the particular work I had been assigned to in the college.

In my travels to continental Europe I could have made better efforts to improve my French and to learn the basics of German and possibly Spanish too. However, after my first trip to Germany in the summer of 1968, I realised that spending time working intensively on a language took too much out of me after a very heavy schedule of lecturing over the previous 9/10 months. I did a lot of sightseeing in Germany, Italy, Spain, France and Belgium, reading guide books and a little history wherever I went.

My visits to East Africa opened my eyes to aspects of the missionary life lived by European missionaries and the great efforts that had been made over the previous 100 years to found the Catholic Church in African countries. At the same time, some of the economic difficulties which these countries were to run into in the 1980s and 1990s were already apparent in 1972 and 1973 but I don't think anyone realised that the decline in education – primary and secondary schools – and in health care – hospitals and clinics – was going to be so disastrous.

My three visits to the United States opened my eyes to the riches of a new continent and to aspects of church life there. The array of Catholic universities from one coast to the other was impressive. In the post-J. F. Kennedy era Catholics were coming into their own economically and professionally. In no other country have I seen Vatican II implemented so creatively in regard to Sunday Eucharist. Even by the mid-1970s many dioceses had made great progress developing a variety of Sunday liturgies, each with appropriate music, training programmes for various ministries, liturgical, social, etc. Priests had started to develop their preaching skills and there was more accountability in all this than I had experienced in England or Ireland. What I was getting, of course, were just snapshots of church life from one state to another. It would have been necessary for me to have lived there in one or other parish for a year or more to begin to get the rhythm of parish life and the bread and butter needs of parishioners. Nevertheless my horizons about possibilities of renewal of parishes were widened and I knew that I had a lot more to learn about church life in the United States.

*Sources of Inspiration*

Apart from learning basic lecturing skills, I also had to cut my teeth in developing leadership skills as Head of the Religious Studies Department and as Superior of the Vincentian community during my last 5 years in Strawberry Hill. At first I would have felt a little insecure in both positions. I was able to develop a reasonably good relationship with the members of the Religious Studies Department and the members of the Vincentian community. I had a good deal to learn about the art and science of challenging and affirming others.

In my last few years in Strawberry Hill, I was certainly overworking and not finding the right balance between work and leisure. This meant that I was physically, psychologically and spiritually exhausted. By the time I was leaving Strawberry Hill it was time to recharge the batteries. I'm not sure that the move to a seminary in Dublin with added responsibilities as the President/Rector and Superior provided me at the time with the space that I needed. However, if I continued on in Strawberry Hill I think I would have been a prime candidate for early burn out.

I had a number of very good friends in the Vincentian community and on the college staff in Strawberry Hill and also former students with whom I kept in touch. The break with Strawberry Hill was very painful for me and I have no doubt that I could have managed much better the process of letting go – especially in making my farewells.

During my 16 years in Strawberry Hill my own spiritual life was nourished by my philosophical and theological reading in the areas I was specialising in, in retreats I took part in or gave to others, through people I met on the staff and student body and groups outside the college. I was also challenged by various individuals I met, such as Jean Vanier, Jan Sobrino, Metropolitan Anthony Bloom of the Orthodox Church, Edwina Gately, founder of the VMM, Jock Dalrymple and others. They challenged me because of their commitment to a life of prayer, to living the Christian life, their commitment to the poor and their passion to promote social justice.

CHAPTER 8

# All Hallows 1982-1995
## A Time of Transition

*Appointment to All Hallows*

When I was appointed to be Rector/President of All Hallows in the summer of 1982 I had very mixed feelings about accepting this appointment. For the previous sixteen years I had lectured in philosophy of religion and moral theology in St Mary's College of Education, Strawberry Hill, London. The world of education was a very challenging one in the Britain of the 1970s. Debates about comprehensive education and equality of opportunity were in full flow. In my lectures I enjoyed walking a tight rope between philosophy and theology. With other members of staff I was engaged in communicating the challenging insights of Vatican II to a young student population. I also enjoyed being involved in implementing the liturgical renewal at the weekend liturgies in the college. Although I knew that seminary formation was changing in the post-Vatican II world, I felt that I was about to enter a closed world and that I was being asked to take on a very demanding ministry. When I crossed over from London to Dublin in late August 1982 I was apprehensive about what lay in wait for me.

There was another reason why I accepted this appointment with quite a degree of reluctance. The number of students in Irish seminaries, as in seminaries in many countries in the Western world, had begun to drop dramatically in the early 1970s. In 1968 All Hallows had over 250 students. This number dropped dramatically through the 1970s. Very serious questions were being asked about the future of the college. I was given to understand that one of the reasons why I was being appointed as an 'outsider' was to try and look dispassionately at the situation and, in dialogue with other members of staff, to come up with some recommendations about the future of the college.

*First Impressions*

Sixteen new students arrived in All Hallows in September 1982, bolstering the overall number of residential students to 65. In addition, there were 20 students attending philosophy and theology lectures from various religious orders. The 16 new arrivals provided a bigger intake than usual over the previous five years and there was hope in the air in seminaries in Ireland that the numbers might start to rise once again. Many thought that the downward slide of student intake into seminaries could be reversed. The enormous crowds of people who turned out to meet Pope John Paul II on his 1979 September visit to Ireland gave some support to this hope. Though the buildings were put to good use, they were a lot of space for the sixty-five resident students and twenty students coming in to lectures from various religious orders. From an economic point of view, I felt very early on that one of the tasks to be faced up to was how to work out of a much smaller space and to economise on the use of buildings.

In Strawberry Hill I was used to a very informal relationship with students. What I found difficult to come to terms with was staff and students dining at separate tables in the large dining room. Coming up to Lent 1983 I suggested to the student Union President that it might be a good idea for the staff and students to join together for lunch on Sundays. After discussions with his fellow students, he returned to report to me that the students did not think that this would be a good idea. One reading of this was that the students wanted to keep a certain distance from the staff, knowing that they had the task of recommending or not recommending them for ordination. Another interpretation was that I was seen as the 'new broom' brought in to change things and the senior students, who now regarded themselves as the guardians of the tradition, were making a point in turning down what was my first overture for change. Whatever the reason was for the students declining my invitation to join together for lunch on Sundays, I was quite shaken by this response. Shortly after Easter the student Union President came back to me and said quite simply, 'I think the students are ready to have lunch together now, Father.'

Through my first year in All Hallows I started to read whatever I could get my hands on about the history of the college. I was fascinated by its beginnings and by what John Hand, David Moriarty and Bartholomew Woodlock had done to get the college up and running, as well as by the crisis that led to the Vincentians being invited to administer the college in 1892. I read systematically through the All Hallows Annals, back to what were known as the Annals, the earliest records of the foundation and development of the college. I was struck by the powerful mission tradition that imbued the founding fathers. It struck me that the 1950s and 1960s were the golden age of the college in terms of the numbers being ordained and the variety of missions the students were going to in four out of the five continents. As I pondered on this one hundred and forty years of impressive mission tradition I kept on asking myself the question, 'Where is the urgency in mission today?', knowing that we were at a turning point in regard to the future of the college.

The November 1st celebration of 1982 lingers on in my mind – the feastday Mass, in which the students pulled out all the liturgical stops, the beautiful banquet which followed, prepared by the matron, Kitty Fahy and her devoted staff, and the distinguished guests who were present from the local archdiocese and University College Dublin – all this highlighted for me aspects of the history and traditions of the college. Archbishop Dermot Ryan and the five auxiliary bishops of Dublin turned up that day. At the end of the evening, I was left with a feeling of glorious past.

As that first year went on, 1982/83, I became more aware of the very good work that was being done by the pastoral department which had just set in motion a new course for deacons. Through a combination of clinical pastoral education and psycho-synthesis formation models and a series of lectures on pastoral or applied theology, a new course was introduced, which was to have quite profound effects on the college in the years ahead. As time went on I began to appreciate more and more the innovative value of this course and its potential to transform life in the seminary at every level. We were moving to a new kind of synthesis of the spiritual, intellectual and emotional formation of the seminarians. This pastoral ministry course was the catalyst that led to the opening up of the doors of the college to laymen and laywomen.

## The 'Curran Report'

In the summer of 1983 Fr Tom Curran visited All Hallows at the beginning of a sabbatical break from his mission with the Columban Fathers in Peru. We asked him to evaluate All Hallows, giving him the following terms of reference:

> Investigate and evaluate the formation for ministry at All Hallows College in relation to the needs of the church today, the developing concept of ministry and the traditional mission of All Hallows to go, teach all nations.

Tom decided that he would interview students and all the staff on the campus. In addition, he interviewed a number of alumni of the college whom he contacted over the following three months. Tom's report was completed by January 1984 and circulated to the staff.

Among the points he made were the following:

- Among the six seminaries in Ireland preparing students for diocesan priesthood, there was increasing competition. Sources of priestly vocations were drying up in Irish society.
- There was considerable support among a number of alumni for the idea that a fundraising campaign should be launched to acquire the funds needed to renovate a number of the buildings in the college.
- The report noted the work that had been accomplished in obtaining state recognition for the courses on offer in All Hallows through the National Council for Educational Awards (NCEA) and church recognition for a pass BD degree from the Pontifical University of St Patrick's College, Maynooth. At the same time, Tom recommended that we should continue to explore the possibility of degree validation from other sources such as Trinity College, Louvain University, or others. The obtaining of university validation for an honours degree was prioritised.
- Tom also commented favourably on the good work that had been done in setting up the Pastoral Ministry course and the blending together of intellectual and emotional aspects of formation with a strong pastoral thrust. A pastoral orientation was one of the traditional strengths of formation in All Hallows.

- The report recognised the considerable resources the college had in the city of Dublin – the availability of part-time and full-time lecturers, and the location of the college in the heart of the city, easily accessible from many places.

As I look back now some twenty years later I think the main significance of the report at that time was that it helped us recognise the opportunities and resources we had to move forward in preparing people for ministry. All Hallows is indebted to Tom Curran for completing this work in a very short time.

### Getting to Know the Past Students

One of the things that Tom Curran said to me in the course of the summer of 1983 was that I would not really know what All Hallows was all about until I touched base with All Hallows priests in different parts of the world. Over the following three years I set aside two months each year to be on the road and to travel to as many dioceses as I could in the United States, South Africa, Australia, New Zealand, England, Scotland and Wales. (I did not get to Newfoundland, Canada, until the early 1990s.) It was an exhilarating and humbling experience to meet the All Hallows priests at the coal-face. It was also a good way to escape two months of the Irish winter.

### The United States: November 1983

My schedule included 21 stops over 28 days. My stopovers included Paterson, NJ, Washington DC, West Virginia, Chicago, Duluth, Los Angeles, Orange, Monterey, San Jose, Stockton, Fresno, Portland, Seattle, Yakima, San Diego, Phoenix, Dallas, Jefferson City, New Orleans, Miami, Orlando, St Petersburg, New York and Boston. I was exhausted when I got back to Ireland but I had a glimmer of the distances the pioneer All Hallows priests had to travel by horse, coach, boat or train in the 19th century to get to their missions. When I sounded out All Hallows men about the future of the college I could sense a good deal of anxiety in their responses. Were we going to close the college? Many of them knew that the college was at a turning point. I was amazed at the vastness of the United States, the variety of scenery and the climate changes from north to south and from east to west. I was also struck by the vitality of the parishes I visited and the quality of the liturgies.

## South Africa: December 1985/January 1986

In the winter of 1985/86, I spent three very exciting weeks in South Africa. Three incidents stand out. The first was being whisked into Soweto on my first afternoon in Johannesburg – two hours after being met at the airport – and being entertained to a concert the following morning in a Soweto parish after the Sunday Mass was over.

The second experience was in Port Elizabeth where again I was brought into a township. At one point our car was surrounded by an angry crowd. A shooting had taken place there the previous day. When my All Hallows companion got out of the car and spoke to the men in their own language, they calmed down straight away and invited us to join the funeral service in a church nearby. Diplomatically we excused ourselves, knowing that it would mean spending the rest of the day in the crowded church. A third experience of South Africa which stands out for me was travelling down to Cape Town from East London, where a contact of mine had arranged for me to meet about twelve of the staff of the Business School of Capetown University, in the house of one of the group. Some of their wives were also present. Being told that I wanted to learn more about the situation in South Africa, they asked me where I had been since I arrived in the country two weeks earlier. When I told them that I had been in townships in Johannesburg, Port Elizabeth and East London, they were amazed. Many of them had never visited these townships and would have felt quite threatened going there. After ten minutes they forgot about my presence and spoke openly about their fears for the future of the country and their own personal fears for themselves and their families. I was a 'fly on the wall' listening to people who felt besieged and paralysed by the apartheid situation. I came away from South Africa realising that the gospel was writ large in this very troubled country at this time, and enthralled by what All Hallows priests were doing in very difficult situations.

*Australia/New Zealand: December 1986/January 1987*

The following year I spent about three weeks in Australia, before Christmas, and ten days in New Zealand after Christmas. When I indicated in a newsletter that I intended visiting all the dioceses where All Hallows men were working ... this amounted to visiting about one hundred priests at that time ... two of them wrote back to say that I hadn't really got an idea of how vast the country was and of course they were right. Eventually I did touch base with the All Hallows men in ten cities – Perth, Adelaide, Melbourne, Sale, Sydney, Wollongong, Bathurst, Canberra, Brisbane and Rockhampton. Again it was a fascinating journey for me. I began to have an idea of the pioneering work that All Hallows men had been doing over the previous one hundred and forty years in both urban and rural settings. Crossing the Blue Mountains on the way to Bathurst I visited a few small churches built by All Hallows priests in the 1860s, including one built by Luke Hand, Fr John Hand's brother. I began to realise that for many of the All Hallows priests who came out to Australia and New Zealand, especially in those early days, it was a one-way ticket. Travelling vast distances on an empty stomach to cover weekend masses must have put a severe strain on both body and spirit. Today we take a more humane approach to the Eucharistic fast but even in 1985, on this my first visit to Australia, I got the impression that many All Hallows priests were still carrying the heats and burdens of the day.

In New Zealand I had three stops, one in Christchurch, one in Wellington and the last one in Auckland. Again I was astounded at the turnout of pastmen to meet me. In one place a pastman had travelled for eight hours to attend the session with me in Wellington. I was beginning to realise the extraordinary work All Hallows priests had done in founding and building up parish communities with scanty resources in New Zealand and elsewhere.

*England/Wales/Scotland*

Over my first five years in All Hallows I picked off English dioceses from time to time, crossing over to meetings in Leeds, Salford, Liverpool, Nottingham, Northampton, Brentwood, Westminster, Southwark, East Anglia, Arundel & Brighton,

Portsmouth, Plymouth, Hallam, Shrewsbury and Clifton dioceses. (I missed out on the dioceses of Lancaster and Middles-
brough and I regret that I did not find an opportunity to visit All
Hallows priests in these dioceses.) These visits to dioceses all
over England made me realise how cut off I was from the parish
scene during my 16 years in Strawberry Hill. Again I was struck
by the variety of parishes All Hallows priests found themselves
ministering in.

I also attended reunions of pastmen in Welsh dioceses. I will
never forget one reunion of All Hallows priests there when
about ten of us were gathered together in a hotel restaurant in
Merthyr Tydfil. The Welshmen and women on neighbouring
tables joined in the singing of the chorus of the *Banner of the Lord*
when the meal was over.

I also visited dioceses in Scotland – Glasgow, Galloway,
Motherwell, Edinburgh and Dundee, and I participated in two
reunions of All Hallows priests in Glasgow, both of which took
place in the late Fr John Hanrahan's parish. I began to understand that the Catholic Church in Scotland has its own unique
flavour.

A number of things stand out for me in all these visits. Tom
Curran was indeed right. It was only when I started to travel
that I began to have an idea of the All Hallows tradition and the
variety of places that All Hallows priests went to all over the
world – urban and rural situations, rich and poor, multi-cultural
and mono-cultural, inner city and stock-broker belt, outback
and township, etc. Secondly, I became aware of the variety of
challenges and opportunities that existed from one diocese to
another, and even inside the same diocese or country. In some
dioceses there were many opportunities for continuing education, in others there were none. In some dioceses there was
good leadership and well worked-out pastoral programmes. In
others there was poor leadership and maintenance rather than
mission. A third thing which came home to me, was the basic
need we all have for affirmation – affirmation for the work
priests have done to build up parishes or dioceses. Bishops
could be good administrators or good theologians but if they
were not listening to and affirming the priests of their dioceses

one could pick this up very quickly. I often felt that bishops underestimated the sacrifices All Hallows priests had made in leaving their own country. Fourthly, I was repeatedly astonished by the spirit of faith that led so many men in their youthful idealism to say yes to a mission in an unknown country or an unknown continent when asked to go to such and such a diocese by the President of the college. And, finally, I was amazed at the very warm welcome I received in every diocese I visited. Shared hardship in All Hallows had bonded priests and students very closely together and I had to learn very quickly how to decipher the nick-names that many of the staff had carried during their time in the college. As time went on, I became fascinated by the oral tradition passed on to me about what was going on in the All Hallows of their day from the 1930s to the 1970s.

And one final comment: I sensed no matter where I went that many of these men were aware of the struggles we were going through to maintain the seminary in All Hallows and at the same time to set a direction for the college into the future. Seminaries in their own dioceses were going through similar struggles, and everywhere I went I received words of support and encouragement. The predominant impression I have from meeting All Hallows priests, through my travels and encounters with them, is of men working in the frontline of parish ministry, doing their best to cope with the tensions in the post-Vatican II church, and giving themselves generously from day to day without counting the cost. I also talked to a number of All Hallows men who had left the ministry. I was impressed by the way they too in a variety of ways were promoting the kingdom of God. Overall, I think there was a consciousness that new opportunities were arising to proclaim the gospel in new ways. I always returned to All Hallows from these visits encouraged to press on with our own efforts to face up to new challenges calling us in new directions in preparing men and women for ministry.

*Vocations to the Priesthood*

The first year intake of students into the seminary in September 1982 was sixteen. In many seminaries and novitiates of various religious orders there was a slight increase over these few years,

1981 and 1982. Some of this was attributed to the euphoria after Pope John Paul's 1979 visit to Ireland. Indeed some people thought that seminaries might start to fill up again. However, Fr Tom Curran had read it right when he wrote in his report that there were 'very few oranges in the trees out there'. We knew that if we were to compete for these students we would have to engage actively in trying to attract them to a mission as diocesan priests in dioceses overseas. Even in those years it was felt that Ireland was very well off for priests. There were still four hundred students preparing for diocesan priesthood for Irish dioceses in St Patrick's College, Maynooth and at least 200 more in other Irish seminaries. We did not see ourselves making inroads into the Irish market, preparing priests for Irish dioceses. The first thing we did was to make contact with the bishops of the dioceses of Tuam, Elphin and Meath, requesting permission to preach in five parishes in each of their dioceses in the spring of 1984. They graciously gave us permission to do so and arranged for us to preach in five of the larger parishes in each of their dioceses. I remember covering my own home town of Glenamaddy in North East Galway, Athlone and Ballygar, where I discovered we had strayed into the traditional recruiting territories of St Patrick's College, Carlow. Other members of staff covered Mullingar, Roscommon, Castlebar, Westport, Kinnegad, Sligo and other sizeable towns. The response to our preaching was disappointing, confirming once again what Tom Curran had said in his report.

The second initiative we took in the summer of 1986 was to invite back to the staff a young priest of the college to engage full-time in priestly vocation promotion. Fr Joe Walsh travelled the length and breadth of the country, using a vocation video and sometimes with the help of students visiting schools and following up on enquiries to advertisements we had placed in newspapers. He also met many priests in his travels. Through these years we were dealing with about thirty quite serious enquiries each year but when we interviewed and followed up the background of many of these candidates we found that they were either unsuitable for seminary formation or too immature to be accepted into the seminary. On the other hand, a small number of very good candidates did come through during those years.

It was evident that priesthood was becoming less and less attractive for young people in Ireland. As I look back now, twenty years later, I can sense that even before the end of the 1980s very serious negative reaction against priesthood as a career option was building up in Ireland. Scandals, which began to break in 1992, certainly deepened this crisis. However, all this had begun in the 1970s and continued through the 1980s and 1990s. The natural supports from family members, or indeed from parish communities, were fast disappearing. A young person needed very firm inner strengths to withstand the strong counter-cultural trends away from celibate priesthood, which were beginning to predominate in our culture.

By the time I was leaving All Hallows in August 1995 the number of enquiries had faded to a small trickle. Moreover, English dioceses who had sent us students – the dioceses of Liverpool, Nottingham, Salford, Leeds and Northampton – were themselves running into trouble in regard to maintaining numbers in their own English seminaries and it was not surprising that this source of vocations in All Hallows also came to an end. The mission statement which All Hallows had formulated in the 1980s was to prepare students for a variety of ministries, including priestly ministry. When we moved to calling the college an 'Institute for Mission and Ministry' in 1988, continuing to prepare students for priestly ministry was an integral part of our vision for the future.

*New Courses for Lay Students*
We did not start off with any blueprint of what an 'Institute for Mission and Ministry' would look like. The changes which took place in All Hallows from 1983 onwards could be seen as 'incremental change' from one year to the next. One development led to another. It was only as we came near the end of the 1980s, when we had already initiated a number of new courses, that we began to realise that the goalposts had shifted and we needed this new title of 'Institute for Mission and Ministry' to include the courses for laymen and laywomen which we had initiated.

I said earlier that the catalyst for this change was the Pastoral Ministry Course, which had been set up for deacons in 1982/83. In the early years we were combining with deacons in Holy

Cross College, Clonliffe and very quickly deacons from various religious orders also joined the course. In 1983/84 the first woman student arrived, a Medical Missionary of Mary, Sr Marie Slevin. Shortly afterwards, more sisters and lay women were accepted on to the course. Central to the dynamic of the course was an intake of men and women, cleric and lay, with an interest in engaging in ministry in the post-Vatican II church. This course blended together the human, spiritual, theological and pastoral formation of the students, deepening their self-knowledge and their sensitivity to the needs of people they would be ministering to in today's world. It also took seriously various aspects of collaborative ministry and the challenges that this would entail for both priests and lay men and women.

By the summer of 1986 other groups of lay men and women were knocking on the doors of All Hallows. As a result of the Summer Schools we had launched – four weeks of courses in theology and spirituality through the month of July – and short courses we had put on in the Retreat/Conference Centre throughout the year, we began to realise that there was a hunger among many laymen and women to deepen their knowledge of the faith and to engage in a variety of ministries at different levels. This led to another breakthrough in regard to student intake. We had a large number of applications for our one-year Pastoral Ministry Course. Having filled the available places, we found that, as there were other good applicants who either did not have the finances or time available to do a full-time course, we decided to launch a two-year 'Preparing for Lay Ministry' course on one evening a week. We consulted ten Dublin diocesan priests about the wisdom or otherwise of running such a course. The responses ranged from being lukewarm to being very supportive – 'People are not ready for this yet' to 'We don't see anybody else doing it so you may as well go ahead.' Overall the responses were quite ambivalent.

Through a certain amount of low-key advertising in parishes we were amazed to find that we had over a hundred people to interview by early September 1986. From our point of view the course would be viable if there were twenty-five people taking it. We had decided to interview everybody because we wanted to exclude people who, we believed, had already covered the basics of pastoral ministry and, secondly, we wanted to focus on people who could acquire basic pastoral skills to contribute to the life of their parishes. As we began the interviewing in September it was our intention to try and bring the intake down to a manageable size. The members of staff who did these interviews were quite astonished at the calibre of people who wanted to sign up for this course and the range of experiences they brought to it. On the first year of the course we accepted about eighty students. Over the following ten years this number was maintained with a minimum of advertising on our part. This course opened the door to a number of the other full-time courses we had on offer in All Hallows which people became interested in as soon as they had overcome their initial fears about engaging in full-time theological and pastoral education.

The launching of the 'Preparing for Lay Ministry' course in September 1986 was a real eye-opener for all of us on the staff about the hunger of lay people for a deeper knowledge of their faith and the desire of many of them to engage in parish ministry. I had a deepening conviction that many laymen and women were living down to the low expectations of many clerics about what they were capable of doing in building up their parish communities. The two-year course we offered tried to take seriously their personal experience and encouraged them to share with one another their experience of living the Christian life. We wanted to avoid launching another 'academic' theology course that might engage them intellectually but do little to engage their hearts and their wills. When I look back now, I can see that this course was for many of the participants a confidence-building exercise in their awareness of being a Christian and a member of the church with a mission to promote God's kingdom in our contemporary world. The feedback from this course was very positive and, like the pastoral ministry course, it brought a certain amount of excitement on to the college campus. The seminarians picked up some of this excitement and in fact in the early years they acted as co-ordinators of the discussion groups associated with this course. There was no better way for them to see first-hand the strengths and gifts of many of the laymen and women they would one day be called to serve and to collaborate with.

*BA, MA and Continuing Education Courses*

By the summer of 1988 All Hallows had obtained validation for a new four-year honours degree course, validated by the National Council for Educational Awards (NCEA). The major component of this degree was theology with a choice of one of three subsidiary subjects – philosophy or psychology or spirituality (some years later English Literature was added to these options). Among the first group of students completing the two-year part-time lay ministry course in the summer of 1988 were some students who had expressed a desire to continue their study of theology. In September of that year about ten of these students joined the seminarians in the first year of this four-year degree. The opening of this degree course to lay men and women was indeed a very significant moment in the life of the college. The response from one of the married women students to the question posed by one of the theology lecturers as to whether she would be able to manage the number of essays to complete the course requirements for the first term was: 'Yes, I think I will be able to manage that.' The awareness that she could do this as well as bring up four children was not lost on the seminarians, and incidents like this had quite a maturing effect on the seminarians. As time went on the students obtained government grants to pursue this four-year degree course in theology and a subsidiary subject. This also facilitated applications from school-leavers, which led to All Hallows joining the CAO entry system for all school-leavers in Ireland, which was their gateway into third level education. Mature students were able to avail of the special entry procedure.

With a BA degree and Graduate Diploma validation with state recognition in place by September 1988, offering MA degrees in pastoral theology was a natural progression. By 1991 a research MA in pastoral studies and by 1993 a taught Masters, were both in place. As with the Diploma in pastoral ministry, applications for these new MA courses came from inside and outside Ireland. Over the years the numbers have continued to build up on all these degree courses.

In the early 1990s All Hallows began to realise the potential for evening courses in scripture, theology and spirituality as well as in other subjects like philosophy, psychology and English literature which we had on offer in the degree course. In the summer of 1992 we appointed one of the newly qualified lay graduates from the BA programme to supervise this development and in a relatively short time students were able to build up units they required to obtain an evening BA degree over an extended period of time. This opened up another gateway for mature men and women to sign on as students in All Hallows. It opened up the possibility also for many people to follow through on adult religious education which they either had no interest in as younger people or did not have the opportunity to pursue. As we opened up theological, scriptural and other courses to lay men and women many of them would ask, 'Why didn't somebody tell us about this before now?'

In the early 1990s the pastoral ministry department was getting more and more requests from religious sisters, brothers and priests – including All Hallows alumni – to follow a three-month sabbatical programme. The purpose of this three-month sabbatical course was to update people on theological developments, but also to offer an opportunity for people who had been engaged in various kinds of ministry to reflect on their experience. Again efforts were made to maintain the pastoral thrust of this three-month course and to provide opportunities for students from a variety of countries to share their experience in ministry. Between forty and fifty sisters, brothers and priests and, from time to time, laymen and women, signed on for this course in the autumn and spring of each year. In the early days the students on this course participated in theology lectures with the BA students, choosing whatever courses they were interested in. As time went on it was realised that their needs were better met by courses tailor-made for them.

*All Hallows as an 'Institute for Mission and Ministry'*
The obvious reason why All Hallows started to refer to itself as an ' Institute for Mission and Ministry' was that it wanted to acknowledge now that it was more than a seminary and that there were laymen and women participating in college life as both full-time and part-time students. But a second and more profound reason was that there was a consensus in our staff that the theology of mission and ministry had gone through some very

fundamental developments in the post-Vatican II church. Some of these changes were reflected in Pope John Paul's *Christifideles Laici* (1988) and *Redemptoris Missio* (1991) and the Roman synods that gave rise to these two documents. A debate continues about the pros and cons of what are sometimes known as the free-standing seminary model, concentrating exclusively on the formation of seminarians, as opposed to the integrated model that is preparing people for a variety of ministries including priestly ministry. By 1988 there was sufficient consensus among the staff in All Hallows to lead us to opt for the integrated model. There continues to be a good deal of discussion in theological circles about the foundation of lay ministry. But what is now patently evident in many parts of the western world is that the continuation of parish communities will depend on the availability of theologically and pastorally educated lay ministers with a strong sense of mission. It is also patently evident that the traditional distinction between mission sending and mission receiving countries is now questionable. The decline of participation in regular Sunday Eucharist in many Western European countries points up the need to put dioceses and parish communities on a state of mission.

*An All Hallows Mission in Munich*

In reflecting on the history of All Hallows through the 1980s, I was constantly struck by the fact that many of the All Hallows missions began through Irish priests following the Irish diaspora all over the world – to the United States, Canada, the Argentine, East and West Indies, Australia, New Zealand, South Africa, England, Scotland, and Wales. In the economic recession of the 1970s and 1980s there was quite a build-up of young Irish people in European cities, especially in Brussels, Paris and a number of German cities, including Munich. We decided to explore the possibility of setting up an Irish chaplaincy in Munich and we were encouraged by one of the Irish bishops on the Episcopal Commission for Emigrants to go ahead and gather information about the situation there.

During the summer of 1987, Joe Walsh, Eugene Duffy and myself, spent three months in rotation in Munich working out of the Peterskirche near the Marianplatz at the centre of the city.

We covered a number of the daily Masses in that church to pay for our bed and board. During the day we contacted as many Irish people as possible living in Munich on either a full-time or part-time summer basis. It was an interesting experience meeting young Irish people in ones and twos, in pubs, restaurants, hotels, factories and campsites. At the end of the summer we recommended the Irish Bishops Conference to set up a chaplaincy and we knew at this early stage that there was a good possibility it would be funded by the Munich archdiocese. We strongly recommended that it would not be an inward-looking Irish ghetto but that it should respond to the needs of English-speaking people in the city of Munich. The Irish Bishops Conference invited All Hallows to take responsibility for setting up and monitoring the running of this mission and we agreed to do so.

In September 1988 an All Hallows priest, Fr Tom Healy, from the diocese of Savannah, was released to take up the post of chaplain and through the following years the chaplaincy itself became a meeting point for many young Irish people and people of other nationalities – English, American and Nigerian. Very good chaplaincy facilities near the main railway station and the use of a church on Sunday evenings, just a few minutes walk from the Marianplatz, were generously provided by the Archdiocese of Munich. A number of graduates from All Hallows filled the post of assistant chaplain, over the past 15 years – Hugh Jones, John Gannon, Gerard Gallagher, Ray Cummins, Pauline Oakley, Kevin O'Regan and Noreen Lynch. Two Irish women, permanent residents in the city of Munich Elaine Stern and Deirdre Cooney-Schmid, became part-time secretaries, providing hospitality to all comers and stability to the chaplaincy itself. In the year 2000 Tom Healy completed twelve years as chaplain and he has been replaced by another All Hallows priest, Bill Buckley from the diocese of Port Elizabeth in South Africa.

The Chaplaincy in Munich has been a place where the faith of young Catholics has been nurtured through the weekend Sunday Mass and other activities, especially during Advent and Lent. A significant number – about a hundred young people – participated in the Sunday evening Mass – very often re-discovering their faith in the secular wasteland of this European city with its rich cultural traditions. Was it that different when Irish priests encountered their fellow countrymen and women in the tough neighbourhoods of cities in the United States, England, Scotland or elsewhere in the 19th century?

When the Iron Curtain lifted in 1989, we began to see Munich as a stepping stone towards new missions to people in a number of Eastern European countries where people had suffered the ravages of Marxist propaganda and religious persecution over fifty years and more and where Christianity had been driven underground. From 1990 onwards a number of students came to Ireland from the Czech Republic, Slovakia and Lithuania to pursue courses in All Hallows. New missions, with the emphasis on mission as an 'exchange of gifts', is waiting to be developed between Europe – East and West. It is often said today that Ireland over the last twenty years has been going through a process of 'enlightenment' – a process of 'secularisation' and a process of 'church marginalisation' which has been taking place in continental Europe for the last three hundred years. Be that as it may, there is no doubt that Ireland has much to learn from how a number of countries, especially countries in Northern Europe, are coping with these processes to preserve and develop our faith resources once again.

*Fr Kevin Condon's History of All Hallows Missionary College*
Kevin Condon was seen by many as the 'guardian of the All Hallows tradition'. From his research on the history of the college he knew more than anybody else about its beginnings, times of crisis and the various missions it had inaugurated. The publication of his book: *The History of All Hallows Missionary College 1842-1892*, in the spring of 1986, was indeed a landmark event. A few months after its publication Archbishop Tom Morris of Cashel wrote to Kevin congratulating him on his publication and saying 'blessed is the college that has archives such as yours and blessed also is the college that has someone like yourself to bring these archives together in a publication such as this'.

Kevin's history was an institutional history. He took great pleasure in outlining the mammoth task facing Fr John Hand in setting up the college and the work done by the four subsequent presidents through the 19th century: David Moriarty (President from 1846 to 1854), a friend of Cardinal Newman who visited the college on a number of occasions during Moriarty's tenure as president and later bishop of the diocese of Kerry; Bartholomew Woodlock (President from 1854 to 1861), Newman's successor as President of the Catholic University, Dublin; and later on bishop of the diocese of Ardagh and Clonmacoise, Thomas Bennett, O Carm (President from 1861 to 1865), who held the post of provincial of his order for some of that time and who walked from Whitefriars St across the Tolka to All Hallows for his round of lectures every day; and finally, William Fortune (President from 1866 to 1891) who lived through the stormy period of dissent amongst the staff and students until the Vincentians took over the administration of the college in 1892. Kevin had explored the archives of the Archdiocese of Dublin, the Seminary of San Sulpice in Paris and Propaganda Fide in Rome, as well as the archives of innumerable dioceses around the world to gather together the material for this book. There are some remarkable tributes to the early All Hallows pioneers and it was one of Kevin's constant refrains coming up to the publication of the book that he could have written four other books about the accomplishments of All Hallows pioneer priests in North America, Australia, New Zealand, Scotland, England, Wales and South Africa. He had spent many of his summer holidays following up and visiting the places where they had ministered gathering information about what they had accomplished.

It was Kevin's intention to write a second volume of the history of the college, from 1892 up to 1962. He often said to us that Vatican II would be the cut-off point for him. This remark I think was very significant. To some extent Vatican II took the wind out of Kevin Condon's sails. Through his scripture studies he was involved in the scriptural revolution of the 1950s. He had anticipated some of the ideas of Vatican II, especially in relation to the notion of revelation as we find it in the Dogmatic Constitution *Dei Verbum*. When the Vatican Council came to an end, a lot of his energies went into researching the history of the college. He had very little time for some transitory fads or fashions in the post-Vatican II church.

I was hoping very much that Kevin Condon was going to

complete Volume 2 of the history of the college. There was so much we needed to know about what had happened from 1892 right up to our own day. One of the greatest tributes that Kevin Condon paid to the alumni of the college was in the speech he gave at the banquet in Orlando in January 1990 – on the evening before he died. He paid a glowing tribute to what the current All Hallows priests had accomplished in the United States. In his summer travelling by Greyhound Bus across the United States, he was acquainted with many of the situations they were working in. One of the guests at that dinner, a priest holding a key post in Orlando diocese, and an alumnus of St Patrick's College, Carlow, was in tears at the end of Kevin's speech. He had grasped, as many others had done, the authenticity of Kevin's tribute.

The heart condition which Kevin Condon had carried quietly for the previous few years, was to take his life on his way back from Orlando to Ireland. He died just when he arrived at Fr Fursey O'Toole's parish in Brooklyn. Kevin had served the college faithfully as a scripture scholar and historian of the college for exactly forty years – January 1950 to January 1990. He had arrived in All Hallows in the middle of an academic year and the reason for this was because the Vincentian Provincial at the time felt that he had stretched his scriptural studies too far into a fourth year in Jerusalem, having already completed three years in Rome. The Provincial instructed him to report for lecturing duties in All Hallows in January 1950.

Through his constant travelling to visit All Hallows priests in far-flung dioceses around the world, through his painstaking research into the history of the college, and through his constant reminders to the staff of its missionary thrust, Kevin Condon left much to be pondered on for subsequent generations of staff and students. In the 1950s, as a young scripture scholar, he had raised many troublesome questions for the dogmatic theologians to ponder on; especially in the use of scriptural passages as proof texts. In the 1970s and 1980s he left a further series of questions for the staff of those decades about the original missionary thrust of the college and how this missionary thrust could be given expression today.

*150th Anniversary Celebrations – 1992*

For the 500 alumni from dioceses all around the world, gathered together and packed into the college chapel for the Thanksgiving Mass on Thursday, 22 July, this was a powerful moment. As the homilist, Bishop Raymond Boland, remarked, this kind of occasion was unlikely to occur ever again. We were celebrating 150 years of a very fruitful mission history and much of this came home to me when I saw priests greeting one another from distant dioceses, many of whom had not met since their ordination day in All Hallows twenty, thirty, forty, fifty, and even sixty years previously. At the banquet which followed the Mass, one speaker described the event as a wake and a wedding – a wake for a mission that was obviously changing and from one point of view coming to an end; a wedding in that new life was beginning in the college with the preparing of laymen and women for ministry. This was highlighted by the fact that a number of these students were on the organising and welcoming committees of this Jubilee celebration. Their presence brought home to the priests that new developments were underway in All Hallows. For many of our alumni, this change of direction was seen as a praiseworthy development – a development which was taking place in some of the parishes and dioceses they were ministering in. However, there was a small group of All Hallows priests who saw things differently. The only future they could see for the college was the one they had experienced when they were students there – preparing exclusively for priestly ministry in dioceses overseas. The talks, speeches and homilies, however, through the week transcended these differences. Afterwards the letters of appreciation from the alumni and from the bishops who were our guests were very positive. The only negative reaction I can remember now is a letter we received later in the autumn after an RTÉ forty minute programme on the event was broadcast. One person who had seen this programme objected to the fact that we had invited President Mary Robinson to visit the college during the Jubilee week. She saw this invitation as a sell-out to Mary Robinson's championing of 'left wing' human rights issues in previous years.

Some of the things which lingered on in my mind afterwards, were:

- Uncertainty about whether or not to move the reception for President Mary Robinson's visit indoors. A black cloud threatened to disgorge its contents on the assembled brethren. One of our students, with a farming background, observed that, yes, the weather was going to break but that it wouldn't come for another forty or fifty minutes. He was right – a downpour did take place immediately after the President and her garda escort drove out the gate.

- The enthusiastic response to Phil Coulter's rendering of *The Banner of the Lord* at the Jubilee Concert in the auditorium of St Patrick's College of Education nearby.

- The logistical solution as to how to accommodate over 500 priests in the college chapel for the Jubilee Thanksgiving Mass, through banking seating at the back of the vast sanctuary space. (In subsequent years when RTÉ wanted to provide an image of a large number of priests gathered together, they often reproduced this scene.)

- The renting of a large banqueting tent, costing £10,000 and provided by a rich investment banker ... The only drawback was that we had to provide a number of guests to attend a polo match in the Phoenix Park on one of the afternoons of the Jubilee week. The racing fraternity among our pastmen obliged!

- The inclusive event on the last day of the meeting in which we welcomed back many students of the college who had opted for other careers, either before or after ordination. This event led to the setting up of the All Hallows Association for the alumni of the seminary who had embarked on other careers, which has gone from strength to strength under the able leadership of Fr John Joe Spring.

The week's events had stretched our resources of staff and students to the limit. We were overwhelmed by the positive response of our alumni and guests to the week's celebrations. We felt encouraged to continue the developments that were now well underway in All Hallows.

Some months later we had a special celebration for the bishops of Ireland. Cardinal Cahal Daly presided and preached, quoting from Cardinal Newman's *The Second Spring* to encourage us to face the future with confidence and with hope. A number of bishops from England and Scotland also attended. We were particularly pleased at the large turn out of Irish bishops. I availed of the opportunity to thank the Irish and English bishops for releasing priests to join the staff in All Hallows – just as earlier in the year at a similar function I had thanked the provincials of various congregations of men and women for releasing their personnel to join the staff too.

Over the years I have often wondered if Irish people and Irish church authorities were aware of the enormous contribution of All Hallows and a number of Irish diocesan seminaries to the founding and development of parish communities in the United States, Canada, Australia, New Zealand, South Africa, England, Scotland and Wales, over the previous one hundred and fifty years, and over two hundred years in the case of Carlow and Maynooth seminaries.

There is a sense in which many in the Irish church were insulated from all of this and did not feel that there was much to learn from what was happening abroad. Perhaps that is beginning to change now as we are challenged to harness all our energies and resources to engage in a mission of re-evangelisation on our own doorsteps.

### Seminary Rectors' Meetings

There were very few meetings of Irish seminary rectors. I can only remember two, convened by one of the Irish Episcopal Commissions in order to respond to a Roman document – known as the *Ratio Fundamentalis* – on seminary formation. However, I attended regularly the annual mid-Lenten meetings of the rectors from Scottish and English seminaries in Britain and their outposts in Rome and Spain. (I missed two meetings over the thirteen years I was in All Hallows at which I was replaced by Eugene Duffy. Eugene took my place as acting Rector of the Seminary over a two year period leading up to the 150th centenary celebration in 1992.) Each meeting lasted for five or six days and it was seen by many of us as a mid-Lenten break from the routine of seminary life and an opportunity to share some of our concerns about aspects of seminary formation.

The first meeting I attended was in the spring of 1983 in

Wonersh. Most of these rectors' meetings took the form of two or three lectures from experts in theology, psychology or spirituality on one or other aspect of seminary formation. Each rector reported on any developments in our respective seminaries. Lastly, we spent a day or a day and a half visiting some interesting historical sites in the neighbourhood of the seminary hosting the meeting. The meeting the following year was in Scotland. At this meeting I had my first taste of a theme that was to keep on recurring at all these seminary meetings: 'Was each of our seminaries viable?' – from the point of view of student numbers, financial resources and availability of qualified personnel. One of the big questions coming up in Scotland in 1984 was a possible merging of the Glasgow and Edinburgh seminaries. Because of the traditional rivalry between these two great cities, the key question was where the new seminary was going to be located. Eventually Glasgow won out. My third rectors' meeting was in Valladolid where I had the opportunity of visiting both the English College and the Scots College. A few years later the Scots College moved to Salamanca. Even then there were very small numbers of students in both these seminaries but both were well endowed and a good case was made for maintaining them. They offered students an opportunity to face up to the challenges of adapting to another culture, and acquiring a facility in speaking Spanish, opening up the possibility of a mission experience in South America later on.

One of my most interesting seminary rectors' meetings took place in 1988, outside Rome, in the summer residence of the English College, located in the Alban hills. Apart from providing an opportunity to visit some of the tourist sites in Rome, this meeting stands out for me because of the meeting of the rectors with Cardinal Pio Laghi, Prefect of the Congregation for Education, the Secretary and other officials of this Roman Congregation. The offices were situated in a well-furnished building on the Via della Conciliazione. After some pleasantries on both sides, the English rectors were called to task for not submitting their response to the Congregation's General Directory on Seminary Formation, the *Ratio Fundamentalis*. One of their number offered the excuse that the English were by nature empirical and pragmatic and not drawn too much to 'blueprint' documents. This did not cut much ice with the Roman officials and the English rectors were urged to complete their work as soon as possible. I began to sense that somebody's knuckles were being firmly rapped.

The second event of that rectors' meeting in Rome that lingered on in my mind was attending a Mass of Pope John Paul II in his private oratory in the papal apartments. We convened in St Peter's Square, outside the Bronze Door, at an unearthly hour of 5.30 in the morning – I had stayed in the Irish College overnight – and we were guided through a few courtyards, up a small lift, into an oratory where the Pope was kneeling on a prie-dieu in front of us, facing the tabernacle. The Pope had his hands over his head and was lost in prayer. The oratory itself was very simply decorated with some beautiful pieces of contemporary art – statues and paintings. The decoration of the oratory was attributed to Pope Paul VI. After about fifteen minutes the Pope, with a slight nod, acknowledging our presence, donned his alb and vestments and began the Mass in English with his back to us. To a great extent it was the private Mass of the Pope which we were invited to attend. There was no homily or bidding prayers. After the Mass was over the Pope again knelt down on his prie-dieu and once again was lost in prayer. Being in his presence like this was indeed a moving experience. Shortly afterwards we lined up in one of the audience rooms nearby and after about ten minutes the Pope arrived and greeted each one of us individually. When he came to me he said, with a smile on his face, 'From Edinburgh?' I smiled back and said 'Dublin.' I was conscious of a very firm handshake from a very strong man with piercing blue eyes and a powerful presence. As we left the papal apartments, the place appeared to be coming alive with secretaries and soutaned officials getting ready for another day's work in Vatican City. We had a Roman breakfast with strong black coffee in one of the cafes nearby. In 1988 Pope John Paul was at the height of his powers and influence in so many church and government circles throughout the world.

In 1990 the rectors' meeting took place in Dublin and it was All Hallows' turn to act as hosts. The rectors were briefed by the members of the pastoral ministry department about courses inaugurated in the college over the previous ten years. I will never forget the look on their faces after the first break on the morning of the first day when they encountered many of our lay students, men and women, in the Coffee Dock. When they returned to the room we were meeting in, there was a kind of awkward silence. The fact that we had opened our doors to lay students, men and women, was quite a shock to a number of them, even though I had been telling them that we had made these moves at the meetings in the previous three years. I believe that some of them felt threatened by this kind of initiative. This I think was because, in most cases, their own bishop trustees would have been reluctant to make this move and secondly a number of the seminaries, because of their location in rural settings, would have found it difficult to go down this road. In organising this meeting we had set aside an afternoon for a meeting between the Irish and English and Scottish seminary rectors around some aspect of pastoral formation. The input was given by Fr Donal Dorr. There was a good exchange at the session and this was followed by a dinner in the college dining-room to mark the occasion of English, Scottish and Irish rectors coming together for the first time. Msgr Jack Kennedy, the rector of the English College in Rome, made a short speech, acknowledging the importance of this first get-together. It was my hope that more meetings like this might take place in the years ahead as I felt that at a time of great challenge for those of us involved in seminary formation it was important for us to pool our insights and experiences. This did not take place. Other events were to overtake us – not least the diminishing number of seminarians in all our seminaries and the competition in both Ireland and England for the ' few remaining oranges' on the trees out there.

In 1994 the seminary rectors' meeting took place in the American College, Louvain. Tom Ivory was the rector of the American College. I had always been impressed by a number of articles he had written in which he stated that seminary formation be brought into line with the RCIA – the catechumenate experience. After some years in All Hallows I had come to the conclusion that there was a kind of short-circuiting in the formation of seminarians. We were encouraging students to take on a priestly *persona* when many of them had not yet gone through the Christian conversion experience – an experience which is at the heart of the RCIA process.

Participating in this Louvain meeting was Sr Katarina Schuth, who had already published research in the United States, comparing different models of seminary formation – free-standing seminaries which concentrated exclusively on the formation of seminarians, and seminaries attached to universities or theological centres, where students mixed with laymen and lay women, taking philosophy and theology courses together. I had met Sr Katarina a few years earlier and had arranged for her to address a seminary rectors' meeting in England as well as in Ireland to dialogue with her about her findings in the American context. Katarina tended to take a neutral stance in regard to the seminary model she herself would have advocated. However, I am fairly sure that her leanings would have been towards the interaction of seminarians and lay people in what is known as the integrated model. On the way up from a meeting in St Patrick's College, Carlow she said to me that it would be better for seminarians to address issues in relation to their psychosexual development in the seminary context rather than later when it might be difficult or too late to do so.

My final seminary rectors' meeting took place in the spring of 1995, during my last year in All Hallows. Now the wheel had turned full circle because this meeting took place in Wonersh where I had attended my first rectors' meeting some thirteen years earlier. At this stage I found myself to be one of the veterans of the group. In fact I was the longest serving rector by that stage. I raised a number of questions about the future of seminary formation in the western world. In the light of so many empty seminaries across Western European countries, the future of priestly formation was likely to be very different to what all of us had experienced. As there was a severe shortage of students in many seminaries, including our own, I tentatively suggested that we might have to look to other ways of calling people to priestly ministry. We would also have to look to other models of formation. Out of the group of 15 rectors I think that there were only three who concurred with me. Many of them did not seem to me to want to face up to the fact that it was the very future of the Tridentine seminary as we had known it that was in question. I could sense that many of the seminary rectors attending these meetings were under very severe pressure because of the shortage of student numbers and diminishing resources of personnel and finance.

Secondly, some of them were faced with polarisation within their seminary staffs, which we escaped in All Hallows. I began to realise that we were in a unique situation to look afresh at the role of the seminary today.

Through my thirteen years in All Hallows, there was a considerable turnover of rectors attending these meetings. Seminary rectors had so many different masters – people they were accountable to – their bishop or bishops who were on their governing bodies, their seminary staff, whom they might have had very little say in appointing, students at many points of the theological spectrum, and priests and lay people in their first assignments who might constantly harp on what kind of priests are you turning out these days. It is not surprising that a piece of research in the United States in the early 1990s revealed that there was a significant fallout of priests in dioceses around the States who had held the post of seminary rector or of vocation director.

## The Transition from a Seminary
## to an 'Institute for Mission and Ministry'

A variety of factors contributed to this development. Through the 1970s Fr Tom Lane had opened the doors of the college to students from various religious orders and obtained the first validation of courses from St Patrick's College, Maynooth and the National Council for Educational Awards. He also turned Purcell House into a retreat/conference centre which offered a variety of renewal courses for religious sisters, retreats for nurses and school leavers and many other groups. With slender resources of income, he kept the college financially viable. The windows of opportunity to offer full-time and part-time courses to lay men and women only came in the 1980s. I would attribute the various developments in All Hallows from 1982 to 1995 to the following:

- There was a latent awareness among the staff in All Hallows in the 1980s that we were coming to the end of one era of mission. Its mission of sending priests to dioceses in certain parts of the world had come or was coming to a natural end. That did not stop bishops coming knocking on our door, asking us

228

if we had students that we could still direct to dioceses in England, the United States and elsewhere. I have no doubt that the quality of priests sent out from All Hallows motivated these bishops to make these requests. However, with the falling number of seminarians through the1980s, a trend that began in Ireland as early as 1968, and the financial pressures in running a large plant, most people on the staff knew subconsciously that we had to move in some new directions.

- Amongst our staff there was a consensus about a developing theology of ministry in the post-Vatican II church – a theology of ministry that was not restricted to priesthood – and a theology of ministry that opened up possibilities for a diversity of ministries based on the sacrament of baptism. With the constant flow of information about what was happening on the ground in many countries, we knew that the building up of Christian communities required the active involvement of as many laymen and women as possible and this of course meant that they needed to be prepared theologically and professionally for this task. There was also a constant flow of information about what was happening in dioceses overseas from the visits of alumni to the college during the summer months. The travels of various members of staff in a number of countries in the summer, and staff exchanges with seminaries overseas, also kept information flowing.

- All Hallows was blessed in having a number of very creative staff members who got a lot of their energy out of mounting new courses to respond to the pastoral needs of parish communities inside and outside Ireland. Mounting new courses meant taking risks – the risk of failing to attract a sufficient number of students to make programmes viable and the risk of not alienating some church authorities who saw ministry in the church exclusively in clerical terms. In nearly every new course that was launched, the number of students arrived from both inside and outside Ireland and as time went on some bishops began to see the value of a number of courses we had put in place. The decreasing number of seminarians in all Irish seminaries highlighted the importance of preparing laymen and women for various ministries at both parish and diocesan levels.

- Parallel with a developing theology of ministry was a growing awareness of new developments in mission theology. A number of theologians were more and more reluctant to divide the world into mission-sending and mission-receiving countries. 'Going on mission' did not necessarily mean crossing a deep blue sea. By the 1980s there were plenty of straws in the wind that what Cardinal Suhard had said about France in the post-war years, as a *pays de mission*, could now be applied to most Western European countries. How to keep mission in Ireland in tension with mission overseas was one of the challenges facing All Hallows when it opened its doors to lay men and lay women in the 1980s. There was a growing consciousness among the staff in All Hallows that a new theology of mission was in the making and that what is said in Pope John Paul's encyclical *Redemptoris Missio* (1991) about re-evangelisation in 'secularised' regions in the heartland of Europe applies in equal measure to the Ireland of our day.
- As each new course got underway our confidence increased about the new directions we had taken. Nevertheless, in the case of nearly every new course we mounted there was a risk of failure. There was only one way to find out if the course was viable and that was 'to have a go'. There was a certain amount of excitement in initiating something new. The positive feedback from students taking the courses gave us the courage to keep going forward.
- The final element in the success of the new courses we had launched was the availability of resources – resources of personnel, financial resources, and a wonderful campus located in the heart of the city of Dublin. We were able to engage teaching personnel from dioceses inside and outside Ireland, religious orders of men and women, and graduates of the college – priests, sisters and lay graduates. Through fundraising and the sale of land surplus to our own needs, we were able to build up our own financial resources and to begin the renovation of a number of our historic buildings. There is no doubt that our physical location halfway between Dublin airport and the centre of the city, and easily accessible from the M50 and other key roads, made access to the college relatively easy for many of the half million people living on the north side of the city of Dublin.

*Three Months' Sabbatical*

From September to December of the first half of the academic year 1994/95, I was on a sabbatical break in Louvain University. I went there to take time out and to reflect on what had happened in All Hallows over the previous twelve years. I also wanted to touch base with a number of theological and pastoral centres that were opening up new ground for ministerial formation and mission outreach. I attended lectures in the theology and philosophy departments and was amazed to learn how much change had taken place since I had been a student in Louvain thirty years previously.

One of the courses I followed was by Herman Lombaerts on Adult Religious Education. Herman had been a frequent visitor to Ireland over the previous twenty years. In conversation with him after one of his lectures about the future of the church in continental Europe, his parting comment to me was that my questions were not radical enough. He left me guessing as to what exactly he meant but I have no doubt that he was pointing up the inadequacy of the present parish structures in transmitting religious faith to the younger generations of our day in Belgium and in countries nearby and the failure of seminaries to attract students.

In the philosophy department, Thomism was completely eclipsed and St Thomas Aquinas was studied as part of a medieval history of philosophy course. The main thrust now was on phenomenology, and an American version of the philosophy of language. There was also a good deal of debate about the philosophical status of psychoanalytic discourse. I began to realise how out of touch I was now with philosophical developments in contemporary European philosophy.

During those three months in Louvain I spent a good deal of time reading various books and journals in their magnificent theology library around four main areas:

- A starting point for a theology of ministry that transcends the division between priests and lay people.
- A theology of mission that transcends the division between mission sending and mission receiving countries, with a focus on what form mission might take in the secularised western world.

- A theology that is pastorally focused, beginning in the religious experience of people of our day and transcending the traditional division between 'dogmatic' and 'pastoral theology' which I have always found unhelpful.
- Finally, some areas of feminist theology where I hoped to find a balanced view of the contributions of both women's and men's spirituality to the understanding of ministry in our time. In this last area, I was disappointed with what Louvain had to offer.

At weekends I travelled to many beautiful towns and cities in the neighbourhood of Louvain – Bruges, Ghent, Antwerp, Aachan, Cologne, Trier, Rheims, absorbing the beautiful Christian heritage of art and architecture in these cities and also participating in Sunday Eucharist. I came away from this three-month sabbatical with alarm hells ringing at the decline of the Catholic Church in countries I had visited. This sharpened my focus on challenges that inevitably would face us in Ireland before very long. The so-called 'Enlightenment' had been kept at bay from our island for a very long time – now it is enveloping us from all sides, having both positive and negative effects and presenting us with a whole series of new challenges for the future.

*All Hallows – Ten Years Later*
Twelve years have passed since I moved on to pastures new in 1995. Being based in All Hallows during the past three years, coming and going to various destinations, I have noticed that considerable developments have taken place since 1995. These developments include:
- validation of degrees by Dublin City University;
- diversification of Lay Ministry courses – with outposts outside the college;
- the refashioning and further development of BA, MA and Graduate Diploma courses with the addition of a new part-time MA in Management: Pastoral and Voluntary Services;
- a part-time BA degree in Humanities – Pastoral Theology;
- the opening of the door to doctoral research students;
- the expansion of the work in the Purcell House Conference

Centre including the development of a very successful Spring Conference on some aspect of parish development;
- the continuing development of the Renewal for Ministry course; the building up of a tradition of an annual musical event highlighting the talents and gifts of the students – which in fact is a rediscovery of a strong college tradition;
- the setting up of an exhibition centre reminding current students and visitors of the 160 year tradition of All Hallows Missionary College;
- linking up with two Vincentian Universities in the United States – St John's in New York and De Paul in Chicago

With over 500 students, full-time and part-time, milling around the campus from Monday to Friday – over 100 of them engaged in post-graduate work – and many conferences, seminars and retreats at weekends and through the summer months, All Hallows continues to be an interesting crossroads of information about mission and ministry. I was amazed at the number of new developments that had taken place in a relatively short period, confirming for me that incremental change year by year amounts to quite substantial change over five and ten year periods.

All Hallows will continue to face many challenges in the years ahead. There will be increasing competition from other institutions, inside and outside Ireland. The external environment is now very volatile in the light of the crisis that has hit the institutional church in Ireland and elsewhere. The college can never sit back on its achievements. There will always be new challenges around about us, which will require a good deal of energy and creativity to respond to - including the challenge of forming new partnerships with other groups and institutions who are thinking radically about re-evangelisation today. The call to 'go, teach all nations' is now a call to our imaginations to envision the mission in all kinds of new ways.

I am very grateful to All Hallows for opening doors and windows in my life – giving me privileged access to the rich experience of many priests all over the world. The lay men and lay women who enrolled as students on our new courses also opened my eyes to the enormous contribution they can bring to the building up of parish communities. I was also privileged during my thirteen years in All Hallows to be working with talented and gifted colleagues who kept the ship moving forward. It could very well be that ministry in the Christian tradition may take many different forms in the future. One thing I feel sure of is that genuine Christian ministry will always involve a voluntary element and a generous spirit. I experienced both of these in abundance among staff and students in All Hallows.

CHAPTER 9

# Provincial Office – a Vincentian World
# 1995-2001

As I began reflecting on my six years in the Provincial Office, I began to realise that I needed distance to see things in some perspective. I have decided to concentrate on a number of points without making any comment.

*Appointment as Provincial*
When Father Bob Maloney contacted me in April 1995 asking me to take on the task of Provincial of the Irish Province I asked for a few weeks to reflect about this. I was 59 years of age and felt myself to be too old for this task. After 13 years of heavy administrative work in All Hallows I felt quite tired and deep down I felt that what I really needed was a long sabbatical break to recharge the batteries, both physical and spiritual. We had nurtured a number of new developments in All Hallows and a good deal of work still remained to be done to consolidate the new courses, to complete the renovation of building programmes, to continue fundraising and to search for new staff. I would be leaving with a number of tasks unfinished.

Having spent nine years on the Vincentian Provincial Council from 1973 to 1982, watching three Provincials in action, I had a fair idea of what the Office of Provincial entailed. With a diminishing workforce I had observed the difficulties from year to year through the 1970s in making appointments and filling various posts. Thirteen years later, the difficulties in making appointments had become even more acute. In April 1995 it was obvious that we would have to continue to close Vincentian houses and withdraw from various works. With no entries in the Irish region for the previous eight years, our situation was quite desperate. We were like many other religious orders and congregations.

I was aware that there could be a good deal of isolation as Provincial. For nine years I had attended Provincial Council meetings, walking away from them afterwards and leaving the implementation and execution of decisions to the Provincial. I also knew that there could be a good deal of challenge and confrontation in asking members of the province to take up new appointments. A very negative *zeitgeist* was developing in Ireland against the church and, of course, the revelations about child sexual abuse scandals had all kinds of ramifications. There was a tremendous loss of trust of priests among a very large group of people.

In All Hallows a good deal of my interest had moved towards the development of lay ministry. I realised that in the post of Provincial I would have to move back into a clerical world and concentrate a lot on the recruitment of students for the Vincentian way of life. Becoming Provincial meant re-immersing myself in a number of Vincentian works in the Province, including education and other ministries where there had been a good deal of tension in the past. It meant re-engaging my energies in works we were phasing out. Maintaining a commitment to the Nigerian region put a very severe strain on our Province with our declining numbers. It put pressure on our Province from the point of view of personnel and financial resources.

The lifestyle of the Provincial as I had observed it, working out of an office in 4/6 Cabra Road and living over the shop, did not enthuse me. The tragic murder of Father James Murphy there in 1981 had left a deep imprint on my psyche. Apart from being in touch with what was happening in St Peter's, Phibsboro, I felt that one was quite isolated from the other works of the Province, if I was based there.

There is no doubt that my wings would be clipped in the amount of travel I would be able to do in the future. I had covered a lot of ground in All Hallows over my 13 years there. However, there would be a good deal of travelling in Ireland, Scotland, England and Nigeria.

The biggest challenge in the Office of Provincial for me was as a spiritual leader requiring a deep commitment to prayer and Vincentian values. I realised that there were other members of the Province who had more to offer than I had in these areas. I lived all of my life as a Vincentian taking very seriously what those in authority had asked me to do and I had seen others taking on difficult appointments. So, weighing up all these reasons, I concluded that I should accept the invitation and I telephoned Fr Bob Maloney, the Superior General, around mid-April to tell him that I had decided to accept the post of Provincial. I detected a certain amount of relief in his voice. He thanked me for agreeing to do so. He emphasised very much the importance of addressing the urgent question of vocations to the Province and indicated that this was one of the strong themes running through the consultation in the Province over the past few months. This decision was communicated to the Irish Province at the end of April 1995.

## Marino Provincial Assembly

The Marino Provincial Assembly took place in June 1995 with the help of Eddie Molloy, a Management Consultant, and an organising committee of five priests. Mark Noonan had prepared a thorough review of the works of the province. The Assembly confirmed my view that we had to concentrate on the development of two or three Vincentian works in the two regions of our Province, Ireland and Britain, that Nigeria be set up as a Vice-Province, and thirdly that we create the slack that was needed to bring about the above. It was a well-run and well-ordered Provincial Assembly and it certainly set things up for me in regard to priorities. Fr Hugh O'Donnell was present at this Assembly as a spiritual animator.

## First Regional Meetings – Dublin and London October 1995

The Regional Meetings were a carry over from the June Provincial Assembly. Eddie Molloy attended both meetings and I indicated that the task now was to apply the Mission Statement marked out at Marino to all our individual houses. I encouraged confrères in each of the communities to have meetings in the autumn to do this. The main issues were:

- What works to concentrate on developing?
- What works to refocus?
- What works to withdraw from?
- What are the theological constructs we are operating out of

now and what theological constructs do we want to operate out of in the future?

I told the confrères in both regions that I intended to keep in existence the Marino Organising Committee and re-naming it the Research and Development Committee, indicating that it would assist me and the Provincial Council in the implement-ation of the Marino Mission Statement. Looking back now I can see that there was no follow through on this. One of the prob-lems was setting up regular meetings with five men who were holding full-time jobs. There was also the question of the rela-tionship of this group to the Provincial Council.

From January 1996 onwards the Provincial Council put in a good deal of time into discussing appointments and to follow through on the recommendations of the Marino Assembly in relation to vocations. The Parish Missions were to be the first priority in both regions. We were eager to strengthen both teams. I started to realise that because of our shortage of person-nel we had very little possibility of taking on new initiatives.

*Withdrawing from Two Vincentian Parishes in England*
Sheffield
In the summer of 1996 I attended a celebration in St Vincent's Church, Sheffield to mark firstly the closure of the church and secondly the presence of Vincentian priests in the parish for 144 years. The celebration brought home to me the long Vincentian tradition that had been built up in this parish. The parish was set up to respond to the needs of Irish emigrants in the 19th century. This beautiful cut-stone church had gone through the cycle of being one of the most important churches, if not the most important church, in the middle of the city of Sheffield to being situated now in the middle of a wasteland in an area that had been depopulated gradually after World War II. It was evident that the church had not been viable for quite a few years and the closure of the church was inevitable.

The final liturgy was very well organised. The baptismal log-books and marriage log-books were brought up in procession and at the end of the Mass the altar cloths were taken from the altar. It was indeed a very sad moment for many of the former parishioners whose singing had filled the church to the rafters on that summer's evening.

Warrington
After the death of Fr John O'Kelly on 3 August 1998 it was evident that we would have great difficulty in finding personnel for this parish and I informed Archbishop Patrick Kelly in Liverpool about this in the autumn of 1998. After a short discussion we agreed to hand over the parish in June 1999.

In the autumn of 1998 I spoke at all the Masses in St Stephen's parish and thanked the people for their kindness to us Vincentians over the 22 years we had spent there. Two or three weeks before our withdrawal in the summer of 1999 there was a celebration Mass in the parish at which Bishop Vincent Malone presided.

*Spring In-Services*
I initiated a Vincentian Spring In-service Conference for most of the years I was in the Provincial Office. It was one way of trying to loosen up the theological constructs we were working out of. The Superior General, Fr Bob Maloney, gave two conferences on priesthood in the Vincentian tradition.

For the first time in 1998 I launched a Spring Vincentian In-Service concentrating on the 'Ministry of the Word' and relying on expertise in our own province. Over two days about 25 confrères attended. With the All Hallows Spring In-service, and talks taking place in Dublin around a variety of topics, it might seem that a Vincentian In-service was superfluous. I wanted to draw confrères' attention to areas that were distinctive in Vincentian ministries and I felt that 'Ministry of the Word' was one that many confrères could participate in. I also wanted to keep the orientation focused on praxis. The purpose of the in-service was to affirm confrères in what they were doing in this area. It was quite a successful session and with a bit of imagination I felt that we could have come up with other topics each year. Exchanges around topics of vital Vincentian interest were important for the morale of confrères.

On a second visit to the Province in 1999, Bob Maloney gave two talks over two days – one on various aspects of world poverty. It was a powe-point presentation. Members of the Vincentian family also attended. The following day he gave another talk to confrères of the province on ten things he had learned in the post of Superior General.

*Harryville*
Some years previously the Provincial Council at the time, had taken the decision to explore a new kind of presence in the North of Ireland to follow up our withdrawal from St Patrick's College, Armagh. One of our men had been working in a predominately Presbyterian area on the outskirts of Ballymena, a place called Harryville, for some time and he was joined by another priest who worked for a year in one of the inner-city parishes in Belfast. In the autumn of 1996 a siege situation developed in Harryville where the church was surrounded every Saturday evening by Presbyterian extremists. There was a lot of pressure on our two Vincentian priests. When the presbytery itself was attacked by fire bombs on one particular night these two men moved to live with the parish priest in the centre of the town of Ballymena. The siege was to continue for well over a year. On two occasions I attended Mass on the Saturday evening, experiencing the tension in the air as Catholics bravely attended the Mass. In the spring, tensions developed between our confrères and the authorities about the appropriate reaction to these events.

In May 1997 the Provincial Council was faced with the decision to continue on in some other parish in the diocese of Down & Connor or to withdraw completely. Later in the summer of 1997 we moved to a parish in West Belfast, St John's, where we supported the parish priest by providing a curate and part-time help over the following four years. Another man acted as a chaplain in a large comprehensive school.

*Visit to the Holy Land*
In the autumn of 1996 Michael Prior had serious heart surgery in a hospital in Jerusalem. He was staying in the Tantur Ecumenical Institute where he was a visiting scholar. I decided to visit him in the first week of January 1997 to find out how he was health-wise and to consult him about his plans for the future.

He introduced me to his Palestinian friends in the University of Bethlehem where he was a visiting lecturer. He also introduced me to the Latin Patriarch in Jerusalem and many other people supporting the Palestinian cause. We had lunch with Fr Jerome Murphy-O'Connor in the Ecole Biblique. I was impressed by the Spartan nature of Jerome's office-cum-bedroom and the evidence of a dedicated scholar's workplace. I had contact with him in Strawberry Hill in 1980 when he came there to lecture on a number of New Testament themes and also the future of religious life. When I was a schoolboy in Castleknock we overlapped for two years. In his comments on various church events, New Testament topics, scholarship etc., he took no hostages. In reading his book on *Paul the Apostle* I was very impressed by his attempt to track down chronologically Paul's movements all through his life. I was also very impressed by his *Guide to Jerusalem* which had very little of the devotional and pious but plenty of archaeological data and reliable scholarship about Jerusalem in the time of Christ.

The most memorable event for me during this week in Israel was an exchange between Michael and a tour guide in the Scottish Hostel in Galilee where we had arrived to spend a couple of days. The evening we arrived about 30 students from a Lutheran College in Minneapolis-St Paul filed into the dining room accompanied by two lecturers, a Jewish guide and a Palestinian driver of their bus. The lecturers, the guide and driver sat down at our table and very quickly a heated discussion took place between Michael and the Jewish guide. Michael took him to task for a number of things he was saying about Israel and an angry exchange took place between the two of them. Gradually everybody else in the room stopped speaking and listened to the heated argument that developed. I was afraid it was going to come to blows. Michael supported the Palestinian cause and the Jewish guide tried to defend what the government had been doing over the previous ten years in setting up Israeli strongholds throughout the country. Michael dismissed in one sentence any justification for all this in terms of the land belonging to Israel based on any biblical grounds. Gradually the conversation subsided and people began to speak again. At breakfast the following morning the two lecturers from this Lutheran

College in Minneapolis-St Paul came up to thank Michael for taking the guide to task. They had to put up with his arrogant claims for the previous couple of weeks and were afraid to challenge him. They pointed out that this group were religious studies students and were studying the nature of religious conflict in three different places in the Middle East. What happened the previous evening was grist to their mill. Needless to say, the Palestinian driver was also delighted with what had happened.

The following day Michael brought me for a tour of the Lake of Galilee, travelling all around it, commenting on the various biblical sites, especially the New Testament ones. The following morning, before leaving the area, we went up to a high point overlooking the lake and there we said morning prayer together, with the marvellous view of Lake Galilee stretching out to the horizon.

When we returned to Jerusalem he brought me to visit the Daughters of Charity in a hospital they were running in Bethlehem. We also visited the Brothers of Christian Instruction, most of them Canadian, who were running the University of Bethlehem. I learned about Michael's sermon on Christmas night when the papal nuncio was present, when Michael interpreted gospel liberation in terms of the Palestinians recovering their land. This sermon was very much appreciated by the Palestinians present but some others felt that he may have crossed the 'diplomatic line', especially some of the staff in Tantur. The papal nuncio did not wait around afterwards.

While I was with Michael in Tantur I read one of his manuscripts which were due for publication, arguing that the Israeli cause had no scriptural foundation and that those who had set up the Israeli state had misunderstood the Jewish leaders of the 19th century, including the philosopher, Martin Buber. Michael wanted to use all his energies to fight the Palestinian cause.

*Three Weeks in the Toulouse Province*

During the summer of 1997 I was keen to learn more about what was happening in other Vincentian provinces on the continent and I decided to link up with Fr Christian Sens, the Provincial of the Toulouse Province. I arranged to stay in the south of France with Toulouse as my base for 3 weeks of that summer. I had many discussions with the French Vincentians in this Province, especially Christian Sens himself, and picked up a good deal of information about the way the Catholic Church in France was coping with the shortage of priests. Four Vincentians were administering a parish with 24 Mass centres, with Catus at the centre covering Masses on a rotation basis through each month. Their parish missions took the form of a presence in a parish for a number of years setting things up and then returning the parish to diocesan priests.

I travelled with Christian Sens to the birth place of John Gabriel Perboyre where a Mass took place in the open air to mark his canonisation. The local bishop of the area was present. It was a very warm summer's day and we all sweltered under the blazing sun. On the way to this place I had a long discussion with Christian Sens about the spirituality of the 19th century. One could say that John Gabriel had a lust for martyrdom. In contrast I was very impressed by the Dominican Archbishop in Algeria who had been murdered a few months previously. It was clear from some of his letters that he had a much more attractive spirituality. He stayed courageously at his post to the end. I became convinced that there was a good deal in the 19th century Vincentian spirituality we had inherited in the Irish Province we could say goodbye to. A reading of Fr Edward Udovic's life of Etienne, Superior General of the Vincentians from 1842 to the 1870s, confirmed my views on this.

Over the three weeks in France I visited the Cathedral in Albi which inspired the architect of St Mary's College Chapel. I also visited the little chapel in the rolling countryside where St Vincent said his first Mass and where I was impressed by the simplicity of the chapel. I stayed for a few days in the Berceau absorbing the atmosphere of Vincent's home and farmland which the family owned.

I also visited Bordeaux, Bayonne, Lourdes and Luchon du Bains near the village of Marignac where I had been chaplain to a 'colonie des vacances' 30 years previously. I spent four or five days in Luchon du Bains exploring the mountains and the spa in the town itself.

On my last evening in Toulouse I had a wonderful dinner with Jean Marie and the local curé. I asked him how the Catholic

Church in France was going to cope with the diminishing number of priests. He said that he did not know but that in his parish there were some excellent lay men and lay women and that he was sure that the Christian tradition would be passed on through them. This remark gave me plenty of food for thought.

*Vocations*

Young Vincentians from other provinces came to Dublin through the summer months to learn English. Many of them stayed in All Hallows. They came from Austria, Italy, France, Spain, Slovakia and South America. This was a great service to other provinces. I usually made a point of meeting these students for a meal in All Hallows or elsewhere and I was always struck by their youthfulness and vitality. Their presence made me realise how different our province would have been if we had managed to maintain a steady stream of young Vincentian life coming through to join the community and moving forward to ordination. We had grown accustomed to living without Vincentian students and it was going to be very difficult to break through the apathy and the fatalism that had developed. One could invoke the apathy of the church in general through this period and the low morale amongst priests because of the scandals that had drawn the priesthood into disrepute. Survival, for survival's sake, was not the question. Did we believe that the Vincentian tradition had something important to offer to the church of our times?

I was not in favour of any large scale advertising campaign. I felt that it would be a waste of money and counter productive. I believed that if we had two or three small communities where a young man could share in the prayer and community life of these houses that this is the most we could do at a time when many people were allergic to mention of church or priesthood. At one point one of the priests who had worked in Castleknock asked a man who had completed his university degree course if he would like to join us – he had shown an interest in priesthood – he responded that his family would be so opposed to this that he could not take this step.

As time went on I began to think that we had to distance ourselves from the present situation before the tide would turn.

Holding on to the few younger confrères we had was to become the priority for us, as it was also for other religious congregations.

*Provincial Assembly – Easter 1997*
In mid-June 1997 a Provincial Assembly took place over three days in All Hallows, facilitated by a Holy Faith Sister. The agenda had been set by the topic chosen for the General Assembly (1998) – The Vincentian Family – which was due to take place the following year. A preparatory committee met through the spring of 1997 and each domestic assembly was encouraged to invite Daughters of Charity, members of the St Vincent de Paul Society and lay men and women, especially those participating in our ministries, to attend these meetings and to come up with suggestions about how we could build closer ties with these groups. These groups were also encouraged to send a number of people to attend the Provincial Assembly itself. Four sub-groups were set up to organise the individual sessions. The first of these was on emergent poverties in which we concentrated on our contacts with the poor, especially the Travelling People. Were we 'listening' to the 'cries of the poor'? The second group concentrated on the changing scene between leadership in parishes – clerical and lay. The third section was a presentation from a Daughter of Charity and a youth retreat team in Damascus House highlighting the ways in which they tried to communicate to the young people who attended youth retreats there. The fourth group was a presentation from boys in Castleknock College. One of the priests on the staff there, as well as a number of pupils, spoke about their work as members of SVP conferences working with Travellers and other groups.

The evaluation feedback was predominately in favour of the assembly being opened up to lay men and lay women in our various ministries. Some said that this enabled us to be much less introverted and to concentrate on some of the real needs in the ministries we were engaged in. We discovered that already there was a lot of collaboration taking place in our ministries.

## Three Visits to Nigeria

During my six years as Provincial I visited the Nigerian Region/ Vice-Province on three occasions. The first visit was in November 1995 when I managed to obtain a visitor's visa fairly easily. I stayed for a few days with Rod Crowley in Lagos and preached to large crowds at Sunday Mass and experienced all the comings and goings from his presbytery. From there I went to Enugu where Timothy Njoku proudly showed me the new building he was putting up for students. I spent a few hours talking to the students who asked me a lot of questions about going overseas to do one or other course. I prayed at James Cahalan's grave which was beside the chapel building. He had spent 15 years working in Nigeria after leaving the Provincial Office.

I visited Oraifite and then the parish of Agpa. In Ogobia I met the recently appointed local bishop and later on that day I enjoyed a beer on the veranda with the confrères in the cool of the evening. From there I went to Ikot Ekpene, where I became aware of the enormous amount of work Paul Roche had done to put up this and other buildings. I returned to Lagos and flew back to Dublin after my short two-week visit. I was very impressed by all the work that had been done by the Nigerian and Irish confrères.

I had found the intense heat quite overwhelming. I visited East Africa on two occasions in the 1970s and South Africa in the 1980s and thought Nigeria would be more or less the same with the heat turned up a little. I found that the intense heat drained me of all energy. Some people said to me that I should have spent a longer time in the country to give my body time to adapt to the heat.

My second visit to Nigeria took place between 19 June and 3 July 1997. This time I flew KLM out of Amsterdam Airport to Lagos. I had waited over six months for my visitor's visa to come through. This time I interviewed all the students coming up for ordination.

At Port Harcourt airport I was challenged by a customs official. I was sitting down in the lounge reading a novel when this lady in uniform came up to me and demanded to see my passport. She said that my visa was not in order and that I would have to go with her to the office. I demurred and said that I would like to telephone the bishop of Port Harcourt first. I had called her bluff. She handed me back my passport saying weakly that she was a Catholic too.

In Ikot Ekpene, I had a meal with the bishop who pleaded with me not to withdraw one of our Irish confrères. I travelled with Matty Barry from Enugu to Ikot Ekpene. He introduced me to the list of slogans he had taken from Nigerian lorries on his various travels. I was very relieved when my two-week mission was accomplished and was quite ill on the way back to Amsterdam with a stomach upset, but recovered after a night's rest in an airport hotel. On the Sunday I took a train down to Paris where I was due to give a talk to Vincentian parish mission groups who were meeting there for a three-week period.

My third and last visit to Nigeria was on 1 January 1998 for the inauguration of the new Vice-Province of Nigeria by Fr Victor Bieler, the Superior General's delegate. Victor linked up with me in Zurich and we flew out together to Lagos, making our way immediately to Enugu, where the Vincentian Provincial Assembly was in progress. Fr Urban Osuji was installed as the first Provincial of the Nigerian Vice-Province. Various matters were discussed – formation of students, new ministries, and financial arrangements with the Irish province. Fr Victor Bieler emphasised that the proposed financial arrangements with the province of Ireland were very generous ones. These arrangements were formally recognised a few weeks later at a meeting in Rome with the Superior General, Fr Robert Maloney, and the Bursar General, Fr Pat Griffin, Fr Urban and myself.

During the previous year I had called a special meeting of all the confrères who had worked in Nigeria and discussed with them the setting up of the Vice-Province. They were unanimous that the time had come to do so. The consultation the Superior General, Father Bob Maloney, had conducted amongst the confrères in Nigeria was less unanimous. There were certainly quite a number of the Nigerian priests who wanted to retain the pipeline to Ireland for personnel and for finances and they had fears that they were going to be set adrift. I came to the conclusion myself that the time had come for the Nigerian confrères to take responsibility for all aspects of the business of their province, including formation. For nearly 40 years the province was in the making and now had a much larger number of personnel than many other provinces around the world. I also felt that the Irish province could no longer afford to send personnel at a time when we were fighting for our future in both the Irish and British regions. Even if we had personnel, I had grave doubts about whether one could ask confrères to work in what would be virtually isolation for many of them. Many expatriate priests were now leaving Nigeria. The time had come for this vibrant group of young Nigerian confrères to make its own way and carve out its own future in the congregation.

When Victor Bieler and myself were going through customs to board the plane back to Geneva, the lady behind the desk asked me if I had a Christmas present for her. I shook my head saying that they were all gone. She kept me waiting for a few minutes and then let me through. Victor and myself went straight to the bar to get a drink of beer and to recover from the hustle of getting to the airport and through the customs. Because of a thunderstorm the Swiss aeroplane was delayed about three hours and the electricity went out in the airport. I was very relieved when that plane finally took off.

*Visit to Slovenia*

Through the month of August 1997 I took a three-week break in Bavaria and Slovenia. Tom Healy made arrangements for me to stay in a student centre near Swabbing in Munich. I had a good opportunity to visit places in Munich itself which I had visited fleetingly ten years previously. I spent a good deal of time in the section of the Deutsches museum that deals with theories about the origin of the universe. Over the years I failed to keep up with all the literature appearing about this and the ways it might all come to an end.

Anton Stres, the Provincial of the Slovenian Province, had invited me to visit him in Ljubljana. I took a plane from Munich to Ljubljana, a beautiful city that was once part of the Austro-Hungarian empire. There was plenty of time to look around this beautiful city, to visit its churches and to walk along the banks of the river at its centre. Anton brought me to visit the Julian Alps which were breathtaking and only a short distance from the city.

He also brought me to visit his sister, a vineyard on the way, and a Vincentian retreat centre about 50 kilometres from the city of Ljubljana.

One of the high points of my visit was a long car journey through some of the troubled areas of the former Yugoslavia. I could see the destruction of houses and buildings as I passed through small villages on the way to the Adriatic. We travelled to a small island where the new Archbishop of Ljubljana, Franc Rode CM, was on holidays. While he was working in the Faith and Culture Department in Rome he used to spend the summer holidays rebuilding a shack on this island. We had two meals together. On both occasions I poured cold water over his suggestion that Europe could return to be a Catholic Europe along the lines suggested by Hilaire Belloc and G. K. Chesterton. He was taken aback by all this. He had fairly negative views about what was happening across Western Europe and gave the impression that we were bringing the decline of the church on ourselves. When I returned to Ljubljana, one of the younger men in the community there came up to me with a smile on his face, saying that I had stood on the archbishop's corns.

Later I learned that he was carrying on quite a battle to retrieve from the government church property which had been confiscated during the communist era. I also learned that his own family farm had been confiscated and that he and his family had emigrated to the Argentine where he spent the first formative years of his life. I began to realise that all this had coloured his views on the church situation in Europe today. Franc Rode was certainly a very different man to the Franc Rode I had met in Madrid in the summer of 1970 when we had an animated discussion about the future of the church in the light of Vatican II. In 2004 he was recalled to Rome and put in charge of the Congregation of the Clergy. A cardinal's hat followed a short time later.

I was very impressed by this small Vincentian province. A number of confrères, including Anton Stres, were working in the philosophy and theology departments of the university. A number of them had degrees from the Institut Catholique in Paris. Many of them spoke English and I got the impression that they knew there were terrific challenges ahead for them in facing up to the 'secularisation' forces which were coming closer to them from Western Europe.

When I got back to Munich I had a beer one morning with a young Irishman who had been thinking of priesthood. He had worked with Tom Healy in the Irish chaplaincy for a year or so. At one point he said to me that in the light of all the revelations coming out in Ireland about bishops and clergy, it would be up to his generation to pick up the baton now.

*Meetings of European Provincials*

Over my six years in the Provincial Office I attended four meetings of European Provincials. The first meeting took place in Germany and The Netherlands in April 1997. We gave the customary reports of what was happening in each of our provinces, especially in relation to CM vocations. The Auxiliary Bishop of Trier updated us on the various funding agencies in Germany, Adveniat, Misereor, etc. In the course of this presentation he highlighted the shortage of priests in many German dioceses, especially in Trier.

We visited Trier where we had a tour of the two Basilicas. On another day we went to Panningen, passing through Aachen. We visited the 'state of the art' retirement facility the Dutch confrères had in Panningen. We had Mass in the college chapel and Wiel Bellemakers gave us a run down of the history of the Dutch province, highlighting the fact that Dutch confrères had been on mission in 34 different countries. The retirement home was for both Vincentians and Daughters of Charity and was run in co-operation with the State, which meant that they had to abide by European regulations in regard to preservation of food. Some of the retired missionaries found it very hard to accept the food prepared for a particular meal. It had to be thrown out afterwards if it was not eaten at that meal. Cooked food could not be kept overnight.

The biggest obstacle to communication at these meetings was the diversity of languages. One could understand the wisdom of Fr Bob Maloney's directives over these years about the importance of every young confrère learning how to speak a second language.

*European Provincials' Meeting, Istanbul and the Lebanon – Easter 1999*
Shortly after Easter 1999 I spent about five days with Franz
Kangler in the German School in Istanbul. It gave me a great opportunity to look around the city. I was very conscious that I was
in a whole new world – Byzantium and the world of Islam. One
of the teachers in the school, Elizabeth, who belonged to an
Austrian Secular Institute, brought me around the city and I
chatted to her about the doctoral thesis she was writing on
Turkish refugees in Austria and Germany. The contrast between
the wealthy European part of the city and the bazaar areas
struck me forcibly. The glories of early Christianity in this part
of the world also struck home to me through visits to various
shrines and churches with beautiful mosaics. The highlight of
the visit was the visit to Santa Sophia, the famous hexagon
church built in the 4th century. It had been turned into a mosque
but now it was a museum.

I flew from Istanbul to the Lebanon with Franz Kangler and
the next ten days were spent visiting various sites in the
Lebanon. We were based in a retreat conference centre of the
Daughters of Charity up in the mountains and each day we visited Vincentian houses, including their famous secondary
school, a famous Orthodox monastery, and Roman temples em-
bodying the state religion. As we left this enormous site, where a
guide had told us about sacrifical rites to various gods, Franz
Kangler said to me, 'Now you can see what St Paul was up
against.' Beirut was just beginning to recover from the disastrous war that had spilt over from Palestine.

As most of the visit was taken up with seeing places in the
Lebanon, we had very little time to discuss Bob Maloney's letter
challenging us as a European Continental group to collaborate
more with one another in various areas, especially in the area of
refugees, representation in the European Union in Brussels,
formation programmes and economic matters.

*European Provincials' Meeting, Madrid and Malaga – April 2000*
In the year 2000 the European Provincial Meeting was very well
organised by the Provincial of the Madrid Province, Fr Felix
Alvarez. We had two interesting talks in Madrid from the leader
of the parish mission team in that province and the brave efforts

they were making to revitalise this ministry, and another talk from the Vocation Director of the Madrid Archdiocese about the vocation situation in Madrid and in Spain generally. From Madrid we visited Toledo and from there we went on to Granada. We spent the last two or three days in Malaga discussing a second letter from the Superior General, encouraging us to follow through on the suggestions he had made a year earlier. We agreed to run a meeting on Vincentian formation issues the following August in Dax. I was given the task of exploring further the possibility of picking up information about setting up some kind of Vincentian desk in relation to the EU in Brussels. I had already visited Brussels on two occasions earlier in the year and given a short report about attending a special conference organised by the leaders of European Religious men and women, which had taken place at Heverlee outside Leuven. Bob Maloney had already suggested to me that when I finished my term as Provincial I might take up this task in Brussels. With this in mind I had started gathering information over the previous 12 months about what various religious groups were doing in Brussels in regard to the European Union and its various offices. The Jesuits had been making the running on the refugee issue and had set up a very well-structured office in Brussels. The Dominicans were active in building bridges to politicians and EU officials. Various other groups were involved, many of them on a lobbying level, in regard to funds, the Third World, etc. I agreed to report back to the European Provincials at the meeting coming up in Dublin the following year.

One of the most memorable aspects of this visit to Spain was the explanation we got of the El Greco painting in a church in Toledo about the burial of Count Cortez, encapsulating a theology of death and resurrection reflected in the Spanish theological world of the 16th Century.

*Closure of Damascus House*
Through 1996/1997 a process was set in place to investigate the future for Damascus House Retreat/Conference Centre in Mill Hill, London. It was evident that a lot of money would have to be invested in the building if work at the Centre was to continue. There was a meeting of the CM and DC Provincial Councils to

discuss all this. We agreed to explore the possibility of another collaborative venture such as a parish mission group, a retreat group or a youth group. After 25 years of very varied activities Damascus House was formally closed at the end of June 1998 with a Mass in the Daughters of Charity chapel and a buffet supper that evening attended by many of the former staff, retreat groups and members of the St Vincent de Paul Society.

The closure of Damascus House was a big loss for the British region and its morale. The three main ingredients in the decision to close Damascus House were:

- A number of the existing programmes and courses were coming to a natural end;
- Qualified personnel from the DCs and CMs were not available;
- An enormous amount of money would have to be invested in the buildings to make them viable and neither DCs nor CMs had this kind of money to invest.

*Retreats*
Community Retreats
For a number of years I recommended strongly that each community should organise its own community retreat at the beginning of the year. It was my hope that communities would get away to another location and that they would take seriously the formation of a community plan for the year ahead. Most communities followed through on this but others pleaded that they could not get away.

Provincial Retreat – June/July 1999
In the autumn of 1998 the Provincial Council decided to try two provincial retreats and break away from the community-based retreats of the previous three years. Tom McKenna was invited to speak at both of these retreats but, unfortunately for us, he was named Provincial of the Eastern Province of the United States around Easter and had to withdraw. His place was taken by John McGoldrick of the same province. The retreat for the Irish region took place in Emmaus at the end of June and the Provincial Retreat in the English region took place in Wimbledon in the autumn.

For the last two years of my Provincialate we returned to community-based retreats in which we had mixed success. A lot depended on the leadership of the superiors in each community and the willingness of confrères to organise it properly and to give quality time to the retreat itself. This usually meant moving away from the house to another location. On the other hand, provincial retreats in the two regions were important in that they promoted networking between the confrères and interaction between houses. As I look back now I think the ideal would have been alternating the two kinds of retreat from year to year.

Millenium Retreat with the Daughters of Charity
To mark the Jubilee year the Retreat In-service Commission recommended that we have a number of retreats during the year in the two regions with the Daughters of Charity. In the British region retreats took place in Canterbury and in pilgrimage sites in the north of England and Wales. In Ireland a group went to Ballintubber. It was my hope to join this group but I was unable to do so. Nevertheless, early in September I spent five days in Ballintubber. Using it as a base I climbed a few mountains in Achill and on the fifth day I climbed Croagh Patrick.

I enjoyed very much the marvellous view from the reek on what turned out to be a sunny afternoon. The rain clouds of the morning had disappeared. I would love to have walked the pilgrimage path from Ballintubber Abbey to the top of Croagh Patrick but an opportunity to do so did not occur during this visit.

*Handing over the Administration of St Patrick's College of Education*
Since its initiation in 1875 Vincentians had been administering St Patrick's College of Education. In the summer of 1998 I had indicated to the Board of Governors that it was not our intention to put forward another Vincentian for approval as President of the college. I had already indicated to the Archbishop of Dublin that we Vincentians felt it was time to withdraw from the administration because of our lack of manpower. I met the Vincentian community in St Patrick's on a number of occasions during the autumn and spring of 1998/1999 to prepare for this.

After the interviewing of six candidates in Newman House

in St Stephen's Green around Easter 1999, Dr Pauric Travers was named the new President. The handing over of the administration went very smoothly with the Archbishop celebrating the Eucharist in the college chapel, followed by a dinner on a Sunday afternoon with speeches being given by Professor Herlihy, Chairman of the Board of Governors, and Fr Sam Clyne in reply.

A few months later I said a few words at the installation of a plaque put together by a sculptor, Betty Ryan, in a prominent place in the college to mark the 124 years of Vincentian administration. It was a very simple piece of sculpture – St Vincent de Paul handing out loaves of bread with the inscription 'food for the spirit and food for the body' underneath.

Over the 124 years 60 Vincentian priests had worked in St Patrick's. The contribution of the 12 Presidents was noted, especially the contribution of Dr Donal Cregan 1958-1974 in the development and the expansion of the college.

*Publications*

During the 1980s and 1990s, a number of confrères wrote books on various topics. Tom Lane on priestly ministry, Joe McCann on teaching science in secondary school, Myles Rearden on various aspects of spiritual direction, Pat Collins continued to turn out collections of articles under various headings, Michael Prior on various biblical issues, especially the Israeli-Palestinian conflict, James Murphy on literature and history in the 19th and 20th centuries, and the liturgical writings of Brian Magee could also be added to this list. And not to be forgotten are the collection of Fr Richard McCullen's sermons and talks through his twelve year period as Superior General. Great credit was due to these confrères who had the courage, the discipline and the tenacity to put these publications together.

*Renovations*

During my time in the Provincial Office, I was involved a good deal in the renovation of a number of houses.

St Peter's, Phibsboro

We decided to renovate the Community House at St Peter's, employing a local architect and a small building contractor. An excellent job was done over the course of the year. During this year some very difficult meetings took place with teachers in the three separate schools, and the corresponding three trustee groups and parishioners in the parish about merging the three schools into one. Now the renovation of these schools is underway.

## St Paul's, Raheny

We employed the same architect and builder for the renovations in St Paul's. New quarters were built above the Provincial Office. In the previous year I had had discussions with a number of confrères interested in archives, especially the Provincial archivist Tom Davitt, about the best location for the archives. We came to the conclusion that St Paul's or St Peter's were the two runners and eventually we opted for St Paul's. By the early summer the confrères in St Paul's community were able to move back into the renovated building and by September the archives and sleeping quarters for the Provincial were ready.

## St Vincent's, Cork

After selling the big property we had beside the church, we used some of the proceeds to purchase a house for a community of four on the opposite side of the street. We also did a good deal of work on the crypt and turned it into a meeting point for the parishioners.

## *Provincial Assembly 2000 – Evaluation Time*

During the spring of 2000 I set up a preparatory committee to prepare for the Provincial Assembly which took place at the beginning of June 2000. I saw this Assembly as a time to evaluate what had taken place over the previous five years to implement the recommendations of the Marino Assembly and especially to concentrate on the Provincial Plan called 'Vincentian Mission 2000'. We had feedback from confrères about the progress of various ministries in the province. I was keen to see all this against the background of what was taking place in the church in Western Europe and for this reason I had invited Michael Paul Gallagher SJ, to speak to us about the crisis in the church across Europe. A few months before the meeting I had circulated the article I had written for *Vincentiana* on this theme entitled 'Crisis for Vincentians in Europe'. Plenty of space was left for confrères to interact during these four days. I harped on the idea that this was evaluation time as I was coming near the end of my six years as provincial. We had not managed to attract young people to us over this period of time. It was the same for many other congregations. At the same time I had to acknowledge that I was uncomfortable about my leadership in this area.

In retrospect I can see now that Vincentian Mission 2000 had run its course and so had the Vincentian Family idea, coming from the General Assembly of 1998. What my own real feelings were about the situation in the Irish Province, and indeed across Europe, could be read between the lines in the article I had contributed to *Vincentiana*. The main thesis of the article was that the two 'foundation' ministries of the Congregation of the Mission were in crisis in Western Europe – parish missions and formation of priests.

*Visit to Beijing*
In January 2000 I travelled with Joseph Loftus to Hong Kong, spending a few hours there and then travelled on to Beijing where we were welcomed at the airport by Padraig Regan. I stayed in a hotel near the university compound and over a period of eight days had a marvellous encounter with this amazing city, visiting the Forbidden City, the Great Wall, Tiananmen Square, the Winter Palace, etc. On certain days, in semi-darkness, I celebrated the Eucharist with Padraig, Joseph and Matthias (an Indian confrère). We had a number of simple meals together and I joined Padraig for the celebration of the Sunday Eucharist in the Irish Embassy. After Mass, over a cup of coffee, I met a number of the Irish people living in Beijing. Maurice Kavanagh had looked after a church in the middle of the city until the communists put him in prison for a few years before releasing him to the West. One evening I was shown an uncensored video of the student demonstrations in Tiananmen Square and the suppression which followed. I listened to some Chinese students who were visiting Padraig. By 10.00 pm they had to leave as this was curfew time for all students to leave the visiting lecturer's compound.

*Superior General's Consultation, January 2001*

For two weeks at the end of January 2001 Fr Bob Maloney consulted every member of the Irish Province in both the Irish and British regions about the post of Provincial. Because it was a crucial time in the life of the province I had asked Fr Maloney to do the consultation himself. After considering some other possibilities, he agreed to do so. Having done the visitation of the Irish Province some twenty years previously and having visited the Province on quite a few occasions since then, I felt that he had the best overall knowledge of the confrères and our needs. From a number of conversations he had with me over the previous two years, he knew I wanted to hand over to another confrère, to someone who could approach our situation with a fresh mind and someone who could initiate a new provincial plan.

During Fr Maloney's visit to the Irish region, a dinner was held in All Hallows in honour of Fr Paul Roche, who had been appointed the first Visitor of the new Province of St Cyril and St Methodius.

*Last Days in the Provincial Office*

A lot of uncertainty entered my life during my last year in the Provincial Office. Towards the end of August in the year 2000 I was informed by a specialist in the Mater Hospital that I had lost the sight in my left eye. The condition was diagnosed as AMD (Age-related Macular Degeneration). My sister Mary had developed this condition two years previously so I had some warning of what the condition was all about. In February 2001 the sight in my right eye also started to deteriorate and by the time I left the Provincial Office in August 2001 my capacity to read was virtually down to zero. I continued to retain my peripheral vision which enabled me to move around with relative ease.

A month or so before I left the Provincial Office in mid-August 2001 I made the decision to donate all my books to the library in All Hallows. This was an extremely difficult decision as I had accumulated an excellent library in certain areas of philosophy, especially contemporary philosophy, moral theology, philosophy of religion, pastoral theology, especially in the area of ministry, psychology of religion and a number of areas in philosophy of education. One of my hopes after leaving the

Provincial Office was to write something on the topic of mission and ministry which I had been reflecting about over the previous eight years. During my short sabbatical break in Leuven, in the autumn of 1994, I had formulated the outlines of a book on this subject. My capacity to do this was now very much in question.

I wrote a short letter to the confrères of the Province thanking them for their kindness to me during my six years in the Office of Provincial. I also thanked the eight confrères I had worked closely with on the Provincial Council and the confrères who had worked on various commissions. I realised at that time that space and distance would be needed to evaluate what had been accomplished during these six years. At a time of retrenchment one of the greatest challenges we faced in our province was seeing the world around us with the eyes of faith and realising that, despite the apparent decline in the church in Western Europe, the kingdom of God was taking root in all kinds of new ways in our 'secularised' world.

On the evening of 15 August I handed over to Kevin O'Shea, wishing him well in his term of office and assuring him that he would have the support of the confrères, as I had.

# CHAPTER 10

# On the Road
## The European Religious Landscape
## 2002-2007

Over the past five years I have had an opportunity to make short
visits to Belgium, The Netherlands, Germany, Austria, Poland
and France. The following are brief accounts of some of these
visits highlighting aspects of the religious landscape in each of
these countries. My purpose is to open a small window on what
is taking place in these countries. Doing this may help us to see
the Irish situation in a larger context.

### I. INNSBRUCK - KARL RAHNER- THE CHURCH OF THE FUTURE
#### AUGUST 1995

In August I travelled by train from Garmisch-Partenkirchen to
Vienna, stopping off in Innsbruck for a few days. It brought back
memories of my first visit to Innsbruck in 1964 when I spent a
few days in the Jesuit House of Studies where Karl Rahner was
living and lecturing in the university close by. I had just read an
article he had written on the first draft of the Constitution on the
Church (*Lumen Gentium*) which had summarised some of the
Council discussions on this document. To describe the idea of
the church as the Sacrament of the Salvation of the World he had
used the image of the morning sunlight breaking over the
mountains. The valleys were still in darkness but through the
course of the morning the sunlight would find its way to these
valleys. This was Rahner's way of portraying the role of the
church in the world. The church, like the sun glittering on the
mountains tops, is the light of salvation to all peoples, especially
to those living in darkness and the shadow of death in the valleys below. As I sat down to breakfast in this Jesuit House of
Studies in Innsbruck that morning and looked out on the sunlight glittering on the tops of the snow covered mountains, I
began to realise where Rahner got this image. It would have

been part of the morning landscape for him at least on the days the mountain tops were visible. It was an image that would have been familiar to the students he lectured to in the nearby university.

Over the last few months as I have searched for ways to describe the situation of the church in Europe today, this striking image of the church has kept coming back to me as has Rahner's often quoted statement that the church of the future will be a diaspora church and a church for mystics. I have come to think that it is one of the best descriptions of the situation of the church in Europe that I am familiar with. Rahner used this imagery and made this statement about the church in the 1960s when the Vatican Council was in full flow. Forty years later, his image and his description of the church of the future seems quite prophetic.

## The Church of the Future – a Diaspora Church

On a number of occasions in the 1960s Rahner referred to the church of the future as a diaspora church. Over the next ten years he kept returning to this theme, especially in a talk he gave to the German Bishops' conference in 1972. This talk was published some years later under the title *The Future of the Church and the Church of the Future.*

We have grown up thinking of the church as one of increasing numerical growth from one era to the next. This may be true in some countries and in some continents but not in relation to the world population as a whole, which is increasing more rapidly. This is particularly true in some Asian countries such as China and India. We also ignore the fact that in many so-called 'Christian countries' many people are Christians in a very loose sense. There are many card-carrying Christians, and this would have become evident to Rahner in his own pastoral work in various parishes in Austria and Germany after the Second World War. Very often the criteria we use for church membership are external criteria. Rahner wants to go beyond this to internal criteria and at the same time he does not want to present the church as a fortress church cut off from the rest of the world. The church is the church of believing Christians and, at the same time, it is the sacrament of salvation for all. Rahner sums up the main reason why the church of the future will be a diaspora church in the following way:

> I want to place myself in the situation of an ordinary Catholic of the future, a layman, and ask him what will strike him in this document (*Lumen Gentium*) about the church in the future. Whether this will come about in twenty, thirty or fifty years does not matter.
>
> In the future there will continue to be Christian communities all over the world though not evenly distributed. Everywhere there will be 'little flock(s)' of Christians. The world population will be increasing more rapidly than the Christian community. There will be little flock(s) because men and women will be Christian not because of custom but because of a personal decision to follow Christ. They will be Christian not because of history or the homogeneity of the social milieu or because of public opinion. They will be Christian because of their own act of faith attained in a difficult struggle and one that is perpetually achieved anew.
>
> This 'little flock' will be a diaspora among the 'Gentiles'. There will no longer be Christian communities who put a stamp on people before they make a personal decision to be Christians. Christians will no longer have an independent historical structure in society. Everywhere Christians and non-Christians will have full and equal rights and together they will give society its character.
>
> The ideology of the state or of the super-state will not be Christian. The Christians will be the little flock of the gospel, perhaps being esteemed, perhaps being persecuted, bearing witness to the gospel in a clear and respected voice ... They will be brothers and sisters to one another because there will be few of them. They will be gathered around the altar announcing the death of the Lord. They will have reached their own personal decision of conscience to stake their hopes on the message of Jesus Christ. The church will have been led by the Lord of history into a new epoch.
>
> There will be no earthly advantage in being a Christian. All dignity and honour in the church will count for nothing in the eyes of the world. Office holders in the church will no

longer constitute a 'profession' in the secular sense. Christians will be brothers and sisters of the same flock, of the same faith, of the same hope, of the same love.

How will Christians as members of these diaspora communities see themselves in relation to the world? They will not see themselves as a church, cut off from others. Living in a vast world of non-belief, the Christian of the future will not see himself as living apart from the world. Neither will he see all these non-Christians excluded from salvation. He will see the church as the sacrament of salvation for all ... The church will be the tangible sign of salvation for all the nations.

Even as early as the 1970s Rahner foresaw the prospect of increasing secularisation in Austria and Germany and in other European countries too. He saw that changes in the relationship between church and state were likely and in both Germany and Austria he put a question mark over the future of the church tax, state support for religious instruction in schools and state support for Catholic and Protestant faculties of theology in state universities. I don't think that Rahner would have been too surprised at the exclusion of any mention of God in the recent EU Draft Treaty.

However Rahner's main point in talking about the church of the future as a diaspora church is that there will no longer be the support from society that there has been up to now and secondly to be a Christian will depend on a personal decision on the part of each person. Support will come from the 'little flock' they belong to.

## The Christian of the Future will be a Mystic

At first sight Rahner's statement that the Christian of the future will be a mystic or he or she will not exist at all is a startling one. However, it becomes apparent that by the word *mystic* in this context he is referring to someone who has had a profound experience of God and someone who has made a personal act of faith. The Christian's faith conviction is linked to an intimate and personal experience of Jesus Christ.

When Rahner says that the Christian of the future will be a mystic, he is not referring to extraordinary experiences such as visions, raptures or ecstasies. In Rahner's view, every Christian is called to a 'mysticism of everyday faith'. This faith is found in ordinary experiences of friendship, decisions of conscience made in the depths of one's being and acts of love and generosity to one's neighbour. He claims that there is only a difference of degree between this everyday mysticism and the mysticism of Teresa of Avila and John of the Cross.

> 'There has to be a personal experience of God. The ultimate decision of faith comes in the last resort not from rational argument but from the experience of God and his Spirit ... It is an inward experience made by the solitary Christian in silent prayer and in a final decision of conscience, unrewarded by anyone.

He goes on to say that this solitary decision of faith usually takes place in relation to an experience of the Spirit in a fraternal community. One is a correlative of the other. In this ecclesial context an experience of the Spirit becomes possible. At the same time, in saying all this Rahner puts himself at a certain distance from the Charismatic Movement and various practices such as speaking in tongues and being slain in the Spirit. On one occasion, when asked why he did not belong to the Charismatic Movement, he replied that there are summer Christians and winter Christians in the church. Summer Christians can appear to be very confident in their faith and radiate joy on all occasions. Winter Christians, on the other hand, have to struggle for their faith. One gets the impression that Rahner put himself in the latter category.

## Some Observations

Have Karl Rahner's predictions of forty years ago been realised? In Europe are we well on our way to being a diaspora church? With the recent depression of the German economy a significant number of Christians withdrew from paying church tax and this has led to financial crises in some German dioceses. Of even more significance, however, is the absence of young people participating in Sunday Eucharist and the shortage of priests to lead Christian communities. I have heard it said that because of the high average age of those attending church at present – which the EVS report says is around 13% for regular church-goers – this may come down to 6% over the next ten years. The greatest problem is, of course, the transmission of the faith to younger generations. If one takes Rahner's view seriously, it means finding ways to help men and women to reach an adult faith and to be able to make a free decision to be a Christian.

Is there a sense in which the church is moving into a new epoch as Rahner suggests?

It has taken us a long time to shake off the mind set of Christendom. We keep hankering back to a time in which the church was a powerful force in society. Indeed we hanker back to a time in which the church had control of education, health care and social welfare as well as control over the legislators and the laws they passed for our societies. Now the influence of the church has been marginalised or privatised. The reality of the church as a collection of diaspora communities is becoming more and more evident and we are beginning to realise that this could very well have certain advantages. We are no longer aligned with political powers and we have to fall back on the strength of the gospel to put forward our points of view. Is there a convergence here between what Rahner said in 1972 and what the French bishops said to Catholics in France in 1996?

Has Rahner's image of the church as the sacrament of salvation to the world been internalised by today's Christians?

Finally, the church does not cut itself off from the world. There is no tendency in Rahner's ecclesiology to see the church apart from the world. The church is the sacrament of salvation for the world. One does not turn the church into a fortress church. The church is not there for its own sake. It is there to be a light that shines in the darkness. It is a beacon that draws people to the light, as Rahner put it so eloquently some forty years ago in using the imagery of the sun rising on the snow-covered mountains and slowly lighting up the darkness of the valleys below.

## II. 'THE CHURCH IN EUROPE IS LIVING IN A BABYLONIAN EXILE'
### JULY 1999

Some years ago I attended a Summer School in the American College, Louvain, to follow up on some scripture and theology courses. One of the invited speakers to the Summer School was Cardinal Godfried Danneels who spent an evening with the group of 30 participants discussing the situation of the Catholic Church in Europe and especially in Belgium. It was the first time I heard him using the expression, 'The church in Belgium is living through a Babylonian exile.' He had just described difficulties he had the previous year when he had to appear in one of the courts to defend himself on how he had handled a serious criminal charge against one of his priests. He had lost the case in one of the lower courts but won it on an appeal to an upper court. I had to admire his honesty in the way he described the positive and negative factors that the church had to deal with in the contemporary European context.

When the time for questioning came, I asked the cardinal where the signs of hope were for the Catholic Church in Belgium today? I was very surprised with his response. He did not refer to any pastoral initiatives the church was taking to counter the secularisation forces at work in Belgian society or to pastoral efforts being made to build up parish communities. Instead he spent about ten minutes describing the extensive religious heritage in Belgium in the spheres of church architecture, music and literature. I was very surprised at this response and when I thought about it afterwards the most positive meaning I could give it was that he was highlighting for the group that 'beauty was the gateway to the Transcendent' for many people of our day. In the years that followed I was to learn more about the strengths and weaknesses of the Catholic Church in Belgium from conference papers Cardinal Danneels gave to various groups in London and elsewhere and from my own visits to Belgium cities – Louvain, Bruges, Ghent, Antwerp, Liege and Namur. A gifted linguist, he has given talks in many countries over the years about the future of the church in 'secularised Europe'. He has been regarded as a moderate voice in the church and one who has advocated dialogue with contemporary post-modern society. After listening to many speeches of his fellow European bishops at the 1999 special Synod for Europe decrying the evils of our secularised society, his speech contained the recurring refrain: 'It is not all negative.'

## *The Church in Belgium Today*

The decline of the church in Belgium is mirrored in many other countries in Western Europe. The 2000 EVS report continues to show a sharp decline in those participating in church life on a regular basis. The percentage given is 19% but many people think that the actual figure is much lower. The number who never attend a church in this traditionally Catholic country of 16 million people is estimated to be 47%.

The intake into seminaries has declined dramatically over the past thirty years. In 2004 there were more seminarians in the Netherlands than there were in Belgium. The seminaries in Antwerp and Ghent are closed. The seminary in Bruges has 12 students and the Archdiocese of Malines-Brussels, the largest diocese in Belgium with over seven million people, has had single figures in the Flemish and French speaking seminaries in recent years. One seminary that has improved its enrolment, is that of Namur where a Neo-Catechumenate seminary stands side by side with the diocesan seminary with a total of 45 students. When Bishop André Léonard was appointed Bishop of Namur in 1991, he brought a number of lay ministry courses to an end, sold a new seminary that had been built some twenty years ago and restored the old seminary which had remained in the ownership of the church. An indication of the church's weakening influence in society has been its failure to counter various kinds of legislation at odds with church teaching including 'assisted euthanasia'.

The euphoria of the post-Vatican II years in Belgium gave way to a time when many priests left the priesthood, so much so that many dioceses lost their 'middle management' and now, like many other countries of Western Europe, Belgium is struggling to maintain its parishes through clustering them. In the diocese of Antwerp, some priests are now looking after five parishes and the focus appears to be on building up parishes where there is a strong nucleus of committed Christians rather than trying to maintain parishes on a geographical basis. The Belgian Catholic Church moved slowly in providing trained pastoral ministers despite the fact that the theological department in Louvain turns out many lay graduates every year. 'The shortage of priests stands like a wall against the future of the church' is how Danneels describes the situation.

*The Challenges Facing the Catholic Church in Western Europe*
On a number of occasions Danneels has pointed out that in a certain sense the church is in crisis in every period of its history. There is a constant dying and rising taking place in all periods. Can we see where the dying is and where the rising is happening in Western Europe today? The crisis today is a crisis of birth pains – new life coming to birth. Our faith perspective leads us to believe that in our lives we reproduce the death and resurrection of Jesus Christ. This is a faith perspective which differs from what sociologists, psychologists, historians have to offer. What is interesting is that Danneels looks at present day realities from both a faith perspective and a perspective of the social sciences. He outlines the positive developments in both the church and society and at the same time he indicates what is inimical to the well-being of both. He knows that the idea of Belgium as a *civitas christiana* is long past. At the same time he resists the temptation to think of the church as a fortress church that cuts itself off from modern society. The church has to take society where it is today and to engage in a vigorous dialogue with what is both positive and negative in our contemporary world.

Danneels lists the following challenges for the church in Europe:

- *The Crisis of the perception of the Invisible*
  We no longer see the invisible. Science and technology have reduced the world to the visible. Sacramental signs and symbols no longer speak to many people. Without this capacity to read these sacramental signs, the Eucharist, and indeed all the sacraments, become meaningless or 'cosy folklore rituals'.
- *Reductive Rationalism*
  We live in a world dominated by rationality. Many movements in contemporary philosophy have done away with

any universal reading of the origin and destiny of the world. The different disciplines have become cut off from one another and all we can know are fragmentary bodies of knowledge. Modernity or post-modernity has deconstructed any universal narratives. Our capacity to reach universal principles in the sphere of knowledge or in the sphere of ethics has been put in question.

- *Wild Religiosity*

  There is an increasing interest in what Danneels calls 'wild religiosity' which he characterises as being self-centred and narcissistic.

  'God is not at the centre of this new religion. It is myself that is at the centre. I don't serve God. God serves me. There is no place or no need for personal conversion. Everything can be obtained without effort.'

  Danneels goes on to say that this religiosity manifests itself in sects of all kinds. He says that in Brussels they come into existence and go out of existence overnight. These sects are a protection of the individual against the anonymity of society and the anonymity that exists in many inner city parishes. 'The sects today are the unpaid bills of the big churches.'

  His critique of wild religiosity is not totally negative. He acknowledges that today it may be the starting point or springboard to obtain real spiritual food and the beginning of a person's journey to the Living God. It is where the church has to begin its dialogue with many people.

- *The Challenge of Islam*

  Fundamentalist Islam is very hard to dialogue with. It is a 'theocracy' like that which existed for many Christians in the Middle Ages. Up to now they have had no French Revolution to help them distinguish between church and state. On the other hand he points out that there is a moderate Islamic tradition that Christians can dialogue with – Islamic intellectuals in the tradition of Avicenna, Moses Maimonides and Averroes – three of the great Islamic scholars of the Middle Ages. Many Muslims have held on to a belief in God as 'transcendent'. They also take religious observances, such as prayer and fasting, seriously.

269

- *The Challenges of Asian Religions*

  Danneels has Buddhism especially in mind in this context. He gives the following reasons why Buddhism has gained a number of followers in the Western World, especially among the well-to-do classes. Buddhism is associated with being self-therapeutic, inculcating a sense of wisdom, providing healing techniques and leaning strongly towards pacifism. He goes on to say that we have to learn how to dialogue with Asian mentalities. The early Christians did it in the first centuries when the gospel came in contact with the Greco-Roman world, especially in regard to their philosophies and thought patterns. We are challenged today to do something similar in regard to the ancient civilisations of India and China.

- *Integrating Faith and Reason*

  Down the centuries the church has tried to dialogue with the philosophical ideas of every age. The church accepts that there will always be a tension between many of these philosophies and Christian belief. Danneels maintains that in recent times many philosophers have moved beyond what he refers to as 'ideological atheism'. Nevertheless theologians are called to enter into dialogue with philosophers of every age. This is, he suggests, what Pope John Paul II was doing in his encyclical, *Fides et Ratio* (1998). This is why Cardinal Mercier set up the Institute of Philosophy in Louvain University over 100 years ago. This continues to be the task that faces theologians in our modern or post-modern era. This dialogue helps to purify religious belief. Rather than shutting ourselves off from these philosophies, many of whom may appear to be alien, the task of the church in our day is to learn what is in harmony with Christian faith and what is at odds with it. The Catholic tradition has always taken the world of philosophy seriously. 'Philosophers help the church to realise that it has not got all the answers.'

### Living in a Babylonian Exile

On a number of occasions Danneels refers to the period we are living through in the Catholic Church as 'living in a Babylonian captivity'. Like the ancient Israelites, we too are living in exile. He wonders if we have tended to be Pelagian in the way we think about the renewal of the church in the post-Vatican II era. 'Did we think we could do it on our own? … Now we know that we need God's help if we are to take things forward.'

> We may not have the packed churches and bulging seminaries that we had in the past but what we do have is a humble and contrite heart. And even in our weakened and minority status we can still sing New Songs as the Israelites did in the Babylonian exile.

### III. LE SEMINAIRE DE PARIS – MAY 2003

In visits to Paris over the last ten years I have had many conversations with people about Cardinal Jean-Marie Lustiger's 'Seminaire de Paris '. Through these discussions I have learned about key elements in its approach to seminary formation. The more I learned about it, the more I began to be interested in the steps Cardinal Lustiger had taken to re-invigorate the traditional Tridentine seminary. And at the same time, I was left with a number of questions about this approach to the formation of priests in our Western European context today.

*A New Beginning*

Before 1984 seminarians for the archdiocese of Paris were educated at the Sulpician seminary of Issy-le-Moulineaux which served not only the archdiocese of Paris but also a number of the neighbouring dioceses too. Cardinal Lustiger had a number of concerns about this arrangement. With declining membership, how long could the Sulpicians be able to administer the seminary in Issy-le-Moulineaux? The archdiocese, like other dioceses in France, was losing a significant number of priests. A number of students and young priests were leaving the archdiocese of Paris to join monastic communities or religious orders. How could 'unity of formation' – the integration of spiritual, human, intellectual and pastoral aspects of formation – be safe-guarded? If one continued as before there was the danger that recruitment for priesthood could peter out as had happened in other seminaries in France.

To counter all this, Cardinal Lustiger took a number of steps to deepen priestly formation for his students and to establish a strong sense of priestly identity. These changes were very carefully thought out and implemented gradually through the 1980s. He took a number of steps to set formation of priests on a new footing and in doing this he ruffled some feathers.

## A Spiritual Year

The setting up of a spiritual year in December 1984 turned out to be the beginning of a ten-year process of formation. The first year students were moved to a new location in December 1984 to begin what came to be known as 'the spiritual year'. The archdiocese took over a vacant Augustinian convent attached to a hospital in Port Royale south of the city centre. Three priests were appointed to organise and to run this first stage of formation. Students followed a very detailed order of day which included lectures in scripture, spirituality and catechetics. This year also included a one month directed retreat and one month's experience of working with the poor. In the course of the year students were encouraged to join young people in pilgrimages to either Lourdes or to Paray-le-Monial.

The spiritual year was seen as an indispensable part of the overall programme of formation. It is basically a year in which students are introduced to methods of prayer, silence and the reading of the Bible. In fact, they are encouraged to read the whole of the Bible during the course of the year. The order of day is very tightly organised, balancing periods of study, prayer, lectures and pastoral activity. They are expected to avail of spiritual direction on a weekly basis. Half a day each week is spent on a pastoral assignment. Access to print and electronic media is limited.

The purpose of this year is to enable students to deepen their spiritual lives and to help them to discern if they have a vocation to celibate priesthood. Cardinal Lustiger wanted men who were prepared to commit themselves with faith and conviction to the formation programme for ministerial priesthood. This year is quite an intensive and demanding one. On average about 30% leave entirely or enter a religious order or a monastic community. At present about 15 students begin this year in early September. In many ways it resembles a traditional novitiate year of a religious order or congregation.

*Living in Small Communities*

When students have completed their Spiritual Year they proceed, not to a seminary as such, but to living in small communities. This is one of the most novel aspects of the *Seminaire de Paris*. They are divided into groups of eight to ten students and live in presbyteries quite near to the Cathedral of Notre Dame. Cardinal Lustiger and his advisers were keen to get away from any kind of institutional living which they believed can run counter to both human and spiritual development. 'Those who live in barrack-like buildings in large groups, such as schoolboys and soldiers, take on a barracks-like mentality.' If seminarians live in small groups there is a better chance that there will be real engagement with one another. They will challenge one another to grow and mature.

In the first two years in these parish communities, students concentrate on the study of philosophy, which is followed by four years of theology. This was a return to the traditional approach of beginning with philosophy over the first two years and then devoting four full years to the study of theology. Through these six years students continue to live in presbyteries with two priests in charge who are also responsible for the parishes they are living in. All these parishes are within striking distance of the École Cathedrale which is located on a side street near Notre Dame Cathedral. Some of these parishes are within walking distance and the others are easily accessible by bicycle, bus or metro. He also wanted men who would be deeply aware of their identity as priests and his hope was that the mutual sharing and support they provide for one another in these communities would forge strong bonds between them and help to strengthen their sense of priestly identity. He also believed that it is this sense of priestly identity that would carry them through the buffeting of a secularised society which inevitably would come their way.

In so far as their studies permit, they participate in the life of their parishes, getting first hand knowledge of the range of parish and apostolic activities going on all around them. Even in the midst of this activity, they are expected to pray for an hour each day apart from Office and Mass. They learn very quickly where the pressures may come from which they will have to cope with later on.

A number of the priests in the formation houses are also teaching in the École Cathedrale or studying for postgraduate degrees or holding down chaplaincy posts in schools or universities. There is one overall rector of the seminary. It is part of his task to make sure that there is a unity of purpose from one community to another. He gives conferences on a regular basis to all the students about aspects of priestly spirituality. He also presides at a weekly meeting of all the priests involved in formation in each of the presbyteries to monitor the progress of each student.

Setting up this new seminary structure has been difficult. It has been seen as a criticism of how priests were formed in the past both in Paris and elsewhere. The priests involved in formation tend to be chosen from the younger cohort of priests in the diocese and this has caused its own tensions. Many 'post 68' priests feel that they have been passed over.

*Post Ordination – Three Years of Continuing Education*
For three years after students are ordained they continue the formation programme. This means that the overall programme is a ten year one. The format of these final three years is worked out between the priest and the parish priest he is assigned to work with after ordination. The tasks assigned to him include working with young people, catechising, preaching on Sundays and in being available for the sacrament of penance in a big city centre church. Each term there is a meeting of each year group in which they pray together and discuss how things are progressing for each of them. At the end of these three years of continuing education, there is a formal end to this post-ordination period after which they receive a new assignment.

*The École Cathedrale*
Cardinal Lustiger founded the École Cathedrale in 1984. This 'school' of theology equipped with lecture rooms, a chapel and a good library is located in the shadows of the cathedral itself. The École Cathedrale was under the direct control of the cardinal and it sees itself as adhering to the authentic interpretation of the teachings of Vatican II. Different categories of courses are on offer for the different groups who use the École Cathedrale – lay

Christians, seminarians, religious and priests. What is known as *The Studium* is mainly for seminarians and those supported by their bishops or religious superiors.

One of the most controversial aspects of the Lustiger seminary model was the setting up of the school of theology. People wondered why one of the existing theological centres could not have been used, such as the Institut Catholique or the Centre Sévres run by the Jesuits, both located near the centre of the city. The fact of the matter was that Cardinal Lustiger wanted control over the theology taught to his students to make sure that there was a unity of purpose in all aspects of priestly formation. He did not want his seminarians exposed to diverse theological views about a number of controversial issues in the church today.

The École Cathedrale is a private institution with no state support. The lecturers are very often priests of the archdiocese of Paris. The emphasis is on a theology that is kerygmatically and catechetically orientated. One gets the impression that running through many of the programmes on offer in the École Cathedrale is a strong thrust towards evangelisation.

*Observations and Questions*

*An expanding seminary* There is no denying the success of *Le Seminaire de Paris* in terms of increasing the intake of students. The number of students for the archdiocese of Paris has doubled, moving from 60 in1984 to120 today. To reverse the decline in the number of seminarians to this extent is a remarkable achievement. The background of many students is that of the New Movements and various charismatic groups that have flourished in or near Paris.

*Distinctiveness of priestly ministry* Running through the formation programme is a strong emphasis on the distinctiveness of priestly ministry. There is no blurring of the distinction between priestly and lay ministry. The idea of belonging to a community of priests is very strong and it is from this brotherhood of priests that one draws on for support and encouragement in the priesthood.

*An evangelising theology in a ministerial context* One detects a strong kerygymatic and evangelical thrust in the courses taught at the École Cathedrale. There appears to be a reaction to theology that is too academic or out of touch with daily living. At the same time, the distinctiveness of priestly formation seems to be safeguarded by the setting up of what is known as *The Studium* where the majority of students are seminarians, in contrast to what are known as the Public Courses which are open to laymen and women from Paris and elsewhere. The beginning and the end of theology in the École Cathedrale is a ministerial one. Apart from wanting to have control over who was going to teach his seminarians, this is another reason why Cardinal Lustiger set up his own theologate rather than avail of the resources of the other theological centres in Paris.

*Living in small groups* There is no doubt that in setting up groups with ten students and two priests in each of these houses there is a very generous commitment of personnel to the formation of these students by priests who are also carrying other commitments. From one point of view, one could argue that what one has are eight seminaries rather than one. The weekly meeting of staff involved in formation, and a weekly Mass and days of recollection together for all students, does try to offset any tendency these small communities may have of going their own way.

*Transcending 'lone ranger' priesthood* There must be plenty of challenges arising in the efforts of each group to live the Christian life together – challenges which arise for both students and priests alike. This approach certainly challenges the 'lone ranger' syndrome that affects many priests. One would like to know what is the ten and twenty year effect of this kind of formation. Are these priests keen to continue this kind of group living later on in life, maintaining a life of prayer together and a life of mutual support?

*The sources of priestly vocations* There are indications that a significant number of students in *Le Seminaire de Paris* are coming from one or other of what is called the New Movements. Would it be true to say that their formation in these New Movements over a lengthy period of time, not only nurtured their desire to become priests, but also gave them the strength to withstand the withering effects of our secularised culture in taking the courageous step to enter *Le Seminaire de Paris*?

*A comprehensive theology of ministry* The most frequent criticism I have heard about *Le Seminaire de Paris* is that there is very little focus in the course of formation on preparing students for collaboration with lay men and women in the running of parishes. I have wondered is this the price Cardinal Lustiger was prepared to pay in emphasising the distinctiveness of priestly ministry in contrast to all forms of lay ministry. We need a theology of ministry that transcends these differences and still at the same time does justice to both the ministry of the priest and of lay ministers. The charge is often made that in many countries what we are doing is 'clericalising lay men and women and laicising clerics'. Surely there are more positive and constructive ways of relating the ministries of priests and lay ministers to one another and outlining the complementary roles they play in promoting the kingdom of God. I get the impression that in *Le Seminaire de Paris* the specificity of ministerial priesthood is emphasised at the expense of the role of lay men and women. At a time when so many parish communities are being carried by committed lay men and women we need a theology of ministry that moves beyond this kind of over-simplification.

*Final Comment*

Last summer as I walked through the Church of St Germain des Prés I picked up a ten-page newsletter from the Paris seminary. I was struck by the upbeat tone of Cardinal Lustiger's successor, Archbishop Andre Vingt-Trois, who was in fact the first rector of *Le Seminaire de Paris*. On average about 20 priests are being ordained each year for the archdiocese and now some of these priests are beginning to help out in neighbouring dioceses. It left me with the question: Is the renewal of the church in France going to come through a reform of priestly ministry as it did in the 17th century and is *Le Seminaire de Paris* a pointer towards how that reform may take place?

IV. LAY MINISTRY IN THE DIOCESE OF AACHEN
NOVEMBER 2003

On a crisp November morning I walked from the Oblate House perched on a hill twenty minutes from the centre of the city of Aachen. This renovated building was a former centre from where Oblate priests went out to give missions and retreats in parishes in the surrounding dioceses. Now it was a place where visitors from third-world countries could stay for a few days when they were presenting their case for funding from *Misereor* or *Caritas International*.

From this hilltop I walked through parks and streets lined with restaurants, catering for the many students who study in a variety of technical institutes in this part of the city. I crossed the ancient Market Square to the historic cathedral. The core of the octagonal shaped building was completed in 800AD. This is where Charlemagne was crowned head of the Holy Roman Empire. The Gothic extension was added in the 14th century. I had plenty of time to look around this ancient cathedral before my scheduled meeting with the director of the lay ministry department in the diocesan offices nearby. This cathedral, which embodied over 1,000 years of church history, made me aware that discussions about new forms of ministry in the church today needed to be seen in an historical perspective in which many changes had already occurred.

*Some Facts and Figures*
Aachen is in a very Catholic part of Germany bordering the Rhineland and contiguous to Catholic regions to the west in Belgium and the Netherlands. The diocese was originally part of the Cologne archdiocese. It was set up as a diocese in 1932.

- The total population is around 1.5 million, of which 60% are Catholics. The number of regular churchgoers is 12%. Since 1950 there has been a steady drop from year to year of those attending church on a regular basis (1958: 48%, 1970: 35%, 1980: 23%, 2006: 12%).
- The total number of priests is 728. This figure includes religious order priests as well as diocesan priests. One has to keep in mind that this figure includes many priests who are

retired. The average age of priests is over 70 years. At present there are four seminarians and two more who are doing their pastoral year in parishes as deacons. In addition to this there are a small number of students studying theology in various universities who have indicated an interest in becoming priests.

- In contrast to this there are 342 lay ministers in the diocese. This breaks down into 225 Parish Assistants and 117 Pastoral Assistants who maintain administrative posts at diocesan and regional levels. As the number of priests declines it is from this group of lay ministers that the vitality and the vision for the future are likely to come.

- In recent years the diocese has come under severe financial pressure which has raised a number of questions about financial viability with consequent anxiety for lay personnel. A plan has just been put in place to cut back the number of parishes from 518 to 72 clusters with two priests and a number of lay ministers in each of these new parish clusters. The diocese hopes to implement this plan over a five-year period. This plan includes a 50 million euro cut back in the diocesan budget. Already a number of salaried lay men and women have been made redundant and others are worried about their pension rights.

*Interview with the Director of the Office in charge of Lay Ministry*
This interview took place in the Director's office in the Diocesan Centre close to the cathedral. Thomas, a married man in his early forties, gave me a friendly welcome. For over an hour he gave very clear answers to my questions.

There are two levels of lay ministry in German dioceses. One group is called Pastoral Assistants (*Pastoralreferants*). They follow a five-year university programme, specialising in theology. This is followed by three years of practical training with placements in parishes and other contexts. The second group is known as Parish Assistants (*Gemeindereferants*). Their course takes three and a half years (seven semesters) of theological studies in either a university or college. This is followed by three years pastoral formation, with placements in parishes. It is interesting to note that the Pastoral Assistants spend the same length of time in training as do seminarians and the Parish Assistants are not far behind. There are two levels of salary corresponding to the two levels of preparation. The Pastoral Assistants receive a salary equivalent to that of a secondary school teacher in Germany. The salaries of the Parish Assistants are equivalent to that of primary school teachers.

In 1987 the German Bishops' Conference brought out a handbook dealing with all aspects of preparing men and women for lay ministry. This handbook contained a set of regulations to govern all that was taking place in German dioceses. There were two reasons why the bishops went down this road. The first reason was to follow through on the implementation of Vatican II's thrust to take seriously the concept of the church as the 'People of God'. A Christian community that is fully alive tries to avail of the talents and gifts of lay men and women to maintain and develop Christian communities and to encourage them to play a part in the building up of the church and the bringing of a Christian influence to bear on society. The second reason was a more mundane one. By the mid-1970s the number of seminarians had started to decline in a serious way. By that time it was evident that the Catholic Church would have a smaller number of priests available in the immediate future. One way to offset this decline in the number of priests was to open doors for laymen and women to study theology and to prepare them to exercise various ministries at both parish and diocesan levels. By the time the handbook was put together in 1987 a number of dioceses had already gone down this road. The Archdiocese of Cologne, under the leadership of Cardinal Hoffner, was one of the first dioceses in Germany to do this and of course the fact that many German dioceses at this time were in a strong financial position helps one to understand why salaries for lay ministry became a common feature of the German Catholic Church. In more recent years, with the decline in the number of priests the second factor has begun to predominate. This does not mean that all German bishops are happy with the involvement of laymen and women in lay ministry. A small number of bishops complain about the lack of a faith commitment or that a number of these lay ministers lack 'a sense of vocation'. However, most of the German bishops are supportive of these developments.

Students who are opting for lay ministry have a 'spiritual mentor' who will keep in touch with them and encourage them to follow courses in spirituality, and to become acquainted with various forms of prayer. Some of the practical formation, which lasts three years, is done in collaboration with priests but the degree of collaboration of seminarians and lay men and women at this level can vary from one diocese to another. At the practical level of pastoral formation, a good deal of emphasis is put on supervision in their pastoral placements in parishes, hospitals, prisons or wherever the students are located.

At the end of their practical formation, both Pastoral Assistants and Parish Assistants are offered contracts by the diocese – that is if they have completed the programmes satisfactorily. Some students opt to work outside an ecclesial context. Some apply for positions advertised in their own or in other dioceses. On being taken on by the diocese, pension arrangements are also put in place. Both groups pay into the state pension fund.

One area of dissatisfaction among the Parish Assistants bears on mobility. Once they make a contract with the bishop and are placed in a certain parish or cluster of parishes, they may find that there is very little opportunity to move on to another parish. Some are happy enough with this situation but others want to get more experience in another situation, especially if they are having difficulties working in a particular team.

*An Interview with a Parish Pastoral Worker*

The following interview took place with Claudia, a married woman in her twenties working in a town of 12,000 people about an hour's journey north of Aachen. Claudia was working in a cluster of three parishes with two priests and a number of lay ministers.

After leaving secondary school Claudia went to a college in Paderbörn where she followed a theology programme over a three and a half-year period. She had opted to be a Parish Assistant. This was followed by three years of pastoral training with placements in parishes where she was carefully supervised and inducted into various aspects of parish life. She specialised in the area of working with children to prepare them for the reception of the sacraments. When Claudia applied for entry to the college in Paderbörn 14 places were available for her own diocese in that particular year. Thirteen students were accepted on to the course.

After six and a half years of training she was given a contract by the bishop and appointed to a parish on the outskirts of Aachen. She spent three years there and then she moved to this town where she was now in her third year. It was her intention to work here for about eight years and then she said that she would be prepared to move on to another parish. All this, of course, depended on her husband's occupation and his willingness to move as well as the school provision for her own children. At present there are about 1,000 churchgoers in the cluster of three parishes in this town. She has a good working relationship with the two priests who are in their forties.

In providing sacramental preparation to children, she was aware that many of them would give up coming to church later on. She saw her task not as trying to fill churches but to 'sow some seeds' that might mature later on. The fact that a lot of Catholics were not churchgoers was a fact of life she had to live with. She seemed to take all this for granted.

Claudia has a diocesan supervisor who comes to visit her from time to time. If she runs into any difficulties in her work she is able to discuss them with this person. She also gets support from other lay ministers, especially the group she graduated with. They meet regularly to give one another support and encouragement.

They were not allowed to preach but they could give what she called 'a faith witness' at the end of Mass from time to time. This appears to be a way of getting around Canon Law on the restriction of preaching to ordained ministers. On the other hand, pastoral workers can hold the post of chairperson of the parish council.

Coming near the end of her course in Paderbörn, the students in her year met for a number of times to discuss what kind of graduation rite they would like. Some groups opt for a religious service in the cathedral of the diocese. Others prefer to have this ceremony in the college where they are graduating. I got the impression that this was an important aspect of their formation and helped to establish their identity as lay ministers.

Claudia acknowledged that the shortage of priests is likely to get worse as time goes on. A number of German dioceses have begun to take priests from other countries, especially priests from India, Poland and some African countries. I was to learn later that the archdiocese of Cologne was going down this road and that plans were in place to set up a two-year programme for such priests so that they could have a reasonable command of the German language and have some knowledge of German culture. However I got the impression that no clear-cut policy has been established in the diocese of Aachen in regard to this.

*Reflections*

Both Thomas and Claudia were very professional in the way they answered my questions. Thomas provided me with the 'nuts and bolts' of the structures for lay ministry in the diocese. Claudia gave me an idea of the kinds of work Parish Assistants were engaged in. She was very loyal to her fellow pastoral workers and the priests she was working with. She gave me the impression of enjoying her work and of being at home with the church as she was experiencing it. She saw her primary task in terms of 'maintenance' rather than 'mission'.

The only negative comment Claudia made was regarding the difficulty she had with an Indian priest in another parish she had worked in. He was not used to collaborating with women in his own culture and this was accentuated in the feminist climate of Germany. A friend who lives in Aachen said to me later that her reluctance to comment on the fact of the shortage of priests in Germany was more a matter of 'perplexity and resignation' about the actual situation, an attitude which was widespread among many priests too.

After going down the road of recruiting and educating pastoral workers for many years, the diocese of Aachen appears to be cutting back on the number of candidates it accepts now. This is coming out of the acute financial pressures the diocese is experiencing at the present time. I sensed some anxiety about job security and the ability of the diocese to maintain pension agreements.

This highlighted for me the debate that is going on in a number of European countries about the pros and cons of salaried lay ministry in contrast to volunteer lay ministry. Comparisons between what has happened in many German dioceses over the past thirty years where financial resources were available, at least up to now, and what has taken place in many French dioceses where financial resources were very scarce and where there was a greater reliance on volunteers, are worth reflecting on. I am not at all sure that the two different approaches can be reduced to the availability or absence of financial resources. The different relationship between church and state in France and Germany plays a part in this. But it also raises questions about the degree of insecurity one is prepared to live with if one is proclaiming gospel values.

I got no sense of any new missionary thrust or efforts being made to draw back people who had fallen away from church practice. Most of the people I had met seemed to be quite happy to live with the *status quo* and whatever efforts were being made seemed to be to look after the 12% or less who were coming to church on a regular basis. It was accepted that most young people who had followed sacramental programmes – Communion, Reconciliation and Eucharist – would fall away as they grew up. I found Claudia's remark that she was 'sowing a few seeds that might mature later on' somewhat fatalistic but her words had the ring of the gospel about them. I could not detect any new sense of mission or a desire to move beyond the *status quo*. I felt that there was much more involved than restructuring parishes or even in training lay men and women to replace the declining number of priests.

My conversations with Thomas and Claudia gave me plenty to reflect on. They both came across to me as dedicated to the work they were engaged in. I came away from Aachen thinking that there was much more to be learned about aspects of lay ministry in the German context.

## V. BOVENDONK – ANOTHER PATH TO PRIESTHOOD
### JUNE 2004

On a summer's evening in early June of 2004, I arrived in the small Dutch village of Bovendonk, just over the Belgian border. I had travelled the 15 kilometres west from Breda, through the flat Dutch countryside with its rows of trees, cultivated fields and well-kept houses. After passing the parish church in the middle of the village we drove up a beautiful tree-lined avenue to an imposing seminary building. I was to discover later that this seminary had been designed by a famous Dutch architect, Petrus Cuypers, who had also designed the Rijksmuseum and the ornate Central Railway Station in Amsterdam at the end of the 19th century. This seminary had served generations of priests in the diocese of Breda for nearly 100 years. Over the next two days I was to learn more about a very interesting approach to the formation of priests in the Netherlands.

*Beginnings*
In the turbulent post-Vatican II years Bovendonk seminary, like other Dutch seminaries, came to an abrupt end. In 1967 the existing seminaries in the country were closed. The leadership in the Dutch Catholic Church had come to the conclusion that seminaries, as they existed, were no longer appropriate places to prepare students for priesthood. Student numbers were rapidly declining. There needed to be some rationalisation of existing centres of formation – diocesan seminaries and theologates of religious orders. It was agreed that from now on five theological centres in Utrecht, Tilburg, Nijmegen, Heerlen and Amsterdam, would provide for the theological needs of seminarians in the Netherlands. These centres would also provide for the increasing number of lay students who wanted to study theology and prepare for the exercise of various ministries including that of 'pastoral worker', a ministry now opening up in the Dutch Catholic Church. Over the following twenty years these centres had varying degrees of success. In 1973 the Bishop of Roermond reopened his seminary and ran it along traditional lines amidst a good deal of controversy about the quality of students and the kind of formation on offer there.

In 1983, Msgr Ernst, Bishop of Breda, decided to open the doors of the diocesan seminary at Bovendonk once again. When the seminary had closed in 1967 it had been purchased by a property developer who had built houses on the extensive grounds. However, because the seminary itself was a listed building he could not get permission to develop it. It had remained vacant for ten years. The property was sold back to the diocese for the princely sum of two guilders. Despite the ten-year period of non-use the building was still in reasonably good condition and it was this building Msgr Ernst decided to use as a centre for a new kind of seminary.

In the 1980s Bishop Ernst had observed that many people in their middle years were changing their occupations and professions. It dawned on him that some of these people might be interested in priesthood. He reopened the seminary in Bovendonk on a new kind of footing. By widening his horizons on the nature of seminary formation, he had a use and a need for this building once again. He was influenced by a seminary for 'late vocations' in Antwerp, over the border in Belgium. However, what Msgr Ernst had in mind was going to be different.

*A Non-Residential Seminary*
Instead of bringing candidates together in a residential setting he decided to leave these candidates at their place of work and asked them to commute to Bovendonk at weekends from Friday afternoon to Sunday lunchtime for lectures and tutorials. So while remaining at work these students attended 21 weekends in Bovendonk each year for four years, covering the essentials of theology, philosophy and spirituality. After the first year, if the students could negotiate it, they could cut down their work commitments to four days each week, using the extra day to read in the library and to prepare their coursework assignments. However, having a job and holding on to it was a condition for entry into the formation programme. Another condition of acceptance was that they be active members of their parish communities. Since the 1960s many forms of both voluntary and salaried lay ministry had developed in the Netherlands. It was taken for granted that to be a member of a Christian community, be it a parish or some other group, one committed one's talents

and gifts to building up and supporting this community. The courses in scripture, theology and related subjects opened up their minds to the riches of the Catholic theological tradition. Participating in these 21 weekends each year for four years put a good deal of pressure on the students. The weekend seminars provided a contrast to the other kinds of work they were engaged in during the week.

In the fifth and sixth year students, gave up their jobs, took up residence in parishes and worked full-time there. They continued to attend Bovendonk to cover various aspects of pastoral theology. A mentoring process was put in place to monitor their initiation into parish life. At the end of the sixth year they were ordained to priesthood.

Having looked carefully at the content of the curriculum for the first four years of this course I was impressed at the amount of theology, biblical studies, and related subjects that were covered on this in-service basis over the 21 weekends each year. The students had to work intensively to keep up with the range of courses on offer and to complete the course work requirements. A variety of adult education methodologies were used. The programme was a demanding one and there was a good deal of pressure on these students to stay the course and maintain their professional work commitments at the same time. Built into the weekends were times for prayer and Eucharist as well as time for socialising in which students had opportunities to get to know one another.

*Staffing*
Apart from the Rector who lives in the seminary and the Director of Studies, a layman, the staff is part-time. They are carefully selected to fit in with the aims of the seminary and to communicate a theology with a focus on Christian living and also to work closely with the students to help them to integrate their theology courses with their experience. A number of staff come from various orders and congregations of men and women, bringing with them a variety of charisms and spiritualities. Particular attention is given to the integration of theology with their life experiences to avoid any kind of dualism. Assisting students on the road to personal integration was an important aim of the staff.

The rector has been in charge for the last 12 years. As a young man he emigrated to Brazil. After a few years he entered a seminary there and completed his seminary training against a background of the intense efforts of the Brazilian bishops to communicate the riches of the Second Vatican Council to both priests and lay men and women. He missed out on all the polarisation of church groups in the Netherlands. He was familiar with a Latin American situation where there was a grave shortage of priests. In Brazil a small percentage of Catholics attend church on a regular basis. The current 10% practice rate among Catholics in the Netherlands is similar to what he had experienced in Brazil. There was also a situation in Brazil where 80% of the services on a Sunday were conducted by laity, 80% of whom were women. In contrast to the Netherlands, he remarked that priests in Brazil were reasonably sure of their identity and roles as priests. Laymen and women were also conscious of their roles in both church and society, not as auxiliaries of priests but with their own distinctive vocation.

The rector lives easily with the notion of a variety of seminaries or theologates to respond to the needs of different kinds of student. Those who are interested in a more 'academic' theology are able to go to university departments of theology in Tilburg or Nijmegen. He spoke about the German seminary model in which a good deal of emphasis is put on intellectual formation and the French model in which the emphasis is on collegial living. I learned that Neo-Catechumenate seminaries have opened their doors in two Dutch dioceses, that of Haarlem and Roermond. Plans were under way to develop a Pontifical University in the city of Utrecht.

*Students*
Between 1983 and 2003, 75 priests had been ordained, the majority of whom are diocesan priests. A quarter of those ordained belonged to religious orders or congregations. There was very little post-ordination fall out and the departure of students during their six years of formation was about thirty percent – a figure well below the usual fall out figure of 50% or more.

In its first year of foundation, 1983, over twenty students enrolled in Bovendonk. This number grew gradually to 47 in the

1990s. However, in recent years the annual enrolment has fallen back to the twenties. A great range of professional backgrounds are represented – health-care workers, a lawyer, a baker, a builder, local government officials, teachers and so on. There is also a great range of intellectual backgrounds – from those with the equivalent of university entrance to those with higher technical qualifications. Some find the academic requirements of the course too demanding and drop out. Students make a contribution to the cost of the course but dioceses and religious congregations cover 80% of the fees.

### Pastores Dabo Vobis

On a number of occasions during our conversations the rector touched on the fact that he was operating inside the framework of *Pastores Dabo Vobis* and especially the opportunities opened up by paragraph 64. This paragraph refers to the fact that many vocations to the priesthood today come from an older age group – men who have been engaged in various professions for a number of years.

> It may not always be possible, and indeed often it is not even to be recommended, that these students follow the programme of the major seminary. A specific programme needs to be provided for them; one that is adapted to their needs. (par 64)

If it is true that the students entering seminaries today in the Western world are predominantly students who are in a much older age group than 18 year-old school leavers, this statement of *Pastores Dabo Vobis* has to be taken seriously. What is happening in Bovendonk points to one possible way forward. The old pattern of students proceeding straight to seminaries after leaving secondary school is disappearing in many parts of Europe. There are good psychological reasons for postponing entry into seminaries of whatever kind until later. At the age of 18 many young people are still trying to find themselves and they are not in a position to make an initial commitment to a way of life such as priesthood. Of course there are exceptions. One could also argue that making even this initial commitment presupposes an adult conversion to Christianity which for many people comes later, often as a result of a crisis in their personal or professional lives. Bovendonk offers some possibilities of thinking beyond the traditional seminary framework.

*Observations*
*Making the decision for priesthood gradually over a four year period*
The fact that students remain in a work situation means that the decision for priesthood is a gradual one. Over a four-year period they are able to explore this calling with the help of a spiritual director instead of making what may appear to be a once-and-for-all decision to enter a residential seminary. This fits in very much with the mentality of the younger generation today who often find it difficult to make a once-and-for-all decision which the giving up of their jobs might imply. They discover gradually if this calling to be a priest resonates with what is deepest within themselves. In this approach there is a much more realistic appreciation of the nature of a religious vocation as the slow dawning of a consciousness of a call from God to use one's talents and gifts in a particular way.

*Remaining in a work situation* Remaining at work and having to earn one's livelihood, like everybody else, keeps these students in Bovendonk rooted in reality. This also means that the theology and philosophy they study at weekends has to pass the test of contact with everyday realities if it is to make sense for the students themselves and people they are interacting with in their work situations. The challenge of remaining at work and continuing to exercise a profession rules out many forms of escapism.

There is also a lot to be said for their remaining close to the local Christian communities that nurtured their Christian vocation in the first place. Perhaps it is there that one would expect them to receive a good deal of the support and encouragement they need if they are to persevere on this road to priesthood.

*Training to be leaders* Bringing students together in a residential situation for a six or seven year period may not be the only way to test a vocation or to find out if students have leadership capabilities. There are more direct ways these days to discover if they have or have not leadership potential and whether or not they can relate easily to men and women of our time. Today when students are usually coming from an older age group the traditional seminary environment may in fact inhibit genuine human and spiritual development of some students.

*Integrating Theology and Life Experiences* There is a good deal of emphasis on one-to-one tutorial work in Bovendonk. Students are encouraged to integrate the theology they are taught from week to week with their own personal experience. An effort is made to counteract any kind of dualism – keeping the world of theology and their own personal lives in watertight compartments. Students are challenged to integrate what they are learning about the Christian tradition with their own spiritual journeys and of course if they do this they are in a position to help others to do the same. I was impressed by the practical steps which were being taken in Bovendonk to bring this about.

In Year 5 and Year 6 this guided reflection process moves into an apprenticeship mode. During these two years students are placed in parishes where their pastoral work is carefully monitored. The two-year placement in a parish in Year 5 and Year 6 is seen very much as a mentoring process to learn the pastoral skills they need to communicate with men and women. To some extent one could say that this is to return to an apprenticeship model of seminary formation which existed before the Tridentine seminary was set up.

## Human Development

A good deal of attention is paid to promoting the human development of students. This is done through one-to-one counselling with both men and women counsellors in the first two years of their course. In this context one has to learn from the lessons of the past in which seminaries paid very little attention to this aspect of formation, sometimes leading to breakdown of one kind or another after ordination. We have to face up to the limitations of an all-male environment in promoting the human development of students.

## The Dutch Catholic Church

The last forty years have been difficult ones for the Dutch Catholic Church. After the euphoric days of the 1960s – the days of the publication of the Dutch Catechism, vibrant student liturgies, especially in the university chaplaincies, and the pioneering days of the Dutch Pastoral Council in which new structures were put in place for laity, priests and bishops, there followed a long period of conflict. The appointment of a number of extremely conservative bishops who could not hold the middle ground polarised the Dutch Catholic Church to a degree that alienated many Catholics. At present the Dutch Catholic Church has moved into calmer waters. It is said that the 10% who are participating actively in the life of the church are deeply committed. The younger generation are no longer carrying the baggage of the post-Vatican II conflicts.

Over the last ten years the conviction has grown in my mind that in Western Europe we are looking for new ways to call people to priestly ministry and we are looking for new ways to prepare them for this ministry in our secularised societies. There are certain ingredients in Bovendonk that offer one way to move forward:

- Belonging to and maintaining a strong link with one's parish community where there are possibilities of deepening one's life as a Christian.
- Remaining in a work situation as the decision for priesthood deepens and matures.
- Introducing a mentoring process or an apprenticeship structure for a significant part of the formation programme.
- Concentrating on a theology that has a practical orientation and is strongly focused on communication with our contemporaries.
- Using a variety of human development processes and adult education methodologies to move beyond the traditional lecture system.
- Avoiding the limitations of an all-male residential context for a six- or seven-year period.

In the context of formulating a theology of mission for Europe, it is important that we begin to think beyond the framework of the traditional Tridentine seminary. Mission and ministry are bound up together. If we see the European context from a missionary perspective, this will have implications on how we call and prepare people for ministry – both priestly and lay ministry.

VI. CHARTRES REVISITED
NOVEMBER 2004

On a visit to Paris in November 2004, I travelled to Chartres. I wanted to recapture some of the memories of a university student pilgrimage I had participated in some thirty years previously. Once again I boarded a commuter train in the Gare Montparnasse and sped through the flat countryside on a cold but sunny winter's day. The train passed through the town of St Piat where the 1972 pilgrimage had begun. For the rest of my journey to Chartres I recalled some of the high points of that pilgrimage in May 1972 and the vitality of the French Catholic church of those years.

When I boarded the train in Montparnasse, on that Saturday afternoon thirty years ago, I was assigned to a group of twelve students – French, German and South American. I remembered in particular the leader of the group, Dominique, who had read John's gospel in preparation for this pilgrimage. Later I was to learn that she had spent some months in hospital the previous year which she said gave her time to reflect on what life might be all about. On the half-hour journey to St Piat we had time to complete our introductions. Dominique briefed us about the themes we would be reflecting on.

After making sure that we had enough food and water to sustain us over the two days, we began walking in silence through winding by-roads, forest pathways and picturesque villages reflecting on the theme, Encountering Christ today. Then we broke into small groups of twos and threes – a multiplicity of road to Emmaus encounters. It was a beautiful sunny afternoon. We walked in silence for the first hour through pathways bordering a river and then through forest roads, pausing every so often for a rest and a drink of water to quench our thirst. At one point I found myself with two Vietnamese students who shared their anxieties with me about their families back in Saigon where the war was still raging. I also remember talking to some students from South America whose main concern was how to escape the grinding poverty that they and most of their brothers and sisters were living in. Their needs were elemental – having enough food for themselves and their families. The main concern of the Europeans was about choosing a good career.

Around 9.00 pm as dusk was falling there was a Penitential Service for a combined group of pilgrims in an old farmhouse courtyard. It began with a number of readings and was followed by a period of reflection during which three students played some haunting music on flutes, oboes and other instruments. A number of priests in white albs were dotted around the courtyard. They spent about ten minutes with each student who approached them. The service ended with a communal prayer for forgiveness and reconciliation and people exchanged a sign of peace.

After rolling out our sleeping bags on a foam-covered barn floor, we slept soundly. Awakened at daybreak we were cold and stiff and we could hear the rain belting down on the galvanised roof. By 6.00 am we were ready to hit the road. As we started we were joined by the girls who had been billeted nearby. They were already drenched to the skin, looking downcast and forlorn. When we were five minutes on the road one of the student leaders began to sing a marching song which was picked up by the group. This had the effect of raising our spirits. The shared hardship brought us all closer together. After an hour or two the sun came out and by midday we had dried out.

A big moment came in the afternoon when suddenly the twin spires of Chartres cathedral came into view. We could see our destination in the distance and as our pace quickened the walls of the town came closer. I can remember walking through the cobbled streets of the town and meeting a few of the thousands of students arriving at the entrance to the cathedral from various directions. The façade of the cathedral was bathed in the evening sunlight. Student pilgrims were arriving from different directions and were engaged in animated conversations about the walk they had just completed. The three great portals were open. As we poured into the church we took up our places. Like pilgrims of old we put our knapsacks in the aisles and sat down on the flagstones on each side of a large table stretching down the centre, decorated with chalices and flowers. We were in the full flush of our post-Vatican II liturgical reforms so all the stops were pulled out for this final part of the pilgrimage. The evening sunlight was streaming through the famous windows and the organ filled every nook and cranny of the vaulted ceiling. The

Eucharist was celebrated with great reverence, the priests standing with each of their groups beside the table which ran from the
sanctuary down the centre of the church.

In reflecting back over all this, I became aware once again
how disciplined and focused this pilgrimage had been. The
main focus was conversion to the person of Jesus Christ. I also
recalled how impressed I had been with the group of students in
my group – impressed by their openness and vulnerability. One
of the memories that remained with me was the intensity of this
expression of French spirituality. There was no preamble to the
presentation of a call to conversion. 'The kingdom of God is at
hand; be converted and believe in the good news.'

When the train arrived in Chartres the spires of the cathedral
dominated the horizon once again. It was easy to find my way
from the railway station to the cathedral square. Just a few
tourists were walking about on this cold winter's day. As I approached the main entrance memories of my pilgrimage visit in
1972 came flooding back … the thousands of students who were
milling around the entrance on that May Sunday. The French
Catholic Church was still living in the euphoria of post-Vatican
II renewal in those years.

The cathedral itself was practically deserted. I enquired at
the bookshop if there was going to be a tour that day and was
told that M. Miller would be leading his usual tour at 12.00 midday. I could hardly believe my ears. I was assured that it was the
Malcolm Miller of old. A few minutes later, the good man himself arrived looking hale and hearty. He was now in his late sev-
enties. With just four American tourists and myself in tow that
day, he told us that he had come to Chartres as a student from
Durham University in the 1950s. As a student of French literature he was doing his year in France and was teaching in a Lyceé
in the town. Instead of writing his dissertation on a literary figure, he obtained permission to write on the history and architecture of the cathedral. Since then he has become one of the great
authorities on Chartres. He is now in his 47th year as a guide to
the cathedral. I heard him for the first time in September 1963 on
my first visit to Chartres. He has lost none of his charm and elo-
quence over the years. For the next hour he gave the four

Americans and myself a marvellous compendium of the history of the cathedral and an introduction to a selection of its stained glass windows and some of the recently restored sculptures over the west door.

At the end of the tour I asked Malcolm Miller if there were many students coming now on the annual student pilgrimage. He told me that at one time there were up to 30,000 students participating over two Sundays in May. Now the number had dwindled to about 5,000 students. However he added that there were about 30,000 'Tridentines', followers of the excommunicated Marcel Lefebvre, coming on Whit Monday each year. I felt that in that remark there was a whole story to be told about the decline or 'restoration' of the Catholic Church in France over the last thirty years.

I marvelled at the way Malcolm Miller had held us spellbound for one hour on that cold winter's day. He had told the story of the cathedral from the point of view of a believing Christian of the 12th and 13th centuries. He had stood above all the political and theological strife of the past 800 years, focusing on the essentials of the story written in stone and multicoloured glass brought alive by the sunlight streaming through the windows. He spoke about the drawing power of the cathedral with its precious relic of the Blessed Virgin Mary, the architectural breakthrough in buttressed high walls, and the way the cathedral became a stopping point on the road to Santiago de Compostella. The cathedral had stood above all the strife of ecclesiastical and state politics over the past 800 years.

*'The Holy Spirit will look after the Church'*
When the tour was over, I repaired to a restaurant a few streets away to recover from the cold and to absorb what Malcolm Miller had said to us. Afterwards I walked around the outside of the cathedral spending a little bit of time in the park nearby looking out over the plain which we had walked across some thirty-two years previously. I stopped outside a well-built 19th century building and asked a senior citizen, standing at the entrance, if this was the seminary. It was the *petit-seminaire* he told me and now it was functioning as a restaurant. If I was looking for the *grand-seminaire* I would find it on the other side of the

cathedral – he told me. And then to anticipate my next question he said that there were very few seminarians around these days. The few they had in the diocese of Chartres were following their studies in the neighbouring diocese of Orleans. The Chartres seminary had been turned into the Archival Centre for the local Department. As he said this a friend of his arrived and as they moved off together in the direction of the restaurant he turned back and said to me, 'The Holy Spirit will look after the church.' As I walked around to the other side of the cathedral to see the new home for the Departmental Archives – it was indeed a very fine building or cluster of buildings – I could not help saying to myself, in the light of recent statistics about the rapidly declining numbers of priests in parishes and the absence of so many French people from any kind of regular Sunday worship, that it was high time for the Holy Spirit to shake things up once again.

As I travelled back on the train to Paris that afternoon I had plenty to reflect on:

- The decline of university students' participation in the pilgrimage.
- The polarisation of the church in France and the increasing influence of Lefebvre groups.
- The declining numbers participating in church life on any kind of regular basis. A recent survey published in *La Croix* put this as low as 8%
- The 2000 EVS report indicated that 60.4 % of French people never go near a church.
- The acute shortage of priests leading to the closure and clustering of parishes.
- The marginalisation of the church in France and its loss of influence in the public forum.

This time was indeed a winter period for the church in France. Moreover, very serious questions were being asked about the capacity of the church to pass on the Christian tradition to the younger generations. All of this contrasted with the glorious heritage of Chartres and the vitality of the church as I had experienced it during and after Vatican II and during the 1972 pilgrimage. How was the church facing up to the challenges of the current situation? Where were the signs of hope in France at this time? I was to learn later that the French Bishops in their 1995 *Letter to French Catholics* outlined a new mission situation in which they saw the church free of any political alignments and proclaiming the gospel in all its purity to those who wanted to make a personal adult commitment to Jesus Christ.

VII. KRAKOW – THE LEGACY OF KAROL WOJTYLA

FEBRUARY 2006

Travelling to Krakow in February 2006 was quite a daunting prospect. Word had come through that Krakow was having its coldest winter since 1939 and that at times the temperature was down to -20C. On the plane there were many young Poles, returning home for a few days' break. As we made our descent the pilot informed us that a snowstorm had enveloped the airport but that conditions were good enough to land. As we taxied to the John Paul II International airport we could see that a blanket of snow had fallen and that snowflakes were swirling around outside. Our driver, who spoke very good English, drove fast through a narrow forest road, which was dimly lit. The falling snow did not seem to worry him. After 15 minutes we crossed the Vistula River and arrived in the old city. Krakow is situated at the most central point of Europe on the ancient trade route between east and west. Over the following ten days I was looking forward to learning as much as I could about this ancient city and the tumultuous events of the last 25 years. In particular I was hoping to learn more about one of the city's favourite sons.

*Some Footprints*

Everywhere I went over the following week people pointed out places where Karol Wojtyla had lived or worked as a priest and archbishop. There was no doubt that for the citizens of Krakow he was their icon and hero – and saint. I hesitated to ask questions about any possible shortcomings. The following are some footprints of Karol Wojtyla I came across during my ten days in the city, brought alive by conversations with Polish priests who showed me around.

*Wooden Clogs*

The convent of Divine Mercy Congregation on the outskirts of the city was one of the first places we visited. Karol Wojtyla used to come to pray in the convent chapel on his way to work in a factory a short distance away, 'wearing his wooden clogs' as he was to say later. Now a magnificent new Basilica stands in the convent grounds. It is beautifully designed in an oval shape with slender columns holding up the roof. There was a lightness about the construction and a lot of sunlight coming through the clear windows that stretched from the floor to the ceiling. As in all the churches we visited there were numerous simple confessionals with priests in violet stoles ready to welcome penitents. The Basilica had been built with donations from Divine Mercy groups all over the world. A large portrait of Sister Faustina was hanging on a wall at the left of the altar. She was canonised by Pope John Paul II on 30 April 2000. The Divine Mercy devotion appeared to be the gateway to the transcendent for many people in Poland today. I learned that many homes in Krakow and elsewhere had a picture of 'Jesus of Divine Mercy' in a prominent place in the house just as fifty years ago a picture of the Sacred Heart would have adorned many Irish homes. Consecrating this Basilica in 2003 was one of Pope John Paul's last actions on his final visit to his homeland.

## Dialoguing with University Students

A few days later, I visited Our Lady of Lourdes parish. A large student population of 10,000 or more were living within the confines of the parish. They were attending courses in university centres nearby. A full-length portrait of a youthful Cardinal Wojtyla hung on one wall of the common room. Fourteen Vincentian priests live and work here. The cardinal at one time spent one month on visitation in this parish during which he visited the sick in their homes. He also met small groups of students in private houses. The authorities at the time forbade him to speak to large groups. Four of the young priests living in this community were acting as chaplains to university students in this part of the city. No longer are they restricted as they were in the past. Polish priests engage intensively with young people in discussion groups and in all kinds of activities to communicate gospel values to the younger generation. This appeared to me to be one of the strengths of the Catholic Church in Poland today.

## An Open Door

One of the surprises for me was to learn that out of the population of 36 million people, 30% practice on a regular basis, 30% are cultural Catholics and 30% are non-believers. I thought that the percentage of regular churchgoers was going to be higher. It can go up to 50% in rural areas, especially in the southern part of the country. In comparison to most western European countries, this is a high figure.

In Krakow, a city with one of the oldest universities in the world, there has been a strong intellectual tradition in Catholic circles. John Paul II's devastating critique of Marxism was built up gradually in the 1960s and 1970s through dialogue with these Catholic intellectuals in Krakow and Lublin. It was said that in his episcopal offices he had an open door policy to anyone who wanted to come and see him, including university professors who wanted to dialogue with him about the origins and claims of Christianity.

## Nova Huta

Nova Huta – an industrial city built on the outskirts of Krakow. The communists wanted to wean people away from adherence to the old religion, which was bound up with the multitude of churches in the old city. Cardinal Wojtyla wanted to put up a modern new church to rival the state of the art communist buildings but the communist authorities would not give him permission to do so. Eventually he was given permission to extend the small church that existed there. By 1977 he had broken through all the bureaucratic restrictions and a marvellous modern church was built, with a famous figure of the Crucified Christ, expressing the suffering of the Polish people and their struggles to break free from the shackles of communism. We tend to associate John Paul with traditional religion but here he backed an ultra-modern design in the shape of an arc. The point, of course, was to show the people that the church too could construct a place of worship in a modern design to compete with all the other new buildings in this area. This church epitomises the thirty years' struggle between John Paul and the communist authorities. What was called the Lenin Highway nearby is now known as the John Paul II Highway. 'As well as being a masterful politician, John Paul was a fighter' is how one Polish priest put it to me. I got the impression that he revelled in his battles against communist authorities and in many ways outwitted them as he was to do so on his various visits to Poland before the fall of the wall. In 1978, when he was elected Pope, the information that Cardinal Wojtyla had been elected Pope earlier that day was the last item on a news bulletin. The TV announcer got international news and local news and the weather out of the way first.

### A City of Churches, Seminaries and Convents

As I walked through areas of the old city I was struck forcefully by the strong presence of the church. Next door to the archbishop's residence was a magnificent Franciscan church with a large compound near by. The Franciscans are one of the largest religious orders in Poland. Next door was their headquarters which included a theologate with 200 students preparing for priesthood. The next building was the headquarters of a women's religious congregation. Next to this building was the diocesan seminary with an impressive façade. As I passed the main entrance four young men came out dressed in their black soutanes and black overcoats and walked unselfconsciously and briskly down the street, one of them with a guitar on his back. I was struck by their youthfulness and vitality.

Around the corner from here, at the foot of Wavel Castle was a Vincentian theologate with a student body of 150 students. In other parts of the city Dominicans and Jesuits ran their theologates. So with the 100 students in the diocesan seminary I came to the conclusion that there was no shortage of priests in this part of Poland. My constant question throughout the time I spent in Krakow was how had they managed to maintain a steady flow of priestly vocations to these theologates in Krakow and also to the seminaries around the country. I was to learn that nearly every one of the 35 dioceses in Poland has maintained its own seminary right up to the present day .

### Mass on the Hour

The Archdiocese of Krakow is very large. It covers a geographical area stretching south to the Tartra Mountains. This ancient diocese was founded in 1000AD. There are about 1,000 diocesan priests running 400 parishes. As I walked in and out of many of the churches in the centre of the city I was amazed at the number of Masses that were being celebrated at all times of the day, morning, afternoon and evening, and the number of priests hearing confessions before, during and after Mass. I learned that it was common practice for priests to spend some time hearing confessions before and after celebrating the Eucharist. Perhaps this explains in part why Pope John Paul donned a violet stole and heard confessions in St Peter's during Holy Week. Inside one of these churches, St Mary's on Market Square, three priests, enveloped in very heavy overcoats and woollen headgear, were sitting in these open confessionals ready to listen to their penitents.

*First Mass in the Cathedral Crypt*
On my last day in Krakow I visited the crypt of the cathedral church of St Stanislaus which was filled with the monumental tombs of members of the royal family and various branches of the nobility going back hundreds of years. The Baroque renovations in the cathedral had made the interior heavy and gloomy as had the 15 dimly lit chapels around the side aisles. When I climbed the seventy steps to the top of the bell tower there was a marvellous view over the city. The snow-capped peaks of the Tartra Mountains some 70 kilometres to the south were faintly visible.

I visited the chapel of St Leonard in the crypt, where Karol Wojtyla had celebrated his first Mass on 2 November 1946. He had been ordained the previous day by Cardinal Adam Sapieha who had invited him into the episcopal residence during the war years to begin his studies for the priesthood. Why did he choose this place to celebrate his first Mass? Was it for patriotic reasons to remember the leaders of church and state over the previous centuries? Was it to remember his father and mother and his brother who had died some years previously? It certainly was a most austere and funereal place to say his first Mass surrounded by the tombs of the dead.

## 'Our Martyrs'

On the Sunday afternoon we visited a Vincentian church on the west of the city. At the entrance there was a large poster with a drawing of Pope John Paul, announcing that a special Mass would take place in this and other churches in Krakow in a few weeks' time to pray for his beatification. Obviously, the new Archbishop, Cardinal Stanislaw Dziwisz, former secretary of the Pope, was promoting this with enthusiasm. I was tempted to question the idea of John Paul being put on the fast track to canonisation. However, I sensed that this would not go down well with some of the Polish priests I was chatting to at the time.

When we entered this church my attention was caught by photographs of 11 Vincentian priests on a notice board. They had been executed during the Nazi occupation. Short biographies and the manner of their execution were written underneath each photograph. These Vincentians, together with priests from other religious orders, had been sent to Auschwitz or had simply been taken out to one of the squares of the city where they were shot by the Nazis who wanted to eliminate leaders in society. I was fascinated by my Polish Vincentian guide referring to these men as 'our Vincentian martyrs'. In Poland today there are many memories of such atrocities committed during the Nazi occupation and later during the period of communist domination which are still alive in the minds of many older citizens and now being passed on to the younger generation. Will these memories fade? Up to now the Catholic Church has played a key role in helping people to come to terms with all this brutality and suffering. One of the reasons why the church occupies an important place in the minds and hearts of Polish people is because church leaders had suffered in these periods of oppression and stood by their people.

## Market Square – Another World

One evening as I walked around Market Square many young people were milling about on their way to discos and cafés. I wondered if this younger generation would remain true to the religion of their parents and grandparents. All the music blaring out from discos was of the rock variety, much of it in the English language. My Polish friends told me that Bono and U2 were well represented. Already there were plenty of signs of the encroaching influence of the West in the fashionable shops with their designer clothes on Market Square and the surrounding streets. Will Polish people be able to resist the lure of Western consumerism? In his seven visits to Poland Pope John Paul kept returning to this theme. Polish Catholics had paid a heavy price in holding on to the faith and now part of their task was to share this faith with the secularised west.

*The Contrast between Poland and many countries in Western Europe*
As I walked around the magnificent buildings of the old city and visited churches, where crowds of people were present at all times of the day, the question kept coming up for me 'How long more will this last?' Will the winds of secularisation begin to blow in Poland as they have done in all the countries of Western Europe? Will Poland too succumb to the same forces that have marginalised the Catholic Church in the west? Will the Catholic Church in Poland undergo a sharp decline as has happened in Ireland over the last twenty years, or a slower decline over fifty years as has happened in Belgium and France? Or will the strong tradition of Polish Catholicism rise above these secularising forces and show us a way forward in the West? Before my short visit to Krakow I would have been opting for the 'decline thesis' but now I am not too sure. The contrast between what we observe in Western European countries and what I was observing in Krakow over these ten days gave me plenty of food for thought.

Up to the fall of the Berlin Wall Poland was cut off from the west. There had been strong and firm leadership from Cardinal Wyszynski in Warsaw and Cardinal Wojtyla in Krakow. By standards in the West, this leadership and leadership at other levels in the church was quite authoritarian. The church had to remain united against communist threats and efforts to eliminate it. There was little room for dissent. Vatican II teaching about collegiality was put on the back burner as were other Vatican II reforms. A strong distinction between priests and laity has been maintained. At a certain level this is expressed by priests wearing distinctive clerical dress. Religious orders of men and women also wear their own distinctive habits. Everything seems to centre on the ministry of priests.

Cardinal Wojtyla was an icon of resistance to communism. On his seven visits to Poland as Pope, he kept reiterating to his fellow countrymen and women that they should make good use of their newly acquired freedom. Their forebears had paid a heavy price in adhering to their church. Their faith had been hammered out on the anvil of suffering over the 20th century and indeed for centuries before that. Will nationalism grow from the faith in the years ahead?

*Final Comment*

There are many different views abroad from one country to another and different views amongst church leaders and theologians about how to plan a way forward. The only point I would like to make is that it will take a good deal of time to work this out and it could very well be that groups may go in opposing directions.

We are looking for a new mission paradigm. The overall impression I have arrived at from my travels in Western Europe is the abandonment by many people of institutional Christianity. Jan Kerkhofs made the following remark about this in an article in *The Tablet* in July 1999: 'It looks as though some sort of mutation, probably much deeper than what occurred after the Renaissance, is accelerating in the depths of Europe's collective consciousness.' Today the Catholic Church is looking for a new mission paradigm at a time of unparalleled change in both church and society. There is a temptation abroad that we will find our way by turning the clock back and resurrecting church structures and ways of evangelising from a previous era. Perhaps the lesson we have to learn from 2000 years of church history is that the way forward may come from sources we have least expected and in ways we have not yet imagined.

# Epilogue

The first lines of this memoir were recorded in the spring of 2002 in Perth, Australia. I am typing these last lines in winter 2007 looking out on Dublin Bay with a view stretching from Dalkey to Howth. Last night's storm has abated and the sea is calm once again.

I have two overwhelming impressions as I come to the end of this narrative. The first is of the variety of opportunities and challenges that have come my way. The second is of a deep sense of gratitude to members of my own family, to colleagues and students in Strawberry Hill and All Hallows, to friends and to Vincentian priests in the Congregation of the Mission, especially the Irish Province.